Ours Once More

Ours Once More

Folklore, Ideology, and the Making of Modern Greece

By Michael Herzfeld

PELLA

Pella Publishing Company, Inc.

New York, NY 10018-6401

1986

Ours Once More

© Copyright 1986
by
Michael Herzfeld

Library of Congress Catalogue Card No. 86-62459

ISBN 918618-32-0

Originally published in 1982 by
The University of Texas Press

Printed in the United States of America
by
ATHENS PRINTING COMPANY
337 West 36th Street
New York, NY 10018-6401

Contents

For my parents, C.T.H. – E.O.H.

Preface

Greece today confronts the visitor with a series of startling contrasts. The ruins and hints of the Classical past mix with the bustle of modern urban life, the warm hospitality with a sometimes overt suspicion of foreigners, the paraphernalia of a functioning national bureaucracy with the omnipresent evidence of patronage and favor trading. Like the early nineteenth-century philhellene, the present-day visitor may arrive in a haze of romantic expectations, only to be thwarted by the importunities of ordinary experience. Generations of travelers have arrived with their baggage of preconceptions about who and what the Greeks were, and many of them soon began to blame the Greeks for failing to fit these uncompromising images. Perhaps the most offensive aspect of this one-sided, soured philhellenism is the insidious conviction that Greeks generally lack any capacity for individual or collective self-criticism.

Yet the reason for these observers' misapprehension seems clear enough: the Greeks see little reason to share their sense of personal and national shortcoming with carping outsiders. Were these critics only privileged to hear the endless agonizing over what one local writer has dubbed "the misery of being Greek" (Dimou n.d.), they might reverse their judgment entirely. The point is, however, that they do not hear such things—not necessarily because they are bent on deliberate misrepresentation but often because they are predisposed to find a very different Greece and because their hosts know this very well.

Indeed, for the Greeks, the persistence of the Classical image in the West poses a painful dilemma: how far should they consciously try to live up to it? There are, after all, two competing views of Greece. One, built from the accumulated materials of European Classical scholarship, looks out beyond the national borders and appeals to those who have championed the Greek cause abroad or yoked it to the service of élitist interests. The other involves reflexive knowledge—a self-portrait that does not always flatter, a Greek's understanding of what it means in practice to be Greek. This second view is an introverted one: visitors may share some parts of it only by taking the Greeks

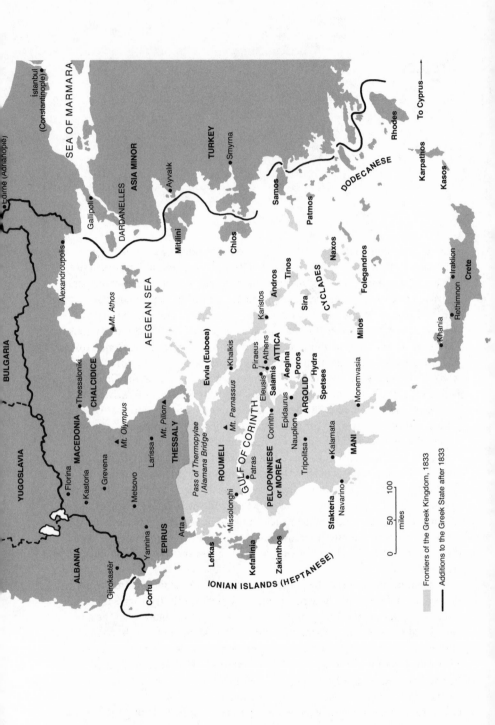

literally on their own terms. Otherwise, were the visitors to insist on the old preconceptions as the price of their sympathy and support, the Greeks would presumably try to disabuse them of such notions only if the foreigners' support had ceased to matter or even to be particularly desirable.

Here, then, is the crux of the matter: we are dealing less with questions of fact (since both images have some claim to a factual basis) than with ideological formulations. Both images, the externally directed and the introverted, are "constructions" of history and culture, and both have become distinct idioms in the effort to delineate a national identity. Each is predicated on certain presuppositions about what makes a "correct" assessment or, in other words, on its own criteria of relevance. The supporters of the extroverted model, for example, point to the "survival" of linguistic and social traits from the Classical era, while their opponents are more likely to dwell on the traces of Turkish values in everyday Greek life. This is not a distinction between "ideal" and "real" so much as a contrast between two "realities," two notions of what matters in the attempt to define Greekness. All descriptions are saturated with presuppositions about what is relevant. To understand the clash of national images is thus to probe each aspect of these descriptions— ethnographic, linguistic, historic, literary—as we receive it, without any imputation of bad faith to the respective authors; it is to identify, not deride, the criteria which shaped both images in their sharply differentiated ways. The central theme of this book, then, is an examination both of the ways in which a sense of national identity was constructed in the young Greek nation-state and, more particularly, of the influence of competing ideologies on the selection of relevant ethnological materials. It is thus a history of history as well as an ethnography of culture theory.

This book also represents its author's shifting personal focus. No scholar can seriously claim to understand the culture of an entire nation in all its complexity. A gentler observation, however, may help put the present work in its proper perspective. I have "lived Greece," as the Greeks themselves express it, and have experienced both the novice's blend of romanticism and bafflement and the later, more reflective curiosity about the conflict of perspectives. As the latter concern became dominant, I tried to gain sharper insight from the many opportunities that came my way. First of all, there are the many Greek friends—urban and rural, scholarly and lay—who responded so generously to my persistent peering and prying. Then, there are the many teachers who guided me at all stages of my constantly intensifying interest in Greek culture. Not least among these were the several teachers of my adolescent years at Dulwich College, who first awakened that interest both through instruction in the Classical languages and literatures and through extracurricular activities that included a richly provocative visit to Greece. Among their successors, I would particularly like to mention the late David L. Clarke, restless critic of taxonomic systems in archaeology and related fields; the late George K. Spiridakis, who supervised my first lengthy acquaintance with academic folklore in Greece; Margaret B. Alexiou, sensitive guide to the literary context of medieval and modern Greek; Ravindra K. Jain, with his knack of constantly asking crucial questions and his infectious commitment to the anthropological study of oral tradition; and J. K. Campbell, whose guidance provided a royal road into the intricacies of Greek ethnography.

John Campbell is also among those whose specific criticisms and comments on versions of this book have helped give it whatever focus and insight it may possess; also influential were Dan Ben-Amos, Gareth Morgan, Loring M. Danforth, and Spyros Stavrakas. I am profoundly indebted to them all. Cornelia Mayer Herzfeld brought her special insight and good sense—an invaluable boon throughout— to bear on many a pertinent discussion as this project began to grow into a tangible entity.

To my former colleagues at Vassar College, I want to express my very real appreciation for a memorably lively anthropology-sociology colloquium at which, with their splendidly argumentative help, I began to hammer this assortment of ideas and materials into a greater semblance of unity. To the librarians of Vassar College—especially to Shirley Maul, presiding genius of their interlibrary loan service—goes much warm recognition of their rare patience and efficiency. And to Vassar College as an institution goes my profound gratitude for its extraordinarily generous financial assistance with the completion of the necessary research and, through its Lucy Maynard Salmon Research Fund, the publication of the present volume. Finally, these acknowledgments would be incomplete without warm thanks to Holly Carver and Suzanne Comer, for their remarkable patience and helpfulness, and to all of their colleagues at the University of Texas Press who helped turn the manuscript into a book.

The issues broached here continue to occupy me in various ways; they have ramifications many of which are barely hinted at in these pages. My personal interest in this cluster of topics has nevertheless already acquired, as in any student's work, certain contours and emphases of its own. That I have always been free to develop my academic interests in various idiosyncratic directions is to an immeasurable degree the gift of my parents. To them, in unstinting gratitude, I am happy at long last to dedicate this book, which is itself very much the child of that freedom.

Note on transliteration. In a book of this kind, it is virtually impossible to be consistent about the transliteration of Greek names and phrases. I have generally adopted a modified phonemic style, except where names are better known in some other guise. The titles of Greek works in the bibliography are given in English translation; these should be readily accessible to those who know Greek, while other readers will gain a sense of the topical coverage.

Ours Once More

Chapter 1
Past Glories, Present Politics

". . . the Europeans as mere debtors . . ."

Cultural Identity as Ideology

In 1821, the Greeks rose in revolt against the rule of Turkey and declared
themselves an independent nation. Their goal was far more ambitious than
freedom alone, for they proclaimed the resurrection of an ancient vision
in which liberty was but a single component. That vision was Hellas—the
achievements of the ancient Greeks in knowledge, morality, and art, summed
up in one evocative word. What was more, the new Greek revolutionaries
went one step further than their forebears had ever managed to do: they
proposed to embody their entire vision in a unified, independent polity. This
unique nation-state would represent the ultimate achievement of the Hellenic
ideal and, as such, would lead all Europe to the highest levels of culture yet
known.

Europeans in other lands, though largely receptive to the attractions of
Classical Greek culture, were not uniformly impressed by the modern Greeks'
claim to represent it. By what token could the latter-day Greeks portray
themselves as the true descendants of the ancient Hellenes? Even if they were
able to do so, had several centuries of unenlightened Ottoman rule not had
any effect on their intellectual and moral condition? Were they still, in any
sense that an educated European could grasp, the same as the Greeks of old?

In a strictly literal sense, of course, they were not. No culture remains
totally unaltered with the passage of time; as generation succeeds generation,
all kinds of changes occur, some abruptly, others imperceptibly but nevertheless with equal persistence. Thus, sameness must in reality be a matter of cultural similarity or continuity. These kinds of connection are unlike the absolute notion of sameness, however, in that they depend on the observer's
criteria of relevance—on a whole set of presuppositions, in other words, about
what traits really constitute acceptable or interesting evidence for some sort
of link. Clearly, then, a premise of cultural continuity cannot usefully be regarded as a question of pure fact. That it is often so regarded in practice is

some indication of the substantial political interests that are vested in it. When cultural continuity is quite obviously a political issue—and in Greece it was never anything else, since it provided the theoretical justification for creating the nation-state in the first place—the observer's personal politics are crucial in determining whether such continuity is admitted to exist.

This book is an attempt to show how Greek scholars constructed cultural continuity in defense of their national identity. It is *not* intended to suggest that they did so in defiance of the facts. Rather, they assembled what they considered to be the relevant cultural materials and used them to state their case. In the process, they also created a national discipline of folklore studies, providing intellectual reinforcement for the political process of nation building that was already well under way.[1]

In their attempt to project a particular view of the Hellenic ideal, moreover, the Greeks were acting no differently than the representatives of other, older European scholarly traditions. The selective character of their research was a well-established trait: Europeans of widely separated times and cultures had long been apt to reconstitute Classical Greece in the terms most familiar to them. The concept of Hellas was already a quicksand of shifting perceptions when the modern Greeks came to it in their turn, bringing with them their specialized nationalistic concerns. Even when Classical scholars could see how much "their" Greece differed from that of some other period or intellectual tradition, their deeper sense of perspective did not necessarily release them from their own time-bound and ethnocentric tastes.

A few examples of European scholarly attitudes will serve to make the point. The early medieval writers are said by one authority to have viewed the Greeks as "more simple-minded and devout, above all more romantic" than they were later to seem (Loomis 1906: 7-8). With the Renaissance, there came a greater respect for the Greeks' intellectual achievements; the influx of Greek scholars to Italy after the sack of Constantinople in 1453 (see Geanakoplos 1962, 1966) produced a rapidly increasing familiarity with Classical philosophy and a general reverence for the wisdom of the ancient writers. As Classical scholarship began to expand and to become more specialized, however, and as philological knowledge was joined by the emergent discipline of archaeology, alternative ways of looking at the ancient world proliferated. By the nineteenth century, Classical scholars had come to pride themselves on a remarkable degree of academic perfectionism, but their views were clearly as much a matter of intellectual fashion as ever. A frankly critical American observer of nineteenth-century European scholarship decried not only the English scholars' "limp Grecism," as evidenced in the excessively "scented, wholesale sweetness of the modern aesthetic school in England," but also the Germans' use of Greek "as a stalking-horse for Teutonic psychology" and their grave concern with minutiae. Scholars of the two nations resembled

each other, he thought, "in but a single trait—the conviction that they understand Greece" (Chapman 1915: 12-13). Nor was this acid commentator entirely free of any such conviction about himself, to judge from the tone of
these remarks. And so, presumably, it will go on. New truths will yield to still
newer truths about the same basic idea, the vision of Classical Greece—the
source, in a commonly held view, of the very practice of historical writing
itself.

Such changes in perception are of interest here for two reasons. First, they
show that through all the divergent interpretations there runs a common
theme: the idea of Hellas as the cultural exemplar of Europe.[2] And, second,
these same contrasts mark the progressive enhancement of that exemplar's
authority, not its dissolution (as we might expect) in the bickering of the
ages. Whatever Greece is or was, the *idea* of Greece—like any symbol—could
carry a wide range of possible meanings, and so it survived triumphantly.
Similarly, the concept of European culture, so stable at the level of mere
generality, has undergone many transformations through the centuries.
"Europe," like "Hellas," was a generalized ideal, a symbol of cultural superiority which could and did survive innumerable changes in the moral and
political order. It was to this European ideal, moreover, that Hellas was considered ancestral. Such is the malleable material of which ideologies are made.

Folklore and History

It is as an ideological phenomenon that we shall treat the twin concepts of
Hellas and Europe here. They provided the motivating rationale for one of
the most explosive political adventures of the nineteenth century, an adventure which claimed thousands of lives and brought many more under the control of a nation-state that had never before existed as a sovereign entity. This
adventure was the Greek struggle for independence of 1821 to 1833. Its
eventual success was by no means certain in the early stages. The Great
Powers were reluctant to commit themselves to the Greek cause until, forced
by public opinion at home, by the Greeks' own successes, and by the fear of
each other's intentions, they began to take a more active part in bringing the
Greek State into existence. That the Greeks did eventually prevail, despite the
enormous Turkish armies with which they had to contend as well as their destructive internal squabbles, is some measure of the evocative power of the
name of Hellas among their European supporters. To be a European was, in
ideological terms, to be a Hellene.

Yet the Hellas which European intellectuals wished to reconstitute on
Greek soil was very different from the Greek culture which they actually encountered there, despite all the western-educated Greek intellectuals' efforts
to bridge the gap. Nowhere were the contradictions more apparent than in

the earliest attempts to provide the new nation-state with an explicit foundation in political theory. In 1822 a national charter, the so-called Constitution
of Epidaurus, was promulgated in a language so archaic that few Greeks could
fully understand it. This language was symptomatic of the idealism with
which the charter had been conceived: it promised a statist democracy in accordance with the principles that were thought to have guided a very different sort of polity, the Athenian city-state of the fifth century B.C. Although
this impracticable blueprint was soon superseded by other constitutions, it
expresses nicely the paradoxical situation in which the new Hellas found
itself.

The paradox, though not openly expressed so baldly at first, was a matter
of immediate concern to the founders of the new state and may be crudely
paraphrased in these terms: how could a modern nation-state survive on the
premise that its citizens were the same as the long-lost inhabitants of the
land?[3] Other, related questions followed in the stream of this first one. How,
for example, could one be a "Hellene"—a term which had meant "pagan" in
the early years of Christianity—while still a member of the Orthodox Christian faith? How could one be considered a Hellene when ordinary conversation was conducted in a language, Romeic, which was conceptually *opposed*
to the ancient ("Hellenic") tongue? What, more generally, were Greeks to
make of all the cultural traits which, though a familiar part of their lives, were
now under attack by their leaders as well as by foreigners as "barbarous" and
"oriental" and therefore as the very antithesis of Greek? Such difficulties
threatened the coherence of the national ideology at the moment of its supreme political triumph.

From 1821 on, the intellectuals had to deal with a large rural population
in the realm of practical politics. The unlettered peasantry presented a potentially embarrassing contrast to the idealized image of Greece which the
European supporters of Greek nationalism—the philhellenes, as they are so
aptly named—had entertained for so long. How were the Greek rural folk to
fit into the grand design? They had almost no documented history which
might connect them, however tenuously, to their ancient predecessors.

The study of folklore provided the most comprehensive answer—hesitant-
ly at first, then with growing confidence as the methods and orientation of
this (for Greece) novel discipline became more and more systematic. The
concept around which the early Greek folklorists organized their enterprise
was precisely that of cultural continuity. This specialized version of the commonly entertained conception of Hellas as the exemplar of all Europe shared
with the latter a similar liability to wide-ranging and ambiguous definition. In
its successive reformulations, it responded to many of the ethnological fashions which sprang up abroad, though often in forms adapted to Greece's
special needs and preoccupations. Against the background of the Greeks' de-

pendence on European patronage, moreover, the role of folklore in fashioning an acceptable external image for the country had political significance right from the start. If it could be shown that the peasants, the largest demographic element, retained clear traces of their ancient heritage, the fundamental requirement of philhellenic ideology would be satisfied, and European support for the emergent nation-state could be based on a secure foundation of historical justification.

An Externally Directed Ideology

For these reasons, folklore was not merely an abstruse academic concern in the early years of Greek independence. It addressed what were perhaps the most sensitive aspects of national identity, and its political implications were widely recognized. Foreigners as well as Greeks, politicians as well as scholars helped launch Greek folklore research on the path along which it was to travel for decades to come. This rise of academic folklore was generated in the interplay between local and foreign interests in the legitimation of the new state.

The nationalist scholar and ideologue Adamantios Koraes (1748-1833), a correspondent of Thomas Jefferson and a close observer of pre- and post-revolutionary France, both exemplified and initiated that process. Koraes could be highly disparaging of the vernacular culture: he once dismissed the Cretan Renaissance verse-romance *Erotokritos* as "the ugly handmaid" of Greek letters, for example (1805). Despite such attitudes, he encouraged Greek scholars to take an interest in vernacular studies and expressed warm admiration for Claude Fauriel, the French historian and compiler of the first substantive collection of Greek folksongs to appear in print (Sainte-Beuve 1870: 202; cf. Llewellyn Smith 1965: 54). Some of the songs in Fauriel's collection had apparently been supplied by Koraes himself, via the good offices of the Greek scholars Christodoulos Klonaris (1788-1849) and Nikolaos Piccolos (1792-1866) (Fauriel 1956: 2). Koraes' own attitude toward folk literature can perhaps best be gauged through his linguistic ideas. In contrast to the neo-Atticists, who wanted to restore the Classical Greek of Plato and the Attic tragedians to daily use, he was willing to retain certain vernacular forms as well as to draw on European traditions of grammatical codification. Whether or not Koraes' moderate stance was what enabled demotic Greek to survive the onslaught of extreme neo-Atticism (Babiniotis 1979: 4), his interest lay less in reviving the Classical glories as such than in locating in the modern Greeks a Hellenic essence which could be refashioned in the philhellenic idiom.

The development of folklore in Greece can be understood only against this background of an externally directed ideology, ever responsive to foreign comment and criticism. Perhaps the greatest period of activity in the history of Greek folklore began with the vehement denial of the Greeks' claims to a Classical ancestry, articulated by the Austrian polemicist and scholar Jakob Philipp Fallmerayer. But, while due regard must be paid to such foreign stimuli, the achievements of the Greek folklorists are not thereby diminished. On the contrary, it was the Greeks' willingness to join battle in the first place which allowed them to recover and preserve so vast a corpus of material; without their efforts, most of it would have vanished long ago. Nor is there any profit in laughing at their methods and theories, outlandish though many of them may now seem. These were partly a reflection of ethnological thinking abroad, partly a response to local political conditions and ideological trends. Above all, the Greek folklorists' methods were intended to guide the earnest search for factual knowledge. These folklorists were actually dogged empiricists, no matter how ambiguous their evidence may seem today. There is nothing to be gained from looking at the early Greek folklorists as an assortment of charming eccentrics, even though the recent treatment of nineteenth-century philhellenes and nationalists (St. Clair 1972; Howarth 1976) may suggest some such course. To understand them, we must instead relate their ideas to the political, social, and moral universe in which they moved.

Toward a National Anthropology

How is such a task best approached? The Greek folklorists were attempting to explain a national culture which they considered to be both internally chaotic and corrupted by foreign influences of many kinds. Their notions about what it meant to be Greek acted as a filter through which only "relevant" data could pass. Indeed, these ideas were often translated into systems of classification. It is by treating such systems semiotically—that is, as a code which embodied and expressed the folklorists' guiding assumptions—that we can most effectively work back to the assumptions themselves.

Every cultural commentary—be it folkloric, historical, or anthropological—is an attempt to convey to an audience of relative outsiders something which already has its own internal forms of explanation and rationale. In the present case, however, it is the commentators themselves that we are studying. The Greek folklorists saw their nation's culture as a unity in which they were themselves fully participating members. In order to examine their relationship to the peasantry whose lore they studied, we cannot afford to accept that assumption uncritically. On the contrary, it is just one of the many distinctive traits of their culture within a culture, of the habits of thought which set them apart from other Greeks. Their willingness and ability to think in terms of *studying* folklore are some measure of the distance which actually separated them from the rural people. In that sense, too, this book is essentially an "anthropology of anthropologists,"[4] whatever its wider implications with regard to modern Greek culture as a whole.

These Greek scholars were anthropologists of a special kind. Most of what they did was in some way a response to the ideological needs of their emergent polity. Indeed, they made a distinctive and important contribution to the making of modern Greece, no less than did the military and political leaders in their respective areas of competence. Their methods and assumptions are thus crucial to our understanding not only of the ideological development of Greece in its first few decades of independence but of the complexities of modern Greek culture as we encounter it today. All too often, our insights are restricted by the boundaries of current academic disciplines. Village-level ethnographies and studies of particular artistic and literary movements are valuable and interesting, but they address comparatively small and isolated segments of the national culture. By examining the Greeks' study of their own national culture, we can at least begin to gain some sense of how these various segments are connected in the national sense of identity.

Attractive though this framework of inquiry is, it does raise two serious difficulties which have to be discussed before we go any further. The first of these concerns the extent to which the folklorists exerted the kind of influence which may have caused the folklore itself to conform increasingly to their preconceptions. The second problem is both more general and more immediate: how can we be sufficiently confident of our own sense of Greek folklore to be able to make a critical examination of the original collectors' work?

The first question—that of the folklorists' influence on cultural change—is hard to answer with any real accuracy. There is no doubt that the folklorists did have some effect on the content of school textbooks, which in turn contributed to the partial dissemination of learned culture (see especially Beaton 1980: 190). Moral censorship, too, seems to have had some effect; what the folklorists permitted themselves to include in their collections may have had greater chances of survival simply because of this semiofficial approval. Yet we should be careful not to overstate the case here; the real difficulty is that our major source of information about the folk culture is precisely the body of material collected over the years by the local scholars, and in fact there is some evidence (e.g., Herzfeld 1979) that the more disreputable forms have survived remarkably well in some areas. Some of the scholars' linguistic emendations may have entered the folk repertoire as the spoken language moved increasingly toward standardization. Here again, however, it is not at all clear how radical the folklorists' influence actually was, and I have been extremely cautious about assuming that they were responsible for any of these kinds of cultural change. It is not necessary to presuppose such input on their part in order to argue that their scholarship represents a highly selective view of the country's popular culture; insofar as such input can be identified, it can only strengthen this overall picture.

As to the second question—the status of our own interpretations of Greek culture—these need not present a serious obstacle provided that we do not use them to "disprove" those of the local scholars whose work concerns us. This proviso, however, is vital. An anthropologist does not try to expose informants' "ignorance" of their cultural universe; it is only possible to say something about how they perceive and articulate that universe. In much the same spirit, our aim here is not to challenge the factual basis of early Greek folklore studies or to treat their motivating principles as somehow erroneous. Since we are treating the scholarly sources as "informants" out of the past, we should no more attempt to debate with them than we would consciously force a living informant to adopt a particular anthropological theory. Of course, there are factual errors aplenty in these sources, and one is sometimes tempted to mutter about poor standards or even fraud. But imputations of bad faith lead nowhere—especially when our aim is to discover why our "informants" thought as they did, rather than to assume the answer in advance.

This is a matter of suiting methods to the purpose of the study. It is one thing to reject an older interpretation as incompatible with current frameworks and interests, quite another to condemn it out of hand. Exactly the same is true of the charge of eccentricity—a word which in Greek means being "off-center." It is to our own conceptual center, not to that of their contemporaries and compatriots, that many of the early Greek folklorists seem marginal. In the context of their time and place, their views, which were by no means crudely uniform, made good sense.

The Premise of Cultural Continuity

The central tenet of cultural continuity provided an organizing principle for the collection, classification, and ranking of all ethnographic items. Although the folklorists' emergent discipline was mainly concerned with nonmaterial artifacts, they were unusually fortunate in the wealth of historical evidence to which they could turn. In many parts of the world, folklorists can often only guess at the stages through which their materials have evolved. In Greece, by contrast, a rich archaeological record enhanced an already surprisingly large assortment of scraps of oral literature preserved (or at least mentioned) in ancient and medieval writings.

The archaeological aspect of this historical perspective was extremely important; indeed, it provided the dominant model for the whole enterprise. Although the phrase "monuments of the word" was first applied to Greek folklore by Claude Fauriel in 1824, it has since enjoyed enormous popularity among local scholars. Apparently an invention of that German philosopher of national identity, Johann Gottfried von Herder (but cf. Nisbet 1969: 100 on Turgot's 1750 formulation), it was extensively used by the Grimm brothers, whose work was to exercise considerable influence on Greek folklore scholarship in the second half of the nineteenth century. The archaeological model is thus not a uniquely Greek concept, but it certainly suited Greek conditions exceptionally well, and it enabled Greek scholars to present their view of cultural continuity in terms to which their European colleagues could respond easily. In describing a present which was also a past, it harmonized with the political aims of a revolution which was also a resurrection.

Superficially, the Greeks were not very different from any other nascent European nation seeking the evidence of its collective character in folklore. Sounding very much like the Greeks on the subject of Turkey, the Finns, for example, contrasted their "European" culture with the "oriental barbarism" of the Russians (Wilson 1976: 148). The Finns, like the Greeks, used their folklore to validate both their national identity and their cultural status as Europeans. Unlike the Greeks, however, they did not speak an Indo-European language and so had even less claim than most European peoples to having "originated" European culture. Greek antiquity, by contrast, was scanned as a prototype for the modern folklores of such countries as Ireland (Dorson 1966: 293) and Finland itself (Wilson 1976: 172). No other country was ever accorded such a generative role in relation to the rest of Europe, and it is this above all which makes the Greek experience the reverse of that of virtually every other European country.

In order to justify their special ancestral status, the Greeks naturally relied heavily upon their archaeological model. Indeed, official endorsement of folklore studies partly rested on the assumption that they were of an archaeological nature. As recently as 1968, celebrating the fiftieth anniversary of the founding of the Folklore Research Center of the Academy of Athens, Academician Anast. Orlandos approvingly described the twin directions of early folklore research in Greece as, respectively, "literary" and "patriotic or archaeological" (1969: 6). A literary essayist might perhaps be a patriot; an archaeologist, by definition, could be nothing else.

Youngest State, Oldest Nation

Although Greece was conceptually the very source of Europe, it was politically one of that continent's youngest member states. As a result, when we compare the history of Greek folklore studies with similar intellectual developments elsewhere in Europe, the sense of inversion is enhanced still further. Before the establishment of the Greek nation-state, the existence of Greek nationhood was an intellectual and political article of faith; the process of ethnological justification, however, was really set in motion only *after* that event. Elsewhere, as in Finland again, folklore studies played an important part in creating a national consciousness long *before* statehood could be achieved. The Greek scholars were unusual in having folklore studies virtually forced on them by events.

There was no local tradition of folklore research as a systematic, autonomous discipline. In early Christian and Byzantine times, folklore attracted attention either as a persistent and subversive paganism, as in the writings of Saint John Chrysostom, or as a source of such curious illustrations as those in the exceptionally perceptive Homeric commentaries of Eustathius of Thessaloniki (cf. Koukoules 1950; Spiridakis 1966: 476-477). Later came rare collections of verbal curios: two fifteenth-century manuscript renderings of the song of Armouris (see Beaton 1980: 82-86), the fourteen song texts with musical notation preserved in a seventeenth-century manuscript from the Iviron Monastery on Mount Athos (Bouvier 1960), and the eighteenth-century compilation of proverbs by the Yannina monk Parthenios Katzioulis (Politis 1899-1902: xxix-xxxv, 69-132). An 1812 manuscript from the island of Folegandros carries a long text of the so-called swallow song, a children's carol that was probably sung on the eve of March 1 every year. But now we are on the threshold of independence.[5]

In general, the foreign contribution to the early stages of folksong research and publication was substantial. The French traveler André Guillet (La Guilletière 1676) had considered making a collection of songs from Greece, but nothing came of the scheme. Claude Fauriel's two-volume compendium, published in France in 1824 and 1825, was followed by the German historian Theodor Kind's shorter effort in 1827. The Greeks, embroiled in a desperate war, also lacked the equipment needed for producing books on their own territory. That matters other than academic publication preoccupied them at this time is quite clear from their unenthusiastic reaction to the gift of printing presses which some Benthamite well-wishers decided to foist upon them (St. Clair 1972: 146-149); it was not until the relative tranquillity of the mid 1830s that such ventures became generally feasible. There were, of course, Greek printers in Venice, where Niccolò Tommaseo published a distinguished collection of Tuscan, Corsican, Greek, and Illyrian folksongs in 1841 and 1842. But the Greek colony in Venice, which had been highly active in the dissemination of Greek learning during and after the Renaissance, was largely composed of literati and wealthy merchants who showed scant interest in the monuments of their rural compatriots' vernacular culture. Fauriel had poor luck hunting for Greek folksongs there (Colquhoun 1954: 173). Only in the Ionian Islands (the Heptanese) were singers and printers to be found in close proximity under conditions of relative peace. Even there, however, the rise of Corfu as the outstanding local center of Greek folklore studies did not begin until the middle of the nineteenth century; by then, the British were on the verge of ceding the Ionian Islands to Greece (1864), and a considerable amount of research had already been done on the mainland too. Thus, the eventual development of folklore studies in Greece seems to owe much more to political and ideological developments than to such purely circumstantial matters as the availability of printing presses.

Although publication was late in developing, the Ionian Greeks certainly showed an interest in folklore from the beginning. One of them, Andrea Mustoxidi, is generally credited with having been the first to voice the need—as early as 1820—for folklore studies in Greece. After the War of Independence, Greeks from many parts of the country became involved in this research, and their publications provided what successive national constitutions had not: a vibrant charter for their *Altneuland*.[6] Unlike, for example, the United States Declaration of Independence (see Wills 1979: 38), the stilted Greek constitutions had hardly served as a focus for allegiance, enthusiasm, and a new mythology. What was needed was a body of patriotic writing which could juxtapose grand ideals with cultural experience. Such a text was collectively created through the development of a national discipline of folklore—or, as some (e.g., Bryer 1976) prefer to call it in order to stress its distinctively local flavor, laography (Greek *laografia*).

Why laography? Ostensibly, folklore entailed the study of the *ethnos*, the nation, yet *ethnografia* has never been a very popular term in Greece. *Laos* denotes the people (cf. *Volk*), *ethnos* the nation qua inheritors of the Classical mantle.[7] In order to justify the creation of the state (*kratos*) in the terms of ideological philhellenism, it was necessary to show that *ethnos* and *laos* were one and the same thing, with the sole difference being that the *laos* did not include the educated élite (cf. Campbell 1976). This meant that there would have to be an independent discipline concerned with the *laos*—laography—from which it would be possible to prove that the common people indeed belonged to the Hellenic *ethnos*. The *ethnos* did not need a branch of study of its own: it was one of the eternal verities, an absolute moral entity against which the *laos* could be matched and measured. Laography was thus politically committed from its inception, and no study of it can ever be anything other than an excursion into ideology.

Quintessential Europeans

If foreigners were among the first to collect Greek folklore, and even to exploit its ideological potential on behalf of the philhellenic cause, they did so as part of a far more extensive commitment. From the outbreak of war in 1821, often at the risk of angering reactionary governments at home, European liberals came to witness and to fight for the rebirth of Hellas. Despite all the twists and turns of the struggle, dedicated foreigners continued to join the affray. Many died in Greece of sickness—like Lord Byron—or of wounds received in battle. Often, expecting to be hailed as leaders and saviors, they found their advice ridiculed or ignored by haughty local guerrilla "captains" who cared little for the much touted advantages of "European warfare" (St. Clair 1972: 75-77). Despite the example set by those who returned home in disgust, others were usually more than eager to take their place.

The Greek cause did not suddenly spring fully formed from the minds of nineteenth-century intellectuals. Among the Greeks themselves, as some authorities have argued (e.g., Vacalopoulos 1970; Xydis 1968), its roots can be traced back at least to the later years of the Byzantine Empire. It seems to have become a major political force only in the second half of the eighteenth century, however, as the rise of nationalist and liberal philosophies in Western Europe began to attract expatriate Greeks with some knowledge of Greek history. The expansion of Russian power in the Mediterranean during this period excited the imagination and ambition of local Greek leaders, who saw the Russians, Orthodox Christians like themselves, as natural allies against the infidel Turks. In 1770, Russia actively encouraged rebellions in western Crete (the revolt of Daskaloyannis of Sfakia) and the Peloponnese but allowed both uprisings to collapse ignominiously when it became evident that Russian interests would not benefit from a protracted involvement.

The Russians nevertheless continued to encourage anti-Turkish sentiment as a means of keeping the Turks damagingly busy in Greece (Kordatos 1972: 59), while the flourishing Greek merchant colonies in South Russia became centers of a swelling national consciousness. It was in Odessa, in 1814, that a group of Greek activists founded the Filiki Eteria ("Friendly Society"), a clandestine organization devoted to spreading nationalist propaganda throughout Greece; this group's work was a major factor in the development of national identity among the rural people.

France and Britain were slower than Russia to take an active role in Greek politics. Once the Greeks had risen in revolt, however, fear of each other's intrigues and of the predominance of the pro-Russian faction among the Greeks eventually forced their hand (Petropoulos 1968; Dakin 1973). The attitude of the Powers toward Greece was thus largely one of step-by-step opportunism, although it was invariably presented as a defense of the Greeks' best interests. The establishment of a monarchical system, designed in part to unite the warring Greek factions behind a disinterested ruler, became the focus of elaborate diplomatic activity on all sides; the eventual choice of Otto, second son of Ludwig I of Bavaria, was a compromise which brought home to the Greeks the impossibility of their taking any major political decision independently of the Powers' collective approval (Couloumbis, Petropoulos, and Psomiades 1976: 19-20; Dakin 1973: 275-290). While the European Powers played no small part in the eventual consolidation of the Greek nation-state, their intention was to form an entity made in their own image and upon their own terms.

It is difficult to know what the rural population thought of these developments. Their scanty acquaintance with Classical culture made it easy for European enthusiasts and western-educated Greeks to promote the ideal of a regenerated Hellas over their heads. Some historians have argued that the rural folk preserved no knowledge or memory of the Classical past at all. The rural Greeks certainly seem to have been puzzled by the expectations which the philhellenes entertained of them, to judge from the accounts of those non-Greeks who returned to tell the tale. If this was the situation at the time of the War of Independence, it seems to have been substantially the same for several centuries before that. While the Marxist historian Yanis Kordatos may be oversimplifying by stating that, at the time of the Turkish conquest in the fifteenth century, "only the learned who of necessity left Constantinople and Thessaloniki and went to Italy and Western Europe spoke of the ancient Greeks and of ancient Greece" (1972: 56, n. 1; cf., e.g., Vacalopoulos 1970), it is likely that few rural folk had any *detailed* knowledge of the ancient culture at that time. Much the same state of affairs seems to have obtained at least until the late eighteenth century, despite the growth of centers of learning in Epirus and elsewhere (on which see Henderson 1970). It was the educated minority who thought in terms of Classical culture, and it was largely in the West that they found the encouragement to do so.

The partially western origins of their vision hardly dismayed the Greek intellectuals, for whom all European wisdom was Greek by definition and derivation. Apart from such rare exceptions as the philosopher Johann Georg Hamann, Herder's mentor, most European thinkers were in general agreement with this position. What they did not endorse quite so readily was the Greeks' nationalistic extension of it. An example of this special attitude is provided by the nineteenth-century Greek historian and folklorist Spyridon Zambelios (1813?-1881), a prominent figure in this account, who proclaimed that Westerners writing their own history "had only consequences to illuminate; whereas, for the Hellene, *consequences* have the lesser rank. His history occurs in an epoch of causes, as a gospel of the genesis and dissemination of ideas, the beginning of fatherland (*patris*) and faith, wisdom, and freedom" (1852: 14).

Half a century earlier, Adamantios Koraes, whose admiration for the French Revolution was tempered by a deep respect for the cultivated ideals of the *ancien régime* (Clogg 1976: 127), had already described the Greeks' cultural primacy in scarcely more compromising terms:

It is France which had the glory of seeing in her own bosom that meet-

ing of philosophers who were the first, in the middle of the past century, to lay the foundations of that vast edifice known by the name
of the *Encyclopédie*. The light which rebounded from that literary
revolution, following the same laws as physical light, had necessarily to
spread clarity far beyond its own environment, in any place where it
encountered no obstacles. We have already seen that, for the Greek
nation, these obstacles had to be large indeed; but we should also have
observed that they were counterbalanced by the sentiments on which a
considerable part of the nation is nourished. The Greeks, proud of their
origin, far from closing their eyes to the lights of Europe, considered
the Europeans as mere debtors who would repay with very great interest a capital sum received by them from the Greeks' ancestors.

(1803: 12)

This is a clearly stated view of cultural relationships, phrased in the language of a philosophical nationalism. Note, first of all, the strong emphasis on
the "natural laws" of human development. The light of the intellect obeys
the same laws as physical light: the poetic conceit serves as an ideologically
powerful metaphor. There is *necessity* in such laws; thus, Greece will find its
just reward. Europe was not entirely unprepared for such a message; indeed,
in the half century following the publication of Koraes' words, Lamarckian
evolutionism had the effect of enhancing still further the general tendency to
place the Greeks at the historical and moral head of human development (cf.
Goodfield and Toulmin 1965). Zambelios' theory of cultural cause and effect, though it owes much to a "historicist" tradition which grew up in opposition to the French natural-law school, converged with Koraes' argument on
this assumption of the Greeks' cultural primacy.

Both arguments, moreover, involve two basic assumptions: the Greeks
constituted a nation, and they had done so before. It is easy to argue (e.g.,
Holden 1972: 22-23) that the Greeks had never previously been united in a
single independent polity, but this misses the point. With their extensive
knowledge of Classical literature, contemporary Greek intellectuals were not
likely to overlook the difference, in scale at least, between Periklean Athens
and a modern nation-state.[8] On the other hand, the Classical Greeks had certainly conceptualized their cultural unity, in opposition to the barbarians
(who were not so much "savage" as, quite simply, "not Greek"). The Greeks
of 1821 likewise had a sense of common religion, language, and customs. Part
of the problem of determining what it means to say that the Greeks were, or
had been, a nation lies in the difficulty of distinguishing *in Greek* between
"nationhood" and "ethnicity." Some such distinction nevertheless has to be
made for present purposes, for, while a shifting sense of collective identity
seems to have existed among Greek-speaking Orthodox Christians long before

1821, it is much less clear how much this constituted a set of national aspirations. Some historians take a critical position. According to Kordatos, for example, the nation (*ethnos*) "is a phenomenon of recent years, a historical phenomenon which had its starting point at the end of the Middle Ages, when feudalism began to be disrupted and the bourgeoisie came into the ascendant" (1972: 33). Whatever the justice of this view in strictly political terms, it should not lead us to assume that other forms of collective identity did not bind Greeks together in the centuries between the Fall of Constantinople and the Greek War of Independence.

Certainly, the formulation of a Greek national identity in terms of cultural continuity was something of a novelty to the largely illiterate country people. No less an observer than Koraes has recorded certain revealing reactions to the Classical revival among unlettered Greeks. It had been only a short while before, he remarked, that "for the first time one saw Greek vessels bearing the names of the great men of antiquity. Until then, only the names of the saints had been known. Today I know of vessels bearing the names of Themistocles and Xenophon" (1803: 44). Koraes was well aware that "in a country where once the wisest laws of Solon . . . reigned supreme," ignorance of the past was now a cardinal problem for the cause of Hellenic regeneration (Clogg 1976: 118-119).

Folk culture, for Koraes, was less a source of proof that the people actively yearned to recover their ancient virtues than evidence of their potential (and need) for extensive reeducation. His own experience, in which a series of lucky chances made it possible for him to acquire some learning at an early age (Clogg 1976: 121-124), may well have influenced his thinking here: the Hellenic virtues could be acquired, given only native diligence and aptitude. That one had to turn to Western Europe in this endeavor was simply a matter of historical circumstance, of the fact that Europe had been the repository of Greek learning during the centuries of Ottoman rule—a time when the Greeks themselves had acquired a shamefully Turkish patina which now had to be scraped away.

Koraes is today remembered most of all for his leading role in the development of *katharevousa*, the neo-Classical form of the modern Greek language which, somewhat ironically in the light of his revolutionary principles, has become closely associated with the political Right and the foreign interests which it represents (Sotiropoulos 1977). *Katharevousa* was always something of a cultural appeal to the West for recognition, an attempt to demonstrate that the ordinary Greeks of today could speak a tongue which was undeniably their own yet no less clearly Hellenic. Such purism naturally demanded that all words of obviously Turkish origin be eliminated. A recent commentator's description of this deorientalization of the language as "beneficial" (Babiniotis 1979: 4) shows how successful Koraes was in establishing a moral standard by which all subsequent linguistic developments could be evaluated. Ideological criteria of culture, if they are to be judged successful, must in some measure become self-fulfilling prophecies—a theme which will recur insistently in the following chapters of this book.

The development of *katharevousa* was part of Koraes' wider, educative view of Hellenic regeneration. Culture, rather than physical descent, still seems to have been the main component of Greekness in his day. Educated people throughout the Balkans called themselves Hellenes; in the Romanian princess Dora d'Istria, we shall later meet one of the latest and most flamboyant embodiments of this conceit. It seems, moreover, that language was sometimes thought virtually sufficient to make people forget that they had ever been anything but Greek—in 1802, there appeared a quadrilingual dictionary published by the priest Daniel of Moskhopolis, exhorting "all who now do speak / an alien tongue rejoice, prepare to make you Greek" (quoted in Clogg 1973: 20). This attitude was to change significantly later on, after the establishment of the new Greek State, when greater emphasis came to be laid on an essentially retroactive claim to descent from the ancient Greeks. Such shifts in the ideology of culture are not uncommon: the United States apparently experienced a somewhat similar switch to a descent-based ideology, with a retroactive attribution of descent "from the same ancestors, speaking the same language" (John Jay, quoted in Jones 1960: 140; see also Lipset 1963: 29), at a comparably postindependence phase. But, while massive immigration into the United States eventually led to the displacement of such ideas by both the melting-pot concept and emergent minority movements, Greek ideology developed in a very different direction: Koraes' cultural proselytizing gave way to claims, in the later nineteenth and the twentieth centuries, of the Hellenes' "racial" predominance throughout the Balkan Peninsula.

One People, Two Histories

The first president of independent Greece, Count John Capodistrias, was assassinated in 1831 by disgruntled Maniat leaders; the ensuing civil strife was brought to an end only with the installation of King Otto by the Great Powers in 1833. The Powers' effective domination of the country's internal politics was in fact generally recognized, the three principal parties being known as the English, French, and Russian (or Napist) (cf. Petropulos 1968; Couloumbis, Petropulos, and Psomiades 1976: 19). Internally, too, Greece was subject to the views of outsiders, for the new king brought with him a group of largely German advisers on whom he relied extensively in the administration of the country.

Ironically, however, under the more peaceful conditions which came with externally imposed rule, the Greeks had more ample opportunity to reflect on the nature of their national identity. With the nation-state an accomplished reality, the intelligentsia now had to come to terms with the obvious discontinuities between Hellenic ideal and Greek actuality. Foreign observers had already shown great interest, most of it benevolent, in the traditions of the Greek countryside: Kind and Tommaseo had published their collections of folksongs to an enthusiastic response from European intellectual circles; Goethe had expressed particular admiration for Greek songs after meeting another collector, Werner von Haxthausen, in 1815 (Kemminghausen and Sonter 1935: 7); while C. B. Sheridan had compounded the dangers of translation by publishing his own English rendering of Fauriel's French! There was thus a receptive audience for Greek folklore in Europe, and the Greeks had a vital political interest in maintaining it. On it depended their ability to convince their benefactors, once and for all, that they were truly the Hellenes of the new age.

What of this designation of "Hellene"? In the traditions of the rural Greeks, it had hitherto played a restricted and ambiguous role. Even those Greek scholars who attempted to demonstrate its survival in the popular memory were unable to show that it had been used by the peasantry as a category of *self*-designation rather than as the name of a mythical race long since vanished from the face of the earth. Its survival was nevertheless of crucial significance to the nationalist ideology, which may usefully be dubbed the Hellenist thesis. To exponents of this ideology, the term's perseverance through the long centuries of foreign domination represented the persistence of the Hellenic ideal itself on Greek soil; it could thus now be cited in retrospect as a supreme symbolic justification for what had been accomplished politically in the shape of the Greek nation-state.

But the Hellenist thesis was not without its critics inside Greece, even in the early years of independence. Their counterargument can be called the Romeic thesis (see also Kiriakidou-Nestoros 1975: 217-234, 1978: 155). According to this point of view, the self-designation of the Greeks had long been that of *Romii*, a name which echoes the Byzantine (East Roman) Empire and hence also the Orthodox Christian tradition to which the overwhelming majority of Greeks still adhered; the Greeks ordinarily called their spoken language *romeika* ("Romeic"), a usage which was even adopted by some of the travelers who visited their country while it was still under Turkish rule. A form of the Romeic name had been applied to all Greeks, and in Asia Minor to virtually all non-Moslems (Dawkins 1916: 641; cf. also s.v. *Hellas*, p. 598), by the Turks.

Most discussion of the relative merits of the two words, Hellenes and

Romii, has been conducted in the terms of an extremely literal sense of cultural history. The choice lies between ancient pagan glories on the one hand and the more immediate and familiar attractions of Orthodox Christianity on the other. Both sides to the dispute claim a strictly factual basis for their respective positions—an excellent illustration, if we need one, of the selective nature of historical explanation and, as such, an ideal introduction to the theme of this book. From a critical perspective, however, the issue is not simply one of selecting a favorite period of history. The Hellenic-Romeic distinction has another role in Greek discourse, one less obtrusive (but cf. Leigh Fermor 1966: 106-115) but nevertheless fundamental to the ideological division in question: the difference between an outward-directed conformity to international expectations about the national image and an inward-looking, self-critical collective appraisal. The outward-directed model is precisely what we may call political Hellenism; the introspective image is the essence of the Romeic thesis.

When a Greek wishes to make an affectionate or a disparaging comment on some aspect of the national culture—in other words, on something very familiar—the object is appropriately described as *romeiko*; this is equally apt for the ills of the bureaucracy, the crafty antics of the shadow-theater antihero Karagiozis, or the stereotype of the sexually aggressive male. Again, the demotic language, *romeika*, is full of acknowledged Turkisms and familiar colloquial expressions.

The Hellenic image is conceptually opposed to all these things. It is not, strictly speaking, a resurrection of everything Classical, as the shade of Aristophanes discovered during the censorious days of the right-wing Papadopoulos regime. It is, rather, a response to the European image of Classical Greece, as this was interpreted by the modern Greek nationalists in their turn. Its linguistic domain is *katharevousa* (although latterly all forms of Greek have been called *ellinika*, "Hellenic"). The Hellenic image is avowedly antiquarian, in sharp contrast to the familiarity of the Romeic. What more eloquent expression of this contrast could there be than the rural Cypriot use of *anttika* (cf. Italian *antico*; Kiprianou 1967: 43) to denote ugliness? Reverence for the ancient past would seem, at least in part, to be an intrusive idea in the culture of rural Greeks.

The linguistic aspect of the Hellenic-Romeic distinction is perhaps the most accessible to analysis. The invention and cultivation of *katharevousa* were consistent both with early philhellenic idealism and, in consequence, with the "outer-directedness" (Sotiropoulos 1977: 27-28) of Greek statecraft. This is a logical expression of political Hellenism (pace Holden 1972: 265), being a way of presenting the nation in a light acceptable to the West. Thus, the Hellenists' academic attempts to burnish the image of the modern

Hellene were expressions of "national pride" (*ethnikos eghoïsmos*; see, e.g., Apostolakis 1929: 57), of a desire to conceal whatever a foreign-educated audience might consider unseemly.

Again, the concern with appearances is especially obvious in the realm of language. At the turn of the century, according to the November 3, 1900 *Spectator*, it was still thought necessary to switch from the vernacular and to conduct conversations, "at least when strangers were present, in a curious jargon modelled upon Xenophon with a strong flavour of Dumas." The writer of these words, a British enthusiast for the demotic language and lore, found the Greeks to have been "eagerly employed for more than a century in the patriotic task of destroying their national language and literature, in order to substitute brand-new articles 'made in Europe' and guaranteed pure and classical by eminent professors." Bitter words, perhaps, but they were echoed by Greek as well as foreign critics of the Hellenist ideology, and they point up the salient paradox of *katharevousa*: this supposedly autochthonous tongue was in fact, to a considerable degree, a response to imported ideals. Greece was unique among the new European nations in not using the vernacular as the language of its *risorgimento*, and this, more than any other aspect of its cultural history, underscores the country's beholden condition (Sotiropoulos 1977: 8-9).

The tension between these mutually opposed images is also reflected in the way Greeks still talk about Europe. They may use the term *Evropi*, either in its geographical or in its cultural sense, to include themselves. This usage carries implicit overtones of the Hellenist ideology, of the view that the Greeks are central to the European entity. When, as they often do, they use *Evropi* to *exclude* themselves, they are in effect expressing the Romeic dimension of their identity. Such oscillation between two models is not the result of some "constant inconstancy of the Greek character" (Holden 1972: 31) but a linguistic and conceptual adaptation to the conflict between an imported ideology and a nativist one.

Local Claims, National Interests

In addition to their ideological preferences with regard to the broad question of national culture history, Greeks also had to decide what kinds of events had been decisive in shaping their recent accession to statehood. To some extent, of course, these two questions are aspects of the same issue. Thus, at its crudest, the Hellenist view equated history with war and war with patriotic joy—a formula further reduced to virtual caricature in recent school textbooks (Frangoudaki 1978: 112-113). Other problems of historical "fact," however, seem to have been determined by ideological elements of a different

order. Such, for example, is the date on which the Greek Revolution is supposed to have begun. This may seem an entirely straightforward empirical
problem. Yet, although Greek historians agree on the year of the outbreak of
war, the day and month are the subject of fierce debate. Why should this
be so?

The date of a national revolution is a momentous symbol of collective
identity. Whether it is literally correct or not may scarcely be relevant to
those who celebrate it, and even a demonstrably inaccurate date may be accepted by those who were involved in the original event; this, to cite an
especially dramatic instance, was the case with Thomas Jefferson and the
signing of the Declaration of Independence (Wills 1979). We can hardly expect that the date of the outbreak of guerrilla warfare in a largely illiterate
and divided land would be any less problematical. The date of a battle, still
more of a protracted and uneven period of war, entails complex questions of
definition and context (cf. Goldstein 1976: 68-70; Austin 1975: 143-144).
As to the *event* which *began* the *war*, the potential ambiguity is enormous.

The date usually selected for the national celebration of this event is
March 25, which is also the Feast of the Annunciation (*Evangelismos*).
Whether by design or not, a parallel is thereby suggested between the regeneration of Hellas and the prophecy of Christ's birth and resurrection. The Greek
term for "revolution" (*epanastasis*), with its strong overtones of "resurrection" (*anastasis*), reinforces that parallel. Local ecclesiastical involvement may
have added still further to the force of the religious analogy, for, on March
25, 1821, Metropolitan Germanos of Old Patras led an uprising from the
Lavra Monastery.[9] Other towns of the Peloponnese were also implicated in
the revolt, however, and several of them claim to have been the place from
which it started, in some cases even earlier than March 25 (Paleologos 1977).
Nor was the social basis of the revolution at all uniform. Even the *kotzam-
basidhes*, wealthy landowners who so feared for their privileges in the event
of a national uprising that Capodistrias was to dismiss them contemptuously
as "Christian Turks," joined the fight for fear of being still more completely
identified with Ottoman interests (Dakin 1973: 60). Thus, many different
groups and motives were represented in the initial revolts, which were hardly
coordinated at all. Various local leaders sought personal gratification and
power, and localist sentiment ran high from the start.

Not only are such allegiances still represented in the competition over the
birthplace of Greek freedom, but they played a significant part—which will be
discussed in a later chapter—in the development of Greek folklore research.
Since they continue to affect the deceptively simple-looking issue of when
and where the Revolution began (Petropulos 1976a), their effects on the
more diffuse problems of folklore should occasion no surprise.

Revolution as Resurrection

Such localist rivalries are also evidence of a wider, transcendent unity. The folklores of various regions are set in competition with each other to determine which of them best approximates pure Hellenism. Local scholars seek evidence not only that their respective regions have proved the most loyal to the revolutionary cause but that they have preserved the ancient customs and values better than any other. Logically, in a revolution which is also a resurrection of the past, antiquarianism and revolutionary ardor go hand in hand; archaeological folklore is the intellectual expression of patriotism.

These associations belong mostly to the Hellenist model. The Romeic alternative was slow to develop; it was perhaps out of tune with the struggle for international recognition in those early years. Admittedly, the theoretical contrast between the two models had begun to develop long before the War of Independence, notably over the language issue (Henderson 1970), but the political implications of the Romeic model were hardly compatible with the country's extreme dependence on foreign support. The premise of cultural continuity—the Hellenists' principal article of faith—suited the times far better.

In the first century of statehood, which takes up the greater part of this book, the Hellenist model was thus dominant politically and academically. Since the Greeks were obliged to build their nation-state under the watchful eye of more powerful countries, circumstances clearly favored the externally directed model over the introspective self-view. By the end of the first century of independence, other events allowed the Romeic model to develop more freely. But by that time, too, ideological Hellenism had done its work, and the modern Greek nation-state had become an irreversible reality of world politics. What follows is an account of the folklorists' contribution to that achievement.

Chapter 2
Extroversion and Introspection

". . . a certain important law of history . . ."

Folklorists to the Cause: Beginnings

The Greek Revolution united only three-quarters of a million people under the new authority (Dakin 1973: 1). Athens, whose temporary recapture by the Turks in 1827 seemed for a while to kill all hopes for the Hellenic regeneration (St. Clair 1972: 317, 330), was a small, economically unimportant town at the outbreak of fighting, with a mixed Greek and Albanian population that was later to attract Fallmerayer's gleeful scorn. It was only after the departure of the Turkish garrison as late as March 1833 that Athens, in succession to Nauplion, became the capital of Greece. As a mercantile and cultural center, it was quite eclipsed up to that point by such places as Thessaloniki, Smyrna, Constantinople, and Yannina—all in Turkish hands—and by the Ionian Islands, most notably Corfu, which were only ceded to Greece by Britain in 1864.

Corfu, indeed, plays a seminal part in the present story. The Ionian Islands were ruled by Venice from various dates, beginning with Zakynthos (Zante) in 1482 until the collapse of the Venetian republic in 1797, when they were annexed by France. In 1800 they were given republican autonomy under the joint protection of Russia and Turkey, an unstable arrangement which led to a two-year renewed annexation by France and thence, in 1809 to 1810, to British control. These islands thus had enjoyed far longer and closer contact with the West than any other part of Greece, and they were the home of a flourishing literary tradition—the birthplace of Dionisios Solomos (1798-1857), author of the Greek national anthem, and also of Count John Capodistrias (1776-1831). The Italian connection never really lapsed, as many Heptanesians went to Italy to study; Capodistrias himself studied medicine at the ancient university in Padua. Venice remained the alternative home of many Heptanesian literati who felt as comfortable with Italian as they did with Greek.

If we begin the Heptanesian part of this story with a character who was not noticeably interested in modern Greek folksongs at all, it is because he epitomizes the mixture of Italian and Greek culture against the background of which some of the first Greek excursions into folklore research must be seen and also, more particularly, because he was taken as a literary exemplar by at least one of the early folklorists, Zambelios. Niccolò Foscolo was born in 1778 on Zakynthos, the son of a Greco-Venetian nobleman and a Greek woman. He grew up speaking both the local form of Greek and Italian. In 1792 he left Zakynthos for Venice, where his mother had already established herself. Three years later, he changed his first name to Ugo, and it is as such that he is still celebrated as one of the major romantic poets of Italy. His friendship with Capodistrias, then an envoy of the Russian court, eventually procured him a safe passage to England, where he fled as a conscientious objector from service in the hated Austrian army (Marinoni 1926: 53-60); there, in lonely exile, he died in 1827, the year in which Athens was recaptured by the Turks and while the outcome of the Greek Revolution was yet in doubt.

Not that Foscolo, who made his name strictly as an Italian poet, had ever shown much commitment to the Greek cause. He was ambivalent on the question of his origins, even going to the point of devising—and publishing—two quite separate etymologies for his surname, one aristocratic and Italian, the other poetic and Greek (Marinoni 1926: 2)! The Italian version, which linked his family with the patrician lines of the Foscari and the Foscarini in a common derivation, was included in his study of the constitution of the Republic of Venice; while the Greek derivation—from *fos* ("light") and *kholos* ("melancholy"), giving the sense of *splendida bilis* "exalted by Horace as the source of great poetry"—appeared, appropriately, in a literary periodical. Such a concern with imaginative etymology is worthy of Vico at his most fanciful, and in fact there is some evidence (e.g., Luciani 1967: 185) that Foscolo was an admirer and imitator of Vico. If indeed he was, his life makes a still more apposite backdrop to the rise of a Vician circle which included Fauriel and Tommaseo, both collectors of Greek folksongs, and which apparently culminated in the work of Zambelios as far as Greek ethnology is concerned.

Foscolo's ethnic ambivalence dramatizes the curious situation of the Heptanesian Greeks, especially during this period when neither the Italian nor the Greek independence movement had come to full fruition. His Hellenism was literary and antiquarian, rather than personal and activist. Indeed, when the Italian ex-*carbonaro* Count Salvatore Santarosa called on Foscolo on his way to join the war in Greece, he found the poet, shattered by poverty and an exceedingly messy love affair, unwilling to share more than his obsession with the problems of translating Homer into Italian. The following description comes from Tommaseo's far from friendly pen. Foscolo "was translating

Homer with very great care.... In his letters he forgot his sadness; in letters and sadness, he forgot his homeland (*patria*). Santarosa went to see him the day before leaving for Greece, [to inquire] whether he wished anything for Greece, the land where he, Santarosa, was going to fight. Foscolo scarcely replied; then—'Hear these lines of Homer, see whether you like them.' This wounded Santarosa's very soul. To hear someone tell the story now is still more moving, when you think that this unhappy Italian was at that moment saying his last farewell to the Greek, ready to die for Greece, while the Greek just kept on fitting Italian grammatical suffixes to a conceit of Homer's!" (1953: 75; cf. 1904: 120). Worse was yet to befall the poor count. The Greeks gave him a more than reluctant welcome, and, in May of 1825, he met a sordid and unnecessary death at Turkish hands in a cave near Sfakteria (St. Clair 1972: 256).

Foscolo's Classicism was certainly "literary" rather than "patriotic or archaeological." It served nevertheless to excite the interest of another revolutionary of Venetian-Greek stock, the Corfiote Emilio de Tipaldo, who put enormous energy into compiling Foscolo's biography; it was to Tipaldo that Tommaseo, in a letter of 1835, wrote his sour account of the poet's encounter with Santarosa. Tipaldo was one of a group of cosmopolitan Italians[1] interested in Vico, especially in the nationalistic filtration of Vico's historical philosophy through the teachings of the Neapolitan historian and revolutionary Vicenzo Cuoco (1770-1823). Among the principal figures of this coterie were the *risorgimento* poet Alessandro Manzoni (1785-1873), the Dalmatian Niccolò Tommaseo (1802-1874), and the Corfiote politician, historian, and bilingual poet Andrea Mustoxidi (1785-1860). Mustoxidi, who was Tipaldo's brother-in-law and fellow philologist (Traves n.d.: 74), incurred Manzoni's eventual dislike; Manzoni, somewhat in the style of Tommaseo on the subject of Foscolo, thought that Mustoxidi's ingratitude to Italy was typical of the Greek revolutionaries (Tommaseo 1929: 12-14). Despite such tensions, however, this group of scholars displayed a considerable degree of intellectual coherence and a common range of interests.

They also enjoyed a close association with Claude Fauriel (1772-1844), who was greatly admired as a historian by his contemporaries and who was sufficiently comfortable in Italian to write competent verse in that language. Fauriel shared with the three Italians an active commitment to the cause of revolutionary nationalism. Manzoni and Tommaseo were in constant trouble with the authorities at home and even, on one occasion, managed to get Fauriel into bad odor with the Austrian police. Not that Fauriel was a stranger to police persecution; in fact, he had experienced it from both sides of the fence. A Jacobin in his early youth, he had managed to escape the excesses of the Terror in France and eventually became personal secretary to the notorious police chief Fouché in 1802. He apparently gave up this position—much to Fouché's disgust—at the insistence of his mistress, the widow of the French philosopher Condorcet; and it was to assuage his grief over her death in 1822 that Fauriel buried himself in work on his celebrated two-volume *Chants populaires de la Grèce moderne* (Sainte-Beuve 1870).

The Greek revolutionary intellectuals had their own share of trouble with foreign authorities. Mustoxidi, who had returned to Corfu from Greece after the assassination of Capodistrias in 1831 and was shortly thereafter made official historian of the Ionian Islands protectorate, was dismissed from his post by the British only four years later on the grounds that he had been intriguing with Capodistrias' Russophile political heirs—an incident which, for a while, earned him Tommaseo's sympathy and admiration (Manesis 1860-61; Tommaseo 1953: 69). In a reverse movement, Andreas Papadopoulos-Vrettos fled to Athens in order to escape harassment by the British. The biographer of Capodistrias (1837) and Mustoxidi (see Tipaldo 1860), this scholar is important in the present context as the author of an early treatise on the persistence of ancient Greek cultural traits on the Ionian island of Lefkas (1825). He claimed to have identified such connections in dances, costumes, marriage and funerary rites, songs, and divinatory techniques as well as in such unlikely or unverifiable features as the veiling of women (which he claimed to have traced to a story recorded by Pausanias).

The activities of this circle suggest the intimate relationship between political interests and the emergence of a serious approach to folklore. Capodistrias himself may have sent folksong texts to Goethe through the good offices of Mustoxidi (Bees 1956: xii). Mustoxidi, again, instructed both Fauriel and Tommaseo in matters relating to Greek language and folklore. Tommaseo was perhaps somewhat guilty of the ingratitude which he was so ready to attribute to others, for, although he requested and received extensive advice on matters of translation (especially with regard to demotic words without obvious Classical Greek antecedents; cf. Lascaris 1934), he claimed that Mustoxidi had great difficulty in speaking Greek; that Mustoxidi could not write his own language, though he sneered at the Venetian dialect of Italian spoken in the Ionian Islands as "a language of harlequins"; and that he wanted to make Classical Greek the ordinary language of conversation in Greece (Tommaseo 1929: 12). Yet the obvious affinity between these quarrelsome friends may be seen in the fact that they both served as ministers of education in short-lived utopian revolutionary governments, Mustoxidi in Capodistrian Greece and Tommaseo in Venice (Petropulos 1968: 115; Tommaseo 1953: 69).

Manzoni was in many ways the dominant figure of this group. He was an ardent admirer of Vico's philosophy, although it has been suggested (Colquhoun 1954: 51) that his understanding of it was restricted; it may be that he was nevertheless able to communicate some of his enthusiasm to the philhellenes and Greeks who came under his influence. Tommaseo and Fauriel were more careful Vicians; the Neapolitan's emphasis on repetitive process in history, his famous *corsi e ricorsi*, must have seemed analogous to the concepts of *risorgimento* in Italy and resurrection or renascence (*anayenisi* or *palingenesis*) in Greece. Tommaseo, especially, devoted critical study to Vico's work and collaborated with Tipaldo on a biography of the philosopher. He also attempted to apply Vico's etymological concepts, particularly the idea of a latent meaning which transcends all later semantic changes of a more superficial kind, to a study of the Illyrian tongue (Croce and Nicolini 1948: 600), an exercise which paralleled in more systematic form what Zambelios was meanwhile trying to do for Greek.

Fauriel, although he professed admiration for Vico's thinking, wrote relatively little about him, but there is some evidence that he and Manzoni discussed Vico's aesthetic views at considerable length (Croce and Nicolini 1947: 485). It is certain, in any case, that this group of romantic nationalists and writers shared a broadly common outlook in which their interest in Vico was a perceived and unifying element. Nor, since Vico had stressed the importance of such ethnographic materials as song, dance, and vernacular language for the understanding of a people's history, is it unlikely that interest in his work should have contributed to the awakening of the nationalists' interest in folklore.

The collecting of folksongs was not unknown among philhellenes even before Fauriel brought out his volumes. The German Werner von Haxthausen (1780-1842) had assembled a collection as early as 1814. Haxthausen, however, kept putting off publication, and in the end it was nearly a century before the compilation appeared in print. It nevertheless circulated in manuscript form among German scholars and writers; when Haxthausen met Goethe in Wiesbaden in 1815 and showed him his collection, Goethe was galvanized into exploring modern Greek folksongs for himself. Haxthausen came to hear of Fauriel's collection, which was rapidly translated into German for publication, and apparently hoped to collaborate with him. But the interest which Haxthausen's collection evinced in Germany, notably on the part of the Grimm brothers, never sufficed to prod him into publication, and it seems that he hoped that others would take on the responsibility of doing something with his material (Kemminghausen and Sonter 1935).

Haxthausen's and Fauriel's collections share one aspect which would probably not be regarded with so much tolerance today: they showed that it was not really necessary to go to Greece itself in order to amass a substantial corpus. Haxthausen collected some of his songs from sailors whose ships docked at British ports; for other material, he turned to Theodhoros Manoussis (1795-1858), a distinguished Greek academic who was then living in Vienna and who joined the first faculty of the University of Athens in 1837

(Spiridakis 1966: 478; Kemminghausen and Sonter 1935: 6 and n. 19). Fauriel obtained his material from Greek exiles in Venice, who were mostly too sophisticated to be of much help, and from the Greek colony in Trieste, as well as from such luminaries as Piccolos, Mustoxidi, and the great Koraes himself. He was indebted to these men of letters for much more than mere materials; as he freely acknowledged, the idea for a collection of Greek folksongs had originally been broached by Mustoxidi in a letter to Dimitrios Skhinas of the Academy of Bucharest (Bees 1956: xiii). Fauriel professed to regard it as nothing more than good fortune which enabled him to be the first to publish such a collection (Fauriel 1824, 1956: 2). In the same antiquarian tradition, in which secondhand materials were perfectly acceptable, Tommaseo likewise included songs gained through his scholarly collections; many of his texts are taken from Fauriel's two volumes, although in such cases he did not consider it necessary to reproduce the Greek originals again. There was apparently a very free exchange of materials among these scholars—Mustoxidi's correspondent Skhinas even possessed a copy of Haxthausen's manuscript (Kemminghausen and Sonter 1935: 22).[2]

These early foreign collectors seem to have been extremely scrupulous in the care which they took over the accurate rendering and translating of their texts. Tommaseo's letters to Mustoxidi bear witness to his industrious determination to make no mistakes. In a passage which may echo his revered Vico in its scorn for the pedant and its respect for the folk poet, Tommaseo writes, "Whoever knows no other poetry than that of printed books, *whoever does not venerate the folk (popolo) as a poet and inspirer of the poets*, let him not rest his eye upon this collection, which is not made for him. Let him condemn it, let him scorn it: we will consider this praise indeed" (1841, I: 5; my emphasis). Later in the same passage, he explicitly denies himself the right to emend Tuscan folksong texts. To do so, he says, would be a "sacrilegious folly"; he was, according to Cocchiara (n.d.: 106-107), equally careful of the Greek texts which he published. Fauriel, too, appears to have left the texts very much as he found them, and his renderings were even used a century later (Apostolakis 1929) as a yardstick with which to measure the textual alterations of Zambelios. The transcriptions of Tommaseo and Fauriel may not be completely faultless, but it is an indication of their austere scholarship that they preferred to leave blank any uncertain passages of the Greek rather than attempt imaginative reconstructions. Of his Tuscan texts, again, Tommaseo wrote that he "would certainly not think of suppressing and condemning . . . any of the sweet wording" (1841, I: 14). As foreigners, Fauriel and Tommaseo perceived as pearls of primitive naïveté textual elements which local folklorists of Hellenist persuasion were to find embarrassingly inconsistent with their loftier view.

It is certainly possible that Fauriel and Tommaseo refused to print texts

which they thought vulgar or bawdy, although their criteria were undoubtedly less stringent than those of their Greek successors. Expurgation (cf. Goldstein 1967) was a feature of Western European scholarship at that time, and
academic detail surrendered more easily to prudery. Robert Pashley's response to some bawdy songs about the sexual antics of monks is at least
honest: "Of such effusions of the modern Grecian muse, every Englishman,
writing in the nineteenth century, must feel it difficult to publish specimens:
and I cannot venture to transcribe those which I heard" (1837, I: 146).
More's the pity, although Pashley does insure that we understand that there is
a lacuna in his account at this point. Over the years, the cumulative expurgation and bowdlerization of folklore were to result in a massively unbalanced
portrait of the rural Greek as a sexual innocent (e.g., Lee 1959), in accordance with the ideological requirements of the outward-directed model of the
Hellenists.

Although there is no clear evidence on the matter, then, it is possible that
Fauriel and Mustoxidi censored their own materials; it is nevertheless no less
likely that their educated Greek informants exercised a certain discretion in
the first place. There is certainly a "moral" aspect (Martellotti 1943: x-xi) to
Tommaseo's classification of the folksongs under four thematic categories:
love, family, death, and God. But this schema, while quite in harmony with
the Hellenists' moral sensibilities, offered them no particular advantage in
their search for antiquarian connections and was never adopted by them.

Despite the conceptual differences between Fauriel and Tommaseo, on the
one hand, and the indigenous Hellenists on the other, all were agreed on the
inherent virtue of the Greek cause. Tommaseo's indignation at the unpatriotic
escapism of Foscolo is matched by the admiration which Fauriel, in the extensive introduction to his *Chants*, expresses for the newly resurgent Greeks.
Fauriel had already published, in 1823, a translation from the Italian of a
poem by Berchet about the flight of the Greek population of Parga, one of
the saddest episodes of the period immediately preceding the outbreak of the
Greek Revolution. Now, a year later, he enthusiastically declared that the
Greeks' own folksongs "would make modern Greece loved and known and
would demonstrate that the spirit of the ancients, the breath of poetry, lived
there yet." And he urged the Greeks "to collect what has not already been
lost of their folksongs. Europe will owe them gratitude for whatever they do
to preserve them; while they themselves will one day be enchanted, because
they will be in a position to acknowledge these products of a wise and cultivated poetry, these simple monuments of the spirit, history, and customs of
their ancestors" (see Fauriel 1956: 86). With these solemn words, the concept of folklore as a repository of verbal *monuments* enters, at an early date,
the intellectual apparatus of Greek folklore studies.

A Greek Reaction

In the eyes of their Greek critics, enthusiasm on the part of foreign observers was not enough. The academic tradition of Europe, so despised by Tommaseo, took root strongly in Greece as a source of legitimation for the Hellenist thesis. What both Tommaseo and Fauriel had presented in their studies was essentially the Romeic view of Greece—a view of the peasantry as it saw and expressed itself. This was difficult for the Hellenists to accept. For, if the Hellenists were outward-directed in terms of their audience, they held strict views as to what was suitable fare for that audience. It was time, they thought, to construct a truly national history of their own.

The first task was clearly to slough off the foreigners' interpretations of Greek history and culture. The philhellenic conceit was now turned against itself. Zambelios states the impassioned subjectivism which this entailed: "The past? Alas! we allow foreigners to portray it to us under the prism of their prejudices and according to the circumstance of their systems and self-interests. . . . Yes! And why should we hide it? Our fathers molded *truth*, a broadly based, vital, genuine truth; whereas we forge myths—myths, moreover, which are not in the least philosophical in the manner of our ancient and ancestral ethos, with suggestions of exalted significance, but foreign ones, disguised in ancient clothing, alien specters, introducing to us the deceptions and distortion of western silliness" (1852: 7-9).

A more extreme and distinctly *ad hominem* version of this attitude is to be found in the attack which George Evlambios launched on Fauriel in 1843. Evlambios' book, *The Amaranth: The Roses of Hellas Reborn*, is a collection of folksong texts evidently intended to supplant Fauriel's. Its title expresses the Hellenist view of Greece as an evergreen plant (*amarandos*) which nevertheless—the essential paradox again—was now undergoing resurrection. It also implies the usual thesis that whatever was good in the vernacular culture was but a resurgence of antique values. And its characteristic outward-directedness is evident in that it was published abroad, in Saint Petersburg, in a bilingual Greek and Russian text.

Even by the time Evlambios attacked him in this work, Fauriel had become firmly established as one of the brightest stars of philhellenic scholarship. The polemic is suitably muted at first: "The effort and labor of Fauriel are exceptionally worthy of respect. But Fauriel, as a foreigner, was not familiar with modern Greek life and was obliged to accept whatever was offered to him as a product of folk creativity. For this reason, in his collection we encounter alterations and distortions—if the expression may be permitted me" (1973: i). Evlambios then begins his specific argument with the criticism that Fauriel had included in his collection of oral poetry verses by Rigas and Solomos. This is patently unfair: Fauriel, far from pretending that these poems were from oral sources, acknowledged and praised their authors' patriotic sensibility (Bees 1956: ix). It is possible, of course, that Fauriel considered demotic poetry sufficiently close to the oral idiom to merit inclusion under the somewhat ambiguous heading of *traghoudhia* or *chansons*, both of which may be used for written verse; his compatriots, Voutier (1826) and Marcellus (1851), were to include many more such literary creations in their published collections.

Evlambios then directs his fire at Fauriel's lack of firsthand acquaintance with Greek customs. He begins by noting that Fauriel's collection of distichs lacks coherence between the texts. This criticism, which has some basis, is the best evidence that Evlambios can muster of his own more intimate knowledge of Greek folkways. Semantic continuity between distichs is considered essential to effective performance in many parts of Greece (Herzfeld 1981c), although only a few folklorists have bothered to explore it (e.g., Aravandinos 1880). It is to Evlambios' credit, and a considerable aid to his credibility, that he observed this characteristic.

But he descends anew into ill-considered polemic when he criticizes Fauriel's textual accuracy. Foreigners, he argues, should not attempt the impossible by seeking to penetrate the mysteries of Greekness—a frequently adopted position among the Hellenists. "I do not know," he observes early in the preface of his book, "whether a foreigner can ever assimilate the spirit (*pnevma*) of another people (*laos*) to the point of daring to correct and alter the people's creations, especially when the Greeks themselves—born and bred in their fatherland, and in contact from childhood on with their customs and language—do not give themselves such a right" (1973: ii).

This would be questionable criticism were it only for the fact that just one collection of folksongs, an anonymous volume produced in Nauplion in 1832 and known to Tommaseo, had so far been published by a Greek and in Greece. Evlambios could not foresee the extent to which later Greek scholars would accord themselves that forbidden "right" of textual emendation, it is true, and this was a habit which he was quite justified in distrusting; in 1865, for example, the scholarly journal *Pandora* published an entire set of folksongs which were later exposed as spurious (Politis 1973: lviii). But the specific complaint which Evlambios lodges against Fauriel in this connection is less than effective. Fauriel had published the text of a short song lamenting the death of the guerrilla leader Zidros (1956: 116-117). Since he thought the text incomplete (for in this respect he was as much of a literalist as any of his contemporaries), he added a fifth line—*in the French translation only*. The Greek text is presented, as far as it is possible to tell, exactly as he received it. Yet Evlambios excoriated this as a "creation of the author's Gallic imagination" (1973: xi). The charge is all the more curious in that Fauriel, who had wanted to print the Greek texts using a strictly demotic orthography (i.e., omitting terminal /n/ where it was not pronounced), had been persuaded not to do so by his scholarly Greek friends (1956: 2)—they were *katharevousiani*, linguistic Hellenists. Only much later (1854: 61) did he recover his self-confidence sufficiently to insist on the autonomy of the demotic forms.

Nor is this all, for the attack on Fauriel's intellectual honesty follows an equally bitter criticism of the French writer's failure to censor his own materials more effectively! Thus, "among many poetical verses," grumbles Evlambios, "the reader suddenly encounters prosaic phrases and even, finally, vulgarities—among the demotic songs are included worthless and coarse compositions. This curious mélange, ornamented with freshly concocted song titles, constitutes an ill-formed edifice, wherein marble ornaments are covered by piles of undressed masonry" (1973: ii). Such examples of "worthless" and "peasantish" folklore as Fauriel is charged with improperly including have since passed muster with folklorists in Greece, although, since they do not meet the canons of "European" poetics, they have attracted little study locally. In any event, Fauriel's alleged vulgarities (1825: 70, 150, 160) were not particularly offensive even by the austere moral standards of his time. In objecting to the use of invented song titles, however, Evlambios does identify a source of future confusion. Just like any other taxonomic device, single-text song titles presuppose that the reader will accept the collector's view of what the song is about and therefore tend to direct all subsequent interpretation (cf. also Herzfeld 1973).

Perhaps the most symptomatic part of Evlambios' diatribe, however, is the passage in which he attacks Fauriel's treatment of funeral dirges. Fauriel experienced some difficulty in obtaining specimens of this genre—not, perhaps, surprisingly, since villagers are still sometimes reluctant to conjure up the specter of death and misfortune for the inquisitive stranger. He did manage to secure one specimen (1825: 262), but, storms Evlambios, "very oddly, he considers that this imaginary dirge was performed by a Turkish woman" (1973: iv). Evlambios' disgust can be understood only in the light of his assumption that "the dirges (*miroloyia*) are the only exclusively Greek form of song" (1973: vi). If sustained, that essentially taxonomic assumption would of necessity either debar Fauriel's specimen from the category of dirges or discredit his attribution of it to a Turkish woman. Evlambios tries to achieve both ends, and it must be said that this was an entirely consistent procedure in the terms of his operative scheme of classification. Fauriel, however, explains quite clearly that the performer was Turkish in what we should today recognize as the broader Greek sense of being a Greek-speaking Moslem. Evlambios, by contrast, took the term in its literal or national sense, and this left him no option but to construe Fauriel's attribution as definitionally impossible. Yet his argument is a curious construction of events on the part of one who claimed to be close to the folk: it entails the imposition of an absolute, literalist classification of ethnicity upon the vernacular idiom.

Evlambios' familiarity with folk customs seems not to have been geographically extensive. Fauriel's remark that his text was improvised by the singer is in agreement with many reports now available (cf. Alexiou 1973). But Evlambios, without the advantage of the accumulated materials which we now have at our disposal, could not believe in the existence of such extemporaneous performances: "The dirges which *I* publish here show how unfounded Fauriel's information is. Dirges were, on the contrary, *specific* songs (*traghoudhia*) which were learned like other popular songs. . . . Upon the experience and the ability of the keener depended whether she might add something of her own to the dirge, something directly connected with the life of the deceased. Those additions were no longer sung but pronounced in a grief-stricken voice" (1973: iv, n. 1). Evlambios here overlooks the fact that vernacular usage makes a somewhat less rigid distinction between "speaking" and "singing" than do *katharevousa* or the Western European languages.[3] His tendency to generalize from restricted ethnographic data to a panhellenic canvas is a logical consequence of the doctrine of Greek cultural unity.

In Evlambios' work, especially in his treatment of Fauriel, certain salient aspects of the Hellenist thesis are apparent. Above all, it is taken as axiomatic that an educated Greek will automatically possess the innate ability to speak for and interpret the entire national culture. The connection with Classical culture, moreover, is a matter of doctrine and, as such, overrides any apparent discontinuities: "The Fates of the modern Greeks are *the same* [my emphasis] as the Fates of the ancients. Here are the names of today's Fates: *Mira, Tikhi, Riziko*; the names of the ancient ones were *Clotho, Lachesis*, and *Atropos*" (1973: cvi). What Evlambios does not point out is that both *riziko* and *mira*, like the cognate Classical *moira*, are generic terms for fate; modern villagers do not give personal names to the three old women who determine their destinies at birth. *Tikhi*, on the other hand, was (and is) also a generic term ("luck") but was personified as a minor deity (Tyche) in Hellenistic times. To establish "sameness," Evlambios has had to give very short shrift to the survival of such generic terms in order to make his case for the more "mythological" survival of the three personified fates. This argument involves an unusually high degree of special pleading to demonstrate some sort of connection with the Classical past; we do not find it reproduced in the more detailed analyses of the mythology of fate by Schmidt, Wachsmuth, or Politis.

But the most diagnostic feature, which Evlambios displays in an unusually raw form, is the view that Greek folklore should be left to the Greeks. By Evlambios' time, the fight to refute the theories of Fallmerayer was already under way. Fauriel, however, seems a comparatively improbable target for

such attacks, unless it is borne in mind that the outward-directed ideology of
the Hellenists logically debarred foreigners in general from prying into Greek
culture on their own account. Not all Hellenist scholars adopted this extreme
position, of course; Politis, in particular, drew upon the modern Greek researches of Schmidt and Wachsmuth, and other Hellenist scholars (e.g., Spiridakis 1966) have acknowledged the contribution of early voyagers' accounts.
Yet Evlambios' more aggressive and xenophobic posture deserves sympathetic
consideration. The philhellenes had fostered an idealized picture of the
Greeks; it must have seemed capricious in the extreme that now, when an independent nation-state had finally been achieved, they should be prepared to
contaminate that picture with their "Romeic" insights. For contamination is
just what the "vulgarities" of certain songs imply, as does the idea that a
"Turkish" woman might sing a characteristically "Greek" genre of song. The
Greekness of the dirges, indeed, was soon to become a more elaborate tool of
the Hellenist thesis in the hands of Zambelios. For, by the time that he took
up his own pen, in his native Ionian Islands, a sophisticated and western-in-
fluenced version of the Romeic model was already in full swing from within.

The Pedant and the People

Corfu, capital of the Heptanese, had long been a center of intellectual activity
when the toga-clad British philhellene, Lord Guilford, established his short-
lived university there in 1860. Unlike Athens, where the overwhelming majority of scholars were committed Hellenists, many of the Corfiote intellectuals were demoticists. Their leading figure was the poet Solomos, a friend and
associate of Manzoni, Tommaseo, and—for a while—Zambelios. Tommaseo
includes some folksongs which Solomos had recorded in his native Zakynthos, and Solomos regarded folk poetry as a rich source of understanding and
documentation for the systematic study of the demotic tongue. Solomos, indeed, advocated a conscious program of nation-forming literary activity, in
which the demotic language would serve as the vehicle whereby the great
works of foreign literature and philosophy would be introduced to the Greek
people. He inspired many imitators and disciples, among whom Iakovos
Polilas (1826-1898) was probably the most fanatical—as Zambelios, after his
break with Solomos, was to discover to his cost.

Another member of Solomos' circle of friends was Andonios Manousos,
whose collection of folksongs was published in Corfu in 1850. Zambelios'
parallel but Hellenist venture appeared there in 1852. Since Zambelios' quarrel with Solomos—and thus with the entire demoticist camp—followed hard
upon the publication of his own collection, the emergence of two distinct
streams of folklore research, essentially the "literary" (demoticist) and the
"patriotic or archaeological" (Hellenist), can be said to have begun in this

period. Zambelios is often claimed by today's Hellenist folklorists as their first major intellectual ancestor (e.g., Spiridakis 1966: 485-487; Orlandos 1969: 6); Manousos, by contrast, is at best cursorily mentioned by them. Midcentury Corfu is thus a watershed in the historical development of two distinct ideological styles of folklore research.

Somewhat in the self-consciously antiacademic manner of Tommaseo, who explicitly denies himself the dubious pleasure of writing a formal introduction to his Greek songs, Manousos refuses to announce his collection with the kind of "methodological" prologue composed by Evlambios and Zambelios. Perhaps this refusal contributed to the relative obscurity into which his work has fallen. Certainly, his comments on individual texts are suitably patriotic and scarcely depart from the Hellenists' position. The references to a common Greek fatherland (*patridha*), the assumption that kleftic songs (i.e., songs of brigandage under Turkish rule) constituted a discrete category of patriotic texts (cf. chap. 3), the treatment of the guerrilla leader Odysseus' death as the result of his enemies' vindictiveness rather than of his own treachery (cf. St. Clair 1972: 190, 239; but also Petropulos 1976b)—all these devices are part of the Hellenists' position, except, perhaps, the charge that the "penpushers" (*kalamaradhes*) were to blame for Odysseus' demise. In Manousos' work, we see immediately that the dispute between the Hellenists and the demoticists was conducted on a considerable area of common ground through the medium of shared concepts and vocabulary. Yet the sharpness of his polemic against academic pedantry certainly does not suggest any sense of compromise.

Manousos' ideological preferences are made especially clear by his substitution of a dramatized discussion for the conventional introduction. This imaginary confrontation is conducted by a wordy pedant, the populace (*laos*), a friend of the author, and the author-editor himself. (It is perhaps significant in this context that Manousos chose to portray himself as an editor [*sindaktis*] rather than in the more actively interventionist role of author, since the point of the whole argument is to decry the excessive interference of pedantic scholars.) The contrast between the pedant's extreme *katharevousa* and the simple demotic of the other characters invests the scene with a piquant irony, foreshadowing a recurrent feature of future Greek scholarship in the humanities by the use of different language "registers" to emphasize ideological distance. The pedant, naturally, gets the worst of Manousos' lampooning. The speech of "your Four-times-secretarial-Penpushership," as he is unctuously addressed, is reduced to the most pompous neo-Classical posturing imaginable. The contrast thereby induced vividly conveys the tensions and confusions which could be generated by the *ghlossiko zitima* ("language question"), as it came to be called.

A clear connection is thus established between linguistic attitudes and the question of the scholar's position in Greek culture. Manousos' disclaimer of any right to emend the texts is phrased in terms of attitudes—particularly the peasants' expectation that the scholars will assert, rightly or wrongly, a privileged ability to explain rural customs—which the ethnographer may still encounter in the Greek countryside. The opening words of the tableau set the tone:

> *Member of the populace:* Excuse me, but would you print our songs?
> *Editor:* You mean that *I* should publish them in printed form? Why? Will you criticize me at all?
> *Another member of the populace:* Not at all! Does it look likely? We're illiterate (*aghrammati*)—that's no job of ours!
> *Editor:* You are mistaken, my friends. These are your own creations, the outpouring of your soul, and nobody can better hear them to correct their omissions and errors than yourselves.
> *Another:* It may be as you say. But we haven't come now in order to correct you but to do our duty and thank you for broadcasting and praising what [we do] in the sweetest hours of our lives, when our souls are at rest with a glass in one hand and love in the other, forgetting their toils and travails and finding comfort and pleasure in song.
> *Editor:* I accept your thanks, as a gift of kindness, not as a duty. The duty is not only my own but that of all Greeks who have had some sort of education and upbringing, who, if they love their nation (*ethnos*) wholeheartedly, must make a careful study of that nation, not leave its brilliant creations unstudied and on the brink of oblivion.   (1850: 3-4)

In a complaint which he shares to a remarkable degree with Zambelios, the editor then compares the sorry state of Greek folklore scholarship with the interest and enthusiasm which foreigners of many nations have shown for the songs of the rural Greeks. But Manousos, lacking the defensive selectivity of the Hellenists, does not at least display any disapproval of the foreigners' role; his criticism is all directed against his compatriots.

The demoticists' respect for the integrity of the oral texts was to remain a canon of their ideology, sometimes to the point where their accusations of meddling fell on dubious grounds (e.g., Apostolakis 1929). Manousos, in this early representation of the ideological choice which confronted an editor in folklore, brings to the reader's attention a besetting ambiguity of the editorial role. On the one hand, Manousos respected the oral character of the texts and said so; on the other, he wished to save them for posterity as a spiritual monument, a task which required that they be frozen on the printed page. As a scholar, he had to confront the peasants' self-abasement as "illiterates"—a term not necessarily meant in an absolute sense but indicating the contrast with his own erudition—yet he championed the superiority of the oral poet over the learned fool. Perhaps the funniest moment in his tableau comes when the pedant ironically praises the editor, in an archaizing style which lacks only the elegance of Attic Greek, for exhibiting "miraculous ingenuity in working with such . . . I dare to say virtually dead material" (1850: 6). The editor, pretending to toady to this overweening pedagogue, asks how he is to save himself from the consequences of such misguided enthusiasm for folk culture."Change the language!" recommends the pedant. The editor demurs: how can one change the language of one's fathers—the immediate, Romaic fathers, as it were? "Write, my dear friend," the pedant tells him, "in a manner totally devoid of meaning, and behold! the problem is solved" (1850: 8-11).

This is a conflict between histories. In the one, the forefathers are those who spoke the same language as the editor and who passed it on to him in turn. In the other, they are the long-dead Greeks of ancient times, whose speech must be pruned of all real significance in order—thought Manousos—to achieve a convincing sense of continuity with the pedantic *katharevousa* of the Hellenists. In the Hellenist view, of course, the "living" traditions must indeed be "dead," as the pedant makes them; in the neo-Classical utopia, they would have no appropriate context of their own. Here Manousos caricatures what he saw as the worst folly of the *katharevousiani*, and he was perceptive enough to realize that the issue had dimensions far wider than those of language alone.

But, in the sphere of language, Manousos makes it fully explicit that his quarrel is with Hellenism. In the concluding speech of the tableau, the editor summarizes the logic of his own argument: "But all those who babble that the Greek (*grekiki*) language becomes better *the more it approaches the Hellenic (elliniki)* seem to me to be doing the same as though they were scheming to correct a naturally beautiful and pretty young woman and to fix her face like that of an old dame so that she might appear to have the beauty she had enjoyed in her youth and no longer possesses" (1850: 14; my emphasis). It had long been usual to distinguish between modern demotic and Classical Greek as *romeika* and *ellinika*, respectively; Manousos' use of the slightly more obscure *Greki* for *Romii* is an Ionian dialect usage, possibly affected here, which hardly disguises the nature of the contrast which he was making. That contrast pitted against each other two cultural ideologies, two Greek languages, two readings of Greek history, two concepts of the Greeks' place in the world and of the Greek scholars' place among their people.

The Greek Past Regained: Zambelios

Manousos' espousal of the Romeic cause is explicit and unqualified. Hardly more compromising is the first major development in folklore studies of the Hellenist ideology by Spyridon Zambelios (1813?-1881), likewise a member of the circle around Solomos until projected into an adversary position by offended dignity and divergent views.

Relatively little is known of Zambelios' life, although what we can glean shows a cosmopolitan Heptanesian intellectual of distinctly hot temper. He was born on Lefkas, the son of a writer of neo-Classical tragedies, and was sent to study at various famous establishments of learning—it is not known which ones—in Western Europe (Zambelios 1902). He eventually inherited an Italian estate in the vicinity of Leghorn (Livorno), and it was here that he appears to have spent a considerable part of his mature life. His last known work, a discourse on the prehistory of the Greek and Latin languages, was published in Paris in 1880, and he died in Zug, Switzerland, the following year. He thus spent much of his later life outside Greece and his native Heptanese, perhaps soured by that failure to achieve recognition which had partially contributed to his break with Solomos (Valetas 1950: xxii). Zambelios seems, in fact, to have been a choleric and demanding person; for example, when his illegitimate son wanted to marry, Zambelios *père* decided that he wanted the young bride for himself, and when the son refused to cooperate the father disinherited him, leaving his entire estate to some Cretan philanthropic institutions instead (Kambanis 1920: 23-25). Similarly, he refused to forgive the equally truculent Solomos for calling him an idiot, although the insult was delivered when the poet was a patently sick man (Jenkins 1940: 196-197), but took up a lonely and embittered offensive against Solomos' reputation until well after the latter's death in 1857.

The initial occasion for their quarrel arose in 1853. In the previous year, Zambelios had published a monumental collection of folksongs, prefaced by an extremely long and solemn "Historical Study of Medieval Hellenism." This combination of archive and essay, probably Zambelios' most substantive work of scholarship, is notable both for the weight of detail adduced in support of the main argument and for its majestic claims of intellectual originality. Solomos, however, derided it for "putting Hegel into a slouch hat"—a strange remark, certainly, when we consider that it was addressed by a self-proclaimed Hegelian to a writer who later (1859) attacked *him* for his heavy reliance on the German philosopher.

Zambelios' indubitable pomposity and his often inaccurate handling of historical materials all too easily obscure the principal merit of his essay, for this work departed significantly from the embryonic tradition of historical writing which then existed in Greece. Its novelty lay in the frank admission, indeed the insistence, that a medieval phase of some importance in its own right connected the Greeks with their ancient forebears. Zambelios eagerly confronted the absurdity of virtually ignoring a millennium of history and pointed out that it was not necessary to do so in order to posit continuity between the Classical and modern periods. Instead, he maintained, it would be more useful to treat the medieval phase as the connecting link (*krikos*) between the ancient and modern cultures. Throughout the centuries of political upheaval, invasions, population movements, and foreign domination, as Zambelios' novel approach would show, the Greeks had retained all their ancient genius and had remained fundamentally unchanged in spirit.

Zambelios proposed to recognize three phases of Greek history: the modern, the medieval, and the ancient, each neatly self-contained. The medieval phase was a time of ethnic regression, during which many signs of an unquenchable Hellenic consciousness were nevertheless in evidence. The tension between the imperial throne of Byzantium and the Orthodox Patriarchate was described, in this connection, as a conflict between "Roman" (and therefore foreign) authoritarianism, on the one hand, and the democratic spirit of Classical Greece which the Greeks had perpetuated in the institutions of their church, on the other. For the defense of the Hellenist model, it was logically necessary to define the "Roman" or "Romeic" element as foreign and, therefore, undesirable. But Zambelios did not scorn peasants in the style of Manousos' pedant, and he did not in any sense dismiss popular lore as either dead or foreign. Instead, he saw folklore and the church as the two great repositories of the true Greek character, and he attributed the almost complete lack of a truly Hellenic documentary history of the medieval phase to the foreign rulers' egotistical control over the court chroniclers.

Zambelios' respect for the vernacular traditions, which contrasts with his own use of a strict *katharevousa*, is solidly evidenced by his very substantial collection of folksongs. These alone could supply the deficiencies of the "Roman" chroniclers, albeit only in a very general way; Zambelios does not elicit specific historical insights from each text separately, as others later tried to do. He also felt free to emend texts without indicating that he had done so, perhaps on the implicit argument that as a Greek he was a participant in the same culture as the singers. In this he made an assumption similar to that of Evlambios, but without the latter's self-restraint in the matter of textual alterations: a Greek was the best-qualified person to understand Greek folklore. He was also, it appears, convinced of his own poetic talents (Apostolakis 1929: 34).

The oral origins of the texts make it extremely difficult to ascertain exactly how much they have been tampered with. Since many of the songs have since disappeared from the living repertoire, there is little reliable material available for comparison. The "Romeic" folklorist Yannis Apostolakis

(1896-1947) attempted a detailed critique of Zambelios' emendations, but his openly avowed subjectivism raises legitimate doubts about his own critical acuity. It must be remembered that by 1929, when Apostolakis' criticisms appeared in print, the Hellenists must have already had a considerable influence on the shape and content of the rapidly dwindling folk repertoire, just as *katharevousa* was progressively infiltrating the demotic language. Apostolakis was also German-trained, so his claim to instinctive knowledge of the folk aesthetic is not wholly reassuring. In his exposition, moreover, there are occasional switches to a more Hellenist style of reasoning, indicating once more how difficult it was for the Romeic scholars to escape the theoretical framework of assumptions which the Hellenists had constructed.

Let us briefly consider Apostolakis' treatment of one of Zambelios' texts, in order to illustrate these points more fully. The song in question describes the departure of a young man for distant parts and his eventual temptation into forgetting his family. "Whereas the son bids farewell in the presence of his mother and his father, his mother at the end bids him not to forget her and her [other] children, while of her husband—his father—not a single word is heard. Such an omission is strange, if not indeed *unnatural*. Well known to us, *and we know on our own account*, are the respect and *tender love with which a wife was wont to look on her husband* in the *Hellenic home*" (Apostolakis 1929: 22-23; my emphasis). Such knowledge of rural conditions and conventions is partly derived from the song texts themselves, with all the editing and selection which they had previously undergone, and seems to conflict with some firsthand ethnographic observations (e.g., Campbell 1964: 151). The constraints which the early collectors set on subsequent perceptions are always, to some extent, inescapable.

Yet some of the evidence for textual interference is more convincing and serves to point up the magnitude of the problem. Apostolakis' criticism is at its most incisive when he finds Zambelios outdoing other Hellenists, rather than foreigners or demoticists, in the patriotic editing of a common text. An example is provided by a song celebrating a guerrilla raid on one of the Zagori villages in Epirus. In one version of the song—not Zambelios'—the robbers calculatingly interrogate their female captives:

> *They were taken and questioned, each in turn,*
> *as to whose husband would turn out to be the best touch for a ransom.*

Zambelios, however, saw these robbers as wild heroes of the national revival. In the text which he presents, no explicit mention is made of anything so despicable as a ransom, although it is a matter of recorded history that extortion of this kind did occur where villagers were wealthy enough to make it a worthwhile proposition:

> *They put them in the middle and questioned them again and again:*
> *which of them had the worthiest husband, the truly brave man?*
> *Angeliki, the daughter of Koumos' wife, has a truly brave husband—*
> *his legs are strong like a Hellene's, his chest like a lion's.*

Zambelios, according to his critic, here found a way to "exhibit the ethnic pride of the robbers and of the women, as well as his own." A text published at a *later* date by a scarcely less committed exponent of the Hellenist thesis (Aravandinos 1880: 87) explicitly spelled out the demand for a ransom, thereby casting serious doubt on the interpretation and perhaps also on the actual text offered by Zambelios (Apostolakis 1929: 57-69). Whether the last line is a forgery, as Apostolakis thought, is less clear; the Hellene may here be a perfectly genuine mythological giant rather than a national stereotype. Zambelios' omission of the ransom episode, by contrast, is more conclusive as evidence of his approach.

This is not to attribute bad faith to him. Zambelios' emendations may indeed have served to show Apostolakis "how peculiar . . . the ethnic self-regard (*ethnikos eghoïsmos*) of Zambelios was, and what misplaced and laughable thoughts it could bring the man to entertain" (1929: 57); but patriotic duty, though probably a sufficient justification in itself in Zambelios' eyes, is far from being the full explanation. Zambelios assumed that, as a Greek, he had a participant role in the shaping of Greek culture, and it is in all likelihood this assumption, so consistent with Hellenist ideology, that most effectively explains the alterations and suppressions of his folksong corpus. In the missionary view which he took of his task, he differed from Solomos in denying the usefulness of foreign learning; it is an ironical consequence of the Hellenist thesis that, although outward-directed, it should in practice be so much more xenophobic culturally than the Romeic. In his subjectivism, more specifically in his assumption that a Greek would necessarily know Greek culture best, he was again not very far from his detractors, particularly Apostolakis. But he differed radically from Apostolakis in the direction that subjectivism led him; and that difference was, in the final analysis, one of ideological orientation.

Tragic Genius Preserved

Zambelios' quarrel with Solomos confirmed the ideological rift. In 1859, two years after the poet's death, Zambelios took the offensive with a highly invidious comparison between Solomos and Foscolo, much, of course, to Solomos' disadvantage. Yet this critical diatribe actually forms a coda, in effect, to a discussion of the true nature of Greek poetry and song, under the cautiously academic title *Whence the Vulgar Word* Traghoudho? *Thoughts*

Concerning Hellenic Poetry. Zambelios' less personal aim in this work is to pursue the demotic term for "singing" back to its Classical origins and, in so doing, to establish the respectably Hellenic character of Greek folk poetry.

His thesis turns upon a linguistic curiosity. Why is it, he asks, that the Classical word *ado* ("sing") was displaced by an entirely different term, *traghoudho*, in the Christian era? Zambelios thought the value of such an abstruse inquiry to be quite beyond question, for, as he explains, "every word, whether living or in desuetude, encapsulates a historical fact which demands special investigation" (1859: 4).

And so he proceeds to a sweeping review of Greek thought and poetry through the ages. At an early date, the greatness of Homer lay in his exaltation of humankind. In Homer, the gods are a product of human creativity; and the heroic ideal is represented by none other than "the Hellene, gloriously fighting for Greece" (1859: 10)—a truly panoptic symbol replacing the petty jealousies of the first city-states. The development of literature in Greece thereafter pursued a progressive course down to the Periklean era: "Ancient Lyric poetry overlooked the earth and only looked up to heaven. Epic introduced into Poetry the element of nationhood (*ethnotis*). But Drama envelops heaven, fatherland, and society *within the mind*, within the heart of the individual" (1859: 13).

Homer did indeed celebrate the deeds of the Achaeans, as Zambelios notes, but the subsequent history of Greece shows how difficult it was to translate a sense of shared distinctiveness as Greeks into practical politics. Zambelios intended his readers to assume that the achievement of a sense of ethnic unity was a watershed from which there was no turning back and that the unification of the modern Greek polity was the culmination of an ideal which had been ever present in the national consciousness (*ethniki sinidhisis*; see chap. 3). He was not so ingenuous or poorly read as to pretend that there had literally existed an ancient Greek nation-state similar to the modern state of his own day.

To his list of literary achievements in the Classical era, Zambelios adds the work of the philosophers:

> It has been said that Christianity emerged among the Athenians in the Academy of Plato. I am of the opinion that it appeared among them still earlier, in the theater of Sophocles and Euripides.
>
> Socrates, Euripides, and Plato, three familiar and inseparable collaborators, stand in relation to the subsequent call of the disciples of Christ as the invention of the compass did to the later discovery of America. (1859: 15)

And he concludes:

> Christianity confirms the promise of Epic, of Drama, of Philosophy.
> In condemning the multiple tyranny of the gods, it makes man the ruler
> of an ordered polity. Established on the throne of this selfsame con-
> sciousness, man speaks forth as a god on earth.   (1859: 17)

Christ on the cross—"a miracle partaking of Epic but at the same time of
Tragedy . . . proclaiming the blessed end of human struggles"—symbolizes this
ultimate achievement, of which the political dimension, the rebirth of the
Greek nation as a political entity on earth, is foreshadowed in the poetry of
the common people (1859: 17).

In his portrayal of this progression, Zambelios has drawn heavily on
Hegel's account of the development of aesthetic religion in Greece and of its
displacement by the absolute religion of Christianity. In some respects, Zambelios' schema closely resembles any outline of Hegel's (e.g., Mure 1965:
104-109). To adapt the Hegelian schema for his own essentially nationalistic
purposes, however, Zambelios had to make a number of changes, notably an
extended discussion of the "lyric" phase of Greek poetry and, most significantly of all, the yoking of Christianity to Hellenism. For him, Christianity
was not in any sense a displacement of one form of religion by another but
the ultimate synthesis of human understanding *in the minds of the Greeks*.
The ecumenical ideal of Christianity was thus represented as the Hellenization
of the entire world; the rise of Protestantism, which Hegel saw as the matura-
tion of revealed religion, was simply another of those secondary effects in
western history whose causes Zambelios attributed exclusively to Greece.
Thus, in the regenerated Greek nation, human understanding would now be
brought to its consummation.

To demonstrate this, it was necessary to show also that the Greeks had
never relinquished their special qualities. The traditions of Classical poetry—
the source from which both Hegel and Zambelios drew material for their respective schemata—had largely been eradicated or transformed by the theological requirements of the new religion of Christ. Folksong, on the other
hand, remained relatively unaffected, Zambelios thought, so specimens of it
from the Byzantine period "may be regarded as the sole evidence for the
sensibilities and sensitivities of the Hellenic people during that long and trou-
bled period of Christian metamorphosis" (1859: 26). It is thus to folksong
that one should look for evidence of continuity in the national character.

And Zambelios did precisely that. Explaining the transference of the Classical word for "tragedy" (*tragōdia*) to the semantic domain of song, he turned
his attention to the traditional dirges (*miroloyia*) for the dead as evidence of
an inherited sense of tragedy in the Greek spirit. It was an ill-advised move,
born of his comparative ignorance of his rural compatriots' terminological

usages, for, as has already been observed (Menardos 1921: 2), these dirges are not usually classified by the Greek villagers themselves as songs (*traghoudhia*). The latter term would, under normal circumstances, be inappropriate for dirges, except in a metaphorical sense (see Herzfeld 1981: 44-53). For *traghoudhia*, as joyful songs or verses, stand in polar and complementary opposition to *miroloyia*; and the corresponding verbs are similarly opposed to each other. Zambelios thus chose a perilously thin support for his argument. That he was almost certainly unaware of this can be inferred from the very considerable detail which he devotes to dirges in order to make his case.

He conceded that the chanting of funeral laments as such was not confined to Greek culture. (It would be somewhat invidious to see in this proof that Zambelios was a better observer than Evlambios, for Evlambios may have meant that the style and content of *miroloyia*, rather than funeral laments in general, were unique to Greece.) Zambelios' interest, however, was caught by a more subtle and, he maintained, distinctive trait:

> What is unique, not to say paradoxical, lies in the climax of lamenting
> for situations which call for anything but sorrow or grief: for example,
> in that most joyful of domestic ceremonies, the wedding celebration,
> that same occasion at which, everywhere else in the rest of Europe,
> harmony and rejoicing prevail.   (1859: 45)

Zambelios witnessed such laments for the bride's departure to her new household on some island, unspecified, in the Cyclades. He was overwhelmed:

> The uncontrived and spontaneous drama which I beheld before my eyes
> gripped my heart strongly. I confess that, before that dramatic aspect
> of the marriage, I too was overcome and could not restrain my tears.
> And yet how often have formal tragic performances left me unmoved!
>   (1859: 49)

Thus did the son of a tragic dramatist join with his ideological enemies in lauding the popular over the pedantic. There is no logical reason, for that matter, why he should not have done so, for he saw in the folk laments the purest evidence of continuity with the Classical genius.

To this material, Zambelios added those traditional dance songs which, though outwardly cheerful in tone, are nevertheless graced with a refrain recalling the inevitability of death. These, too, he considered as distinctively Greek and as further evidence that the tragic sense had survived among his people.

Having disengaged the tragic spirit from modern folksong, Zambelios then turns briefly to the other repository of Hellenism, the ecclesiastical. In the Greek Orthodox funeral service, he finds the analogue of the *miroloyia* and is moved to exclaim:

Everywhere and forever is Death, beloved of the Soul. Life, Death,
and the resurrection of the dead, inseparable.

Behold Hesiod, Theognis, Phocylides! Behold the poetry of Mimner-
mus! Behold the Gospel! Behold the hymns of the burial service! Behold, in like manner, the source from which there flowed, and from
which still flows, everything fine and original in modern Greek poetry!

(1859: 50)

For Zambelios, cultural continuity was continuity of the spirit (*pnevma*), and
the originality of an individual artist could be apprehended only within that
context.

This continuity of the spirit provides the solution to the linguistic conun-
drum with which he began the essay. The essence of the art form, *tragōdia*,
had been maintained by the common people in their *traghoudhia*, their poetry and song. The sterility of the Romeic, monastic learning of early Christianity could not quench the poetic inspiration of the Hellenes—for whom,
what is more, Christianity "confirms the premonitions of Epic, of Drama, of
Philosophy. Rejecting the multiple rule of the [pagan] gods, it makes man
the leader of the rational polity. On the throne of the selfsame consciousness
is seated man, proclaimed as God on earth" (1859: 17); and, since the new
Christian ideal "is not simply Attic or at most Hellenic but entirely ecumenical" (1859: 18), Hellenism has finally, in this new and sublime embodiment,
been brought to all humankind. This is the logical completion of Zambelios'
1852 answer to the eastern origins of so much of Greek culture: the assimilation and perfection of half-formed eastern philosophies, Christianity now included, were themselves definitive characteristics of the Greek genius. In a
century when educated Western Europeans saw a precursor of Christ in Socra-
tes and the essence of Christian religiosity in the writings of the Classical
Greeks generally, when Oscar Wilde could seriously find satisfaction in the belief that Jesus' language had actually been Greek (Jenkyns 1980: 69, 91-93,
158-159, 229), such claims as those of Zambelios did not seem especially
preposterous.

Zambelios in a European Context

Zambelios' 1859 essay on the etymology of *traghoudho* has not generally received the recognition which was accorded both his history of medieval Hellenism and an intermediate essay, published in 1856, on the Byzantine phase
of Greek ethnicity. It is possible that this has something to do with its intemperate comments on Solomos, who was already coming into his own as
the acknowledged national poet of Greece. Zambelios' remarks were countered in a sharp, satirical essay by Solomos' ardent disciple Iakovos Polilas

only a year after they appeared in print (see Valetas 1950). Yet the linguistic aspects of Zambelios' essay, although extravagant by present-day standards, deserve a more generous hearing than they have been given so far. Not only are they a useful source for the development of the continuity concept, but they indicate something of the intellectual background of Zambelios and his Heptanesian peers, and they are not without ingenuity.

The essay is admittedly not of a kind where one can say that its author belonged to a single identifiable school of thought. Zambelios was careful to acknowledge no foreign roots and to condemn what he saw as the humiliating imitation of foreign philosophers by his contemporaries. He was, however, well acquainted with various aspects of foreign scholarship, and his Hellenism is palpably, and predictably, directed toward the refurbishment of the Greeks' *external* image. To have assimilated and perfected foreign teachings in his own mind, and to have labeled the result as both Greek and his own, would have been entirely consistent with his theory of Hellenic cultural primacy: the wisdom of the West was Greek by origin and by right, while that of the East could be valued only in its Greek distillation. If there are distinct suggestions of Vico in his writings, as well as of the neo-Platonic tradition, and if we also sometimes meet in them the ideas of Herder and Hegel, there is yet nothing to be gained by labeling Zambelios as a plagiarist or as a poor imitator. Whatever elements of foreign philosophy he absorbed were assimilated to an overall design of some originality, one which provided its own argument against acknowledgment.

Zambelios' references to national consciousness, moreover, do not necessarily reflect the direct influence of Herder or his German successors. The concept of *Volksgeist* was far from new when Zambelios appeared on the scene. Its connection with folk traditions, furthermore, had an alternative source in the writings of Vico, who was to exercise considerable influence on the development of folklore in his native Italy (cf. Cocchiara 1952: 278) and on the thinking of some of the Greek and Italian scholars already mentioned above. Zambelios must have had some contact with Vico's ideas, however indirectly, through the Heptanesian intelligentsia. His linguistic reasoning, moreover, does not recall the grammatical concerns of the Herderians' *Sprachphilosophie* (cf. Berlin 1977: 170) so much as it does Vico's analyses of etymology.

Vico had argued, and tried to demonstrate by a distinctive combination of historical detail and intuitive guesswork, that etymology could be used to reveal the peculiar histories of cultural institutions. Zambelios' announcement of "a certain important law of history," whereby "every word . . . encapsulates a historical fact," sounds suggestively like a summation of several Vician formulas (see especially Vico 1744: nos. 154, 167, 354). Whether the connection between Vico and Zambelios was anything more than an indirect one, however, is an open question.

Certainly, Zambelios did not plagiarize the specific details of his disquisition on the etymology of *traghoudho* from Vico. There is no evidence to suggest that it was derived, at that level, from any other source. Tommaseo, in fact, came much closer to plagiarizing Vico when he adopted the Neapolitan philosopher's (probably accurate) proposal (nos. 910-911) of a connection between *tragōdia* ("tragedy") and *tragos* ("goat")—an indication, according to both Vico and Tommaseo, of the Dionysiac origins of the drama. In a passage which, without acknowledgment, more faithfully reproduces Vico's cyclical *corsi e ricorsi* than anything Zambelios wrote, Tommaseo notes that "*traghoudho*, from 'tragedy,' to the Greeks of today means cheerful song: almost returning to its origin in *tragos* and the Bacchic songs" (1842, III: 140, n. 3). And then Tommaseo properly notes that the term is contrasted in Greek usage with the word for funeral laments—the point which Zambelios evidently missed. This shows that Zambelios almost certainly did not take his Vician ideas, if such they are, piecemeal from Tommaseo but developed for himself a version which is more faithful to the methodology than to the examples of Vico's thinking.

Because of its assimilated nature, Zambelios' seeming Vicianism never emerges more unambiguously. There are possible hints of it in his treatment of Homer (although, unlike Vico, he accepted Homer as a single, real person), in his respect for folk traditions ancient and modern, in the correlation of symbolism (Vico's *fantasia*) with social changes, and in the acceptance of a divine Providence as the guiding principle of cultural evolution. But he differed from Vico in praising the institutions of democracy, just as he parted company from Hegel on the question of monarchy (Zambelios detested it). He also shows little of the cyclical sense of history that one expected from a committed Vician—not that he should be criticized for failing to adopt what Berlin has described as "the least interesting, plausible, and original" of Vico's theories (1977: 64).

The exact relationship between Zambelios and Vico is opaque. Zambelios did not represent his own ideas as derivative, but this may have resulted from a desire to avoid associating himself too obviously with foreign philosophies, especially after quarreling with Solomos on just that account. Opportunities for reading Vico must have existed both on Corfu and abroad, and Vico's ideas were current in the circles in which Zambelios tried to make his name. The obscure style of the *Scienza nuova* encouraged haphazard mining rather than systematic perusal, and Zambelios' use of ideas which may have come from that source certainly suggests a much more restricted range of interests. By Zambelios' time, much of Vico's thinking had been more generally diffused or, as with Herder, paralleled in the independent conclusions of others. But the resemblance between Zambelios and Vico is striking, to say the least, when we examine their approaches to etymological reconstruction. Zambelios' "important law of history" is well-nigh indistinguishable from the cardinal *degnità* ("axiom") of Vico's imaginative linguistics (cf. also Zambelios 1880: v).

Ecumenical Ethnocentrism

The argument that the modern Greeks' destiny was to perfect the philosophies of East and West carried certain responsibilities and consequences. To illustrate these, we conclude this chapter with an essay which, whether or not it was directly inspired by Zambelios, pushes his argument to its logical extreme. In this particular essay, the comparative lack of attention suffered by Greek folklore research in the wider European context becomes easier to understand—not because the essay is representative of scholarly standards in Greece but quite simply because it indicates, in exaggerated form, the isolating effects of a methodology and a philosophy that were clearly stated to be national rather than global in scope.

For Greek folklore remained, for the most part, a strictly national discipline. Even the term *laografia*, when it was eventually coined in 1884, denoted the material and the discipline more or less indiscriminately. And, since Greek folklorists were generally disinclined to take a sustained interest in the folklore of other lands, except insofar as it provided insights into their own (and not always then), the discipline itself rarely achieved more than purely domestic importance as a scholarly activity. In consequence, Greek folklorists are rarely given more than a passing mention in international studies of folklore epistemology. Cocchiara's wide-ranging historical study of European folklore scholarship (1952) does not name a single Greek folklorist, although it accords warm recognition to both Fauriel and Tommaseo for their Greek and other studies. It is not necessary to invert Zambelios' view of the cause-and-effect relationship between European cultures in order to perceive how radically the Hellenist ideology inverted the international perspective of ethnology and, thereby, prevented the Greek scholars from making a more ecumenical contribution to methodology. Such examples as Finnish (Wilson 1976), Russian (Oinas 1961; Sokolov 1950: 40-155), and Serbo-Croatian (Karadžić, in Cocchiara 1952) folklore studies also indicate that a language barrier cannot provide a sufficient explanation of so high a degree of isolation. The reasons for this isolation lie, rather, in the interests and presuppositions of the local folklorists themselves.

While later folklorists, working in the tradition of Politis, were at least prepared to use foreign materials in illustration of their Greek data, Zambelios and his immediate contemporaries, though often well versed in the literary works of other countries, were unwilling to do more than refer in the most general terms to their folk traditions. The result was to create an intellectual cul-de-sac in the midst of an already closed academic environment. Exemplifying the extreme development of this trend, at a time when Politis had already begun to publish his comparative essays on Greek folklore and world ethnology, is the disquisition which the Athens lawyer Stamatios Valvis published in 1877. This essay is an attempt to see in the dying words of one of the revolutionary guerrilla leaders a philosophical refinement which surpassed the best work of even the Classical Greeks or the modern Europeans. The argument, which particularly recalls Zambelios in its identification of the ancient literati with the largely unlettered population of the modern countryside, adds to this the more dynamic notion of an autochthonous spiritual evolution among the folk themselves.

Valvis' dissertation consists of twenty-three pages devoted, ostensibly, to the study of a single folk distich. The couplet in question is that said to have been uttered by Diakos when he was led off to execution after his hopeless defense of the Alamana bridge against overwhelming Turkish odds. To this day, it has remained a well-known verse with intense patriotic associations:

> *But see what a time Death has chosen for taking me,*
> *now that the trees are blooming and the earth is sprouting grass!*

But it takes Valvis slightly more than half his essay to come to the point of actually quoting the verse itself. The earlier pages are resplendent with philosophical musings on the admiration which sensitive human beings feel for nature and on nature's own insensitivity to the feelings of humans. Saint Matthew, Sophocles, Virgil, Goethe, and the modern Greek poet Alexander Soutsos are all quoted in witness against nature's callousness toward human pain. The ancient tragedians' words are held to be especially moving in this connection, partly because of "the serene beauty of nature in Greece": the contrast between human suffering and the serenity of nature is especially painful.

After finally quoting the couplet, Valvis declares his ideological focus:

> We may say that this couplet does far more honor to that much sung hero than his own Leonidian heroism, because it shows that that great-hearted fighter had a sensitive and wholly pure heart, a heart which nurtured feelings such as those which stirred in the breasts of those noblest of men, educated in the highest of cultures, whose sentiments we have noted above.   (1877: 143)

Diakos, however, not only exemplified the finest of the virtues extolled in Attic tragedy and Holy Writ alike but actually surpassed these sources of wisdom as well as their intellectual offspring, the European philosophers: "We know nobody else to have thus mourned for himself, in other words because of *the circumstances* under which he was dying and not *because* he was dying or because *a person such as himself* was dying" (1877: 145; Valvis' emphasis). The hero of Greek liberation thus succeeds not only to the martial glory of Leonidas, whose finest hour came in similar fashion at nearby Thermopylae, but also—and, for Valvis, more significantly—to the intellectual heritage of the philosophers, tragedians, and Gospel writers. Where Zambelios had sought to demonstrate such spiritual continuity in the persistent relationship between language and concept, Valvis found it in the realm of concept alone.

Valvis' argument brings out more starkly, perhaps, than Zambelios' writings a fundamental problem of the Hellenist thesis. The more extreme Hellenists' claim to an ecumenical vision grew naturally from the transplantation of philhellenism to the intellectual soil of Greece itself. If renascent Greece represented the ultimate vindication and triumph of European culture, who but the Greeks should be best qualified to interpret that larger entity? This, as one might expect, reverses the broadly phenomenological subjectivism of European philosophers by granting the Greeks an intuitive understanding of culture at large. Elsewhere in Europe, the ideas of Hamann (Hammel 1972: 4), Herder (Dorson 1968: 91; Wilson 1976), and Vico (Cocchiara 1952: 278) were being interpreted as defining the distinctiveness and autonomy of each and every people's national character. They were not understood to accord the modern Greeks such intellectual catholicity on the basis of past glories. Not even Vico, with his rapt admiration for Classical culture, mentions the modern Greeks specifically. Hamann actually disliked Classical Greek culture, at least as it was interpreted by his contemporaries; and, while Herder did not absorb this prejudice along with the rest of his mentor's teachings, he opposed the pseudo-Classical posturing of his fellow Europeans as a violation of their inherent national characters (Berlin 1977: 182-192).

What we may call the ecumenical ethnocentrism of Zambelios and Valvis thus came at a time when Europe was little disposed to listen. Other intellectual currents were now abroad in Europe; Max Müller, for example, was in the process of exciting his contemporaries' imagination by reversing Vico's view of the relationship between mythology and language (cf. Cocchiara 1952: 314). The new ethnological fashions quite passed the older Hellenists by, and it was now a new generation of Greek scholars (with Nikolaos Politis at their head) who turned to these developments for their own researches. Yet Zambelios should not be forgotten. His intermediate paper of 1856 (see Spiridakis 1966) spurred the periodical *Pandora* into folklore publication, giving the very youthful Politis one of his first platforms, and it also galvanized the Greek Parliament into providing regular funds for folklore research. While Zambelios' intellectual path led in the direction of such writers as Valvis, his own observations were full of insight as well as ideologically directed exaggeration, and his energy and enthusiasm brought about the earliest official recognition in Greece of the importance of the folk traditions.

Chapter 3
National Character, National Consciousness

". . . the virile habits of the Europeans . . ."

National Character in a European Context

Zambelios' repeated references to "national spirit," to "race" and *ethnos*, and to concepts of national consciousness all reproduce the definitive concerns of nineteenth-century ideological nationalism in Europe. The terminology itself represents a gloss, possibly at more than one remove, on the language of Hamann and Herder; these German philosophers' ideas had been disseminated throughout the European continent, notably in France by Madame de Staël (Cocchiara 1952: 278-303), and had received further application by Fauriel and many others. That this broad tradition should have influenced Zambelios in no way contradicts his apparent adherence to Vico, for Herder himself came to admire Vico greatly and to recognize that the Neapolitan's thinking was at times startlingly similar to his own (Berlin 1977: 91). By the middle of the nineteenth century, the language and concepts of the German romantic nationalists were in general use throughout Europe, often in a more aggressive and explicitly statist frame of reference than Herder, at least, had found palatable.

It is thus difficult to estimate the range of Herder's influence in Greece. Recall, too, that Greek folklore studies began in earnest only after the founding of the state, as a source of a posteriori exegesis. This contrasts radically with the situation in Finland, where, long before the prospect of national re-demption had become at all immediate, such leading early students of folk-lore as Sjögren and Poppius could point to Herder as the wellspring of their ideological formation (Wilson 1976: 3). By the time Herder's thinking came to affect the direction of ethnological thought in Greece, there were several modern intermediaries (including the brothers Grimm) from whose works the Herderian idiom could be absorbed by folklorists and others; by midcentury, moreover, the broad concepts of *Volksgeist* and *Zeitgeist* had been too gen-erally disseminated for their appearance in Greek writings to be attributable to a specifically Herderian source.

What Cocchiara rather contemptuously calls "the myth of *Volksgeist*" (1952: 278) encouraged the development of academic folklore throughout Europe, as scholars scurried to find empirical evidence that such a spirit really existed. To call it a myth, moreover, is to miss its *ordering* potential. The notion of a Greek national consciousness became a kind of cognitive map (cf. Geertz 1973: 220) wherein cultural similarities, common language and religion, and a burgeoning restiveness with Turkish rule were given a certain unity of meaning. While it has been argued (St. Clair 1972) that few rural Greeks were in a position, in 1821, to predict what national politics would do to their values and allegiances, they clearly already recognized the principle of nationhood; such proselytizing agencies as the Odessa-based Filiki Eteria had already done much to bring this about. National consciousness has been defined by a Greek folklorist as "the conscious knowledge of every individual that he is part of a nation, partaking to [*sic*] the strong groupal [*sic*] aspirations that bind him to the other individuals around him, creating thus the common will of all to belong to this and not to any other nation" (Kiriakidis 1955: 11). Whatever the mystical possibilities of the *Volksgeist* concept, it emerges in this admirably specific definition as a form of collective self-identification.

The definition is useful, too, in that it stresses the aspect of individual self-knowledge in relation to the larger entity of the nation. As an abstraction, however, it is very much a product of learned rather than folk discourse. The Greek term for "consciousness" in this context, *syneidēsis*,[1] is the New Testament and ecclesiastical term for "conscience" or "self-knowledge" (cf. Latin *con* and *scientia*). When this word appears in village usage, it tends to be conflated with the phonetically similar but etymologically noncognate word for "custom" (*synētheia*; see Herzfeld 1980a: 346–347).

Such a lack of fit between scholarly terminology and village usage is an indication of the pedigree of "national consciousness." *Syneidēsis* seems to be a convenient gloss on the French *conscience*, which conflates the ideas of "conscience" (German *Gewissen*) and "consciousness" (*Bewusstsein*). Representative of the Europeans' "very great debt" to Greek culture, this particular repayment, indeed, probably owes something to Koraes' own writings. It is a Western European notion, dressed up in the language of early Christianity and put to work in the service of the European nation-state ideal. Not only was the *concept* of national consciousness a European conceit, but that consciousness itself was increasingly perceived as a definitively European possession. In consequence, moreover, the various distinctive nationalities of Europe derived from this shared proclivity a sense of transcendent unity, and the increasingly comparativist perspective of folklore studies fostered that perception of unity in diversity. "Folklore, indeed, pressed the learned into thinking in German, in English, in French, in Russian, or in something else, but it also simultaneously pressed them, to use an expression of Madame de Staël's, into 'thinking in European'" (Cocchiara 1952: 303). Given this background, and given also the pattern of reversal which stemmed from its origins in philhellenism, the Hellenist thesis could only benefit from the development of folklore. If Greece had been the *fons et origo* of all Europe, then Greek folklore would enshrine the quintessence of the European spirit.

D'Istria and the Premise of European Character

Although Dora d'Istria was not of Greek origin, it was she who launched this methodological perspective on Greek folklore into a wider, European perspective. Zambelios and other Greek writers had already developed it in their own researches, but d'Istria expounded it to a more international audience, and it is instructive to see how much her views converge with those of the indigenous Hellenists.

A brief review of her life may help explain her intense involvement in the description and defense of the Greek national character. She was born in 1828 in Bucharest as Helen Ghikas, a Romanian princess of Albanian extraction. Her father, Prince Michael Ghikas, was a provincial governor who had been among the first of his circle to adopt western dress and who, throughout his life, took a deep interest in the study of archaeology; from him, presumably, the young princess first absorbed the idiom of European antiquarianism. Her mother was the first Wallachian woman to write in the Romanian language, thereby setting her an example combining female emancipation and linguistic nationalism. D'Istria was educated according to principles of supposedly Classical Greek derivation. These included admitting a respected place in the curriculum for physical training—which proved fortunate one dark Moscow night in 1854 when her younger sister's governess, who could not swim, fell into a pond! In 1849, she married a Russian prince but soon left him for an independent life of travel, adventure, and the wars of the pen.

Despite her enthusiasm for the various forms of Balkan nationalism, d'Istria chose to reside in Italy. She wrote principally in French, the language of diplomacy. For her vocal endorsement of Greek aspirations, especially of the ill-fated Cretan insurrection of 1866, she was granted Hellenic nationality by a special decree of Parliament. In expressing her gratitude for the honor, which was unprecedented for a woman, she remarked that she had "always considered Greece as a second fatherland"—a reference to that superior education, perhaps, which made many Balkan aristocrats of the period refer to themselves as Hellenes.

Such affectations of Hellenic identity were neither literal nor absolute. They certainly did not prevent d'Istria from exploiting her Albanian ancestry when, in 1860, she wrote to Prime Minister Dimitrios Voulgaris (Boulgares)[2] to solicit support for her plans to conduct research in Greece. She told him, among other things, that she had been deeply moved on a visit to the island of Hydra by the memory of the Hydriote sea captains' heroic participation in the War of Independence (cf. Dakin 1973: 122-123), recalling that the Hydriotes, *like Voulgaris as well as herself*, were of Albanian origin.

Her interests spanned the entire Balkan area and beyond. Her published work, which draws extensively on folksong as a repository of national character, deals with the Greeks, Albanians, Bulgarians, Magyars, eastern Turks, Romanians, and Serbs. She died in 1888, a revered and internationally recognized authority on Balkan nationalism as well as on the position of women in Balkan and other societies (see Anon. 1860-61; Cecchetti 1868, 1873; Pommier 1863; Mandouvalou 1969).

Dora d'Istria's instatement as an honorary Greek citizen coincided with the broader sense in which she chose to regard herself as a Hellene. Her conception of modern Greek nationality was primarily antiquarian and so did not conflict with her more literal claims to Albanian and Romanian identity. Some allowance must be made, in considering her letter to Voulgaris with its references to their shared Albanian origins, for the polite rhetoric of diplomacy; but the same provision applies equally to her letter of thanks to the Greek Parliament, in which her Hellenic feelings, of course, take center stage. Yet her multiple sense of nationality was much more than a diplomatic conceit, to be manipulated according to circumstances. Her extensive writings show that she fully subscribed to the philhellenic view of Greece as in every sense the continuation of its ancient predecessor. Her gracious acceptance of Greek citizenship was above all a confirmation, in personal terms, of a consistent ideology.

D'Istria subscribed wholeheartedly to the twin concepts of national character and national consciousness, although it is in terms of the first of these that her ethnographic studies are principally organized. She portrayed individuals as capable of behaving only in accordance with the social values, the character, of the cultures to which they belonged. The cultures themselves were subsumed under the larger opposition between European and Asiatic peoples; and, adopting a convention widely accepted by her contemporaries, she attributed to the former the prize of absolute superiority. For the Albanians, she maintained, the sight of the Greek flag fluttering over Corfu after that island's cession to Greece "appeared to the sons of Skanderbeg as the symbol of Europe's definitive triumph over Asia" (1866: 417).[3]

In like manner, too, d'Istria was able to "explain" the failure of the Serbs to achieve rapid independence:

> Had the Turks been the sole adversaries of the Serbs, the latter might have had grounds for hoping that the Asiatic mores, enervating influ-

ences that they are, would have delivered them sooner or later; but the
Moslem Serbs and Albanians [who fought for the Turks], having con-
served the virile habits of the Europeans, are far more redoubtable
enemies for them than is the entire Ottoman army.   (1865: 360)

Striking a somewhat backhanded blow for her fellow Albanians, she anticipates prejudices still far from uncommon in Greece, to the effect that the
Turks, as Asiatics, are worthless in battle against Christians and Europeans.

Within the generality of European peoples, d'Istria sought to make finer
discriminations. She discerned, as it were, different grades of European character, different degrees of adherence to the absolute ideal. Her comment
on the folksongs lamenting the Fall of Constantinople in 1453 is extremely
revealing:

> Whereas the ruin of the Serbian Empire at Kossovo inspired the popu-
> lar poets of Serbia to their best works, the collapse of Constantine's
> empire did not provoke from the mouths of the people a single cry
> worthy of retention for posterity. The fact is that great poets are not
> always born, in each country, at the moment of great disasters. On the
> other hand, it is also true that the Serbian Empire was struck down in
> its prime, that of the Greeks when in full decline. There is perhaps a
> further reason for the difference: *the Serbs have the somehow com-
> munistic influence of the Slavs* and are interested above all in those con-
> flicts where the nation as a whole is itself the hero; by contrast, the
> Greeks, *whose genius is entirely European*, seek in the multitude for an
> Ajax, a Ulysses, an Agamemnon, for great figures who vigorously stand
> out from the confused, misty masses and strikingly describe, to some
> extent, their character and passions.   (1867: 590; my emphasis)

These lines were written before the Greek folklorists had come to make the
popular laments for the Fall of Constantinople an object of their especial
interest and veneration (see chap. 6). D'Istria was herself evidently unac-
quainted with them, to judge by her view of the Greek folk poet's style, for,
when the emperor appears in those laments at all, he does little to earn a
hero's distinctive lineaments.

In d'Istria's scheme, the Serbs—even when Moslem by religion—are more
European than the Turks, but the Greeks are the most European of all. Their
distinguishing mark is that penchant for individualistic character drawing,
that seeking "in the multitude . . . for great figures," which links the Greeks
of today both with their ancient forebears (especially as represented by the
Homeric heroes) and with contemporary Europeans. That national characteristic, moreover, had survived the vicissitudes of foreign domination. Like
Zambelios, d'Istria regarded the Byzantine imperium as a foreign growth on

true Hellenism (1867: 592), but, perhaps because she felt no need to "justify" Christianity, she dismissed the church as a destructive foreign influence too. Only the heroes of the folksongs entirely escape these effete sources of corruption, for they "are new men, in many respects more like the rude companions of Achilles than they are like the timid subjects of the last [Byzantine emperor] Constantine." The heroes of the songs to which d'Istria refers here are the so-called klefts (*kleftes*), or brigand-guerrillas. It may seem oddly contradictory to use these klefts as symbols of spiritual continuity with the heroes of Homer while fixing the earliest date of their activities in the eighteenth century (d'Istria 1867: 592), but in fact this pair of apparently incompatible propositions is also contained in the work of indigenous folklorists, where we shall shortly examine them more critically.

D'Istria's attribution of "communistic influence" to the Slavs, some eight decades before they officially adopted Marxist constitutions, curiously foreshadows the modern Greek convention of condemning political communism as an imported Slavic doctrine (cf. Kofos 1964). Certain events, notably the hostile relations between Greece and the neighboring countries during the Greek Civil War, have reinforced that attitude. For d'Istria, as for her contemporaries in general, continuity between Classical and modern Greek culture was the best proof that there was indeed such a thing as a Greek national character, which contrasted so strongly with the national characters of neighboring peoples. Thus, while praising Fauriel for having "taught an astonished Europe that bards still existed in the land of Homer" (1867: 587), she did not so much as mention his useful work on Slav folk poetry (cf. Ibrovac 1966). It was not until many decades later that Parry and Lord introduced to the scholarly world the possibility that the techniques of the Yugoslav *guslari* could help penetrate the complexities of Homeric composition and style (see Lord 1960; Finnegan 1977).

Pagan Heroism

The premise of national character enabled the early nationalist writers to extract a measure of continuity from what could otherwise be presented as an exceptionally radical break in the cultural history of Greece. This was the religious change from the worship of local deities and the Olympian pantheon in Classical times to the centralized unity and doctrinal monotheism of the Greek Orthodox church.

Dora d'Istria had only contempt for the influence of the church and its leadership:

> The reaction is such that the kleftic poems were soon to seek inspiration in the vague recollections of a free, pagan Greece, rather than in

the craven teachings of a theology fashioned over the centuries to suit
the tastes of autocratic rulers. Outlaws and fugitives gathered in the
mountains: Olympus was once more to open its miraculous flanks to its
old children . . .   (1867: 591)

But this scornful formulation was not a happy one for those resident in
Greece itself who, unlike the peripatetic princess, had to achieve a balance between their religious affiliations and their pagan ancestry. Zambelios, as we
saw, viewed the Orthodox church as the very means whereby democracy survived in the Greek spirit. This argument was better suited to the needs of the
new nation than d'Istria's, since the priesthood and the monastic tradition
had maintained necessarily close social connections with the rural population;
the lower clergy, unlike the senior hierarchy, had supported the revolutionary
movement actively.

But, if the relationship between Classical paganism and Orthodox Christianity was a dangerous subject, d'Istria concentrated her analysis on aspects
of the Greek *Volksgeist* over which the Hellenists could comfortably agree
with her. Stressing the ethnic purity of the Greeks, she argued that this was
revealed in a unique combination of heroism and, as the quoted passages
show, individualism. That the Greeks had indeed fought hard for their independence was indisputable. That the Greek guerrillas thought it generally
more prudent to abandon hopeless confrontations and could not understand
the last-ditch heroism of their philhellenic supporters (St. Clair 1972: 35-40)
is no reflection on their commitment to the cause as such but conforms to a
code of combined bravura and prudence which still has some currency in
rural areas. A Cretan or Sarakatsan shepherd may, for example, be forced on
moral grounds to defend his reputation with his fists or a knife but prefers to
confront his enemies in the presence of others who will intervene—being
killed over an insult is foolish, since it leaves one's family exposed to poverty
and ridicule (Campbell 1964: 196). The Greek revolutionary guerrillas fought
hard when there was reason to hope for a successful outcome or when there
was no alternative, but they did not see any reason to throw their lives away
for no obvious practical end. Some of the philhellenes who came to fight with
them were dismayed at what, to European gentlemen, looked like cowardice;
but cowardice, like collaboration (cf. Petropulos 1976a), is a term which does
little justice to the indigenous values and circumstances against which the
guerrillas' performance should be interpreted.

One recognized component of the guerrillas' behavior was an aggressive
idiom of self-assertion. Such self-assertion is not individualism in a psychological sense. On the contrary, the indigenous terms for it (*eghoïsmos, pallikaris-
mos*) denote conformity to an ideal.[4] The conventional stance of the guerrilla, which was dismissed as mere swashbuckling in the *post*-revolutionary

brigand, was a socially validated norm. When d'Istria compared this to the "communistic influence of the Slavs," she seems to have read institutional values as psychological attitudes on both sides; Slavic "communism" probably refers to the structure of the *zadruga*, which, significantly, has been treated as discouraging "individualism" by some Yugoslav writers (cf. Winner 1977)! Whether individualism and heroism are discovered is a function less of what is really there than of the principles of descriptive selection involved, and we find the dispute over the respective national characters of Greeks and Bulgarians expressed in strikingly similar terms (cf. Colocotronis 1918; Jireček 1891; Kiriakidis 1955; Kofos 1964; Megas 1946). By refusing the Bulgarians their claim to having originated heroic songs and a national epic of their own, the Greek folklorists were able to deny them the trait of heroic individualism which they had accorded themselves on the strength of their own, Greek folklore.

Heroes or Brigands?

The Greeks' claim to that trait was thus an important argument in support of the overall Hellenist thesis. It combined in a single formula the recent struggle and the ancient glories. That the trait was especially evident among the heroes of the struggle in the countryside, that it was celebrated in rural songs, meant that the incorporation of the *laos*, the folk, into the historical *ethnos* could be placed on a solid scholarly basis. The essays of Zambelios, Valvis, and d'Istria, while substantially different from each other in style and content, are all elaborations of this seminal idea.

D'Istria, in particular, dwelt on the activities of the Greek guerrillas as the embodiment of Hellenic valor. Her views were widely shared, both in Greece and elsewhere. Yet this enthusiasm for the category of fighters who called themselves *kleftes*, and who made such a signal contribution to the cause of Greek independence, did not extend to those of their compatriots who continued to bear arms once that independence had been achieved, for by this time their activity was mostly directed not against the Turkish enemy but against the representatives of the Greek State. Those guerrillas who might have challenged the politicians' authority but had died too soon could be apotheosized, since they no longer constituted a threat; even that archenemy of the political establishment, Odhisseas Androutsos, appears on schoolroom posters to this day, resplendent in his Classical helmet. Others, however, many of them only minor figures in the recorded history of the war, lived on to continue their more parochial battles, performing acts of brigandage whenever opportunity arose. They posed a serious problem not only for the representatives of law and order but, more generally, for the proponents of ideological Hellenism: they undermined the image of the valiant Hellene who fights only to defend hearth and homeland.

At this point, it will be necessary to move away from our examination of individual folklorists' work, in order to explore the more general issues posed by these fighters and their traditions. For they were not of interest only to those scholars, like Zambelios and d'Istria, who attempted to construct a generalized picture of the Greek national character. On the contrary, the very widespread concern with them among Greek folklorists of the period is only part of the commotion which they caused among the intellectual and political leadership of the nation. We shall see that they were retrospectively coopted into the national mythology wherever possible and that this necessitated the development of a formal taxonomic category suitable for such a task. Furthermore, the definitively Hellenic character that was attributed to them gave them a special interest for folklorists who wanted to make a case for the cultural supremacy of a particular region. For all these reasons, the following discussion of the phenomenon will provide a bridge between the *Volksgeist* models we have been considering so far and the development of a more empirical kind of culture history which we will consider as we return in the remaining chapters to the work of particular scholars.

Kleftism and the Constitution of History

The category of kleftic songs appears early in the writings of foreign observers. Fauriel found it useful, while Kind (1827: v, x, 1), following Fauriel's lead, explained that since the klefts were not mere brigands (*Räuber*) the songs about them deserved special consideration. By the time the German philologist Arnold Passow assembled his critical compendium of Greek folksongs in 1860, the kleftic category had become a vital part of the classification of Greek folklore. D'Istria's airy reference to "kleftic poems" shows how familiar the category had become even outside the immediate world of Greek philology. Nor was any challenge mounted to the historical and chronological status of "the klefts." While their patriotic motives were later questioned to some extent, or at least substantially reinterpreted (Kordatos 1972; Lambrinos 1947; Katsoulis 1975), and while the concept of nationalism in the Greek context has been considerably refined (see Petropulos 1976a; Vasdravellis 1975), only occasionally do we find "the klefts" replaced by the more careful "kleftism" (e.g., Petropulos 1968: 31-34).

That very definite phrase, "the klefts," suggests a historical movement with clear chronological boundaries. The duration of the kleftic period, apparently accepted by even so iconoclastic a writer as Lambrinos (1947: 78-79), is given as the century immediately preceding the Revolution. In this determination, the dearth of documentary evidence has resulted in great prominence being given to certain personal names which recur in the folk-songs; these names, interpreted with varying degrees of credibility as belonging to particular klefts whose activities are suggested by the thin documentary sources, do not carry us back to before about 1720.

The literalist interpretation of these names, the assumption that they referred to specific personalities, is symptomatic of the archaeological view of oral transmission. This view assumes that historical names will provide chronological markers for the whole text of a given song, much as a coin or a potsherd can perform the same service for an archaeological stratum. The stemmatic approach to textual comparison, whereby a series of copyists' manuscripts is located on a philological *Stammbaum*, was thus applied to oral texts despite the fact that these materials can go on changing right up to the moment they are recorded. When Evlambios attacked Fauriel's use of invented song titles, he very accurately pinpointed one of the major sources of the problem: such titles as "The Siege of Rhodes, 1522" (cf. Herzfeld 1969, 1973) or "The Death of Zidros" imply that the songs to which they are attached are literally *historical* texts to which dates can be attached with great precision. "Kleftic songs" seemed particularly amenable to such treatment because of their frequent mention of personal names.

Names, to the more literalistic among the folklorists, meant dates. In extreme cases, the evidence might even be fabricated, perhaps on the usual reasoning that the folklorists and the folk shared a common culture; this seems to apply to some of the references to the major guerrilla leader Theodhoros Kolokotronis (e.g., Lelekos 1868: 21–25). Of course, not all named references to Kolokotronis are necessarily forgeries. On the contrary, his name was without doubt a familiar one in the Greek countryside: he lived on after the war until 1843, and his memoirs are an important contribution to the historical literature of the period. His family name, at least, does appear in songs of apparently genuine rural provenance. The addition of Classical motifs in the forged texts is another matter—an extreme consequence, it would appear, of treating folksongs as "historical" and "national."

Often, moreover, Kolokotronis appears in song texts under his baptismal name of Theodhoros, sometimes in the affectionately diminutive form Thodhorakis. It was common practice to extol a guerrilla by his baptismal name in this way; occasionally, too, a widely used hypocoristic (*paratsoukli*) might be employed instead.[5] This use of common names instead of distinctive surnames, however, had the effect of eroding rather than preserving a man's posterity as an identifiable individual.

This erosion of identity in folksongs is not, of course, confined to personalities. Places, dates, even the course of particular events are all liable to the same process. Thus, the more distant in time that historical events are, the less factually specific do popular verse accounts of them tend to be. The

1822 fall of Nauplion to the Greeks is recounted in far more graphic detail
(presumably by Greek-speaking *Moslem* singers again!) than the Turkish capture of that city in 1715, and with still more circumstantial and factual elaboration than the 1522 siege of Rhodes by the Turks, even though all three
verse accounts share a common pool of motifs and expressive devices. Probably no nineteenth-century villager could have recounted the exact details of
the sixteenth-century siege; what was of interest, to judge from the extant
corpus of such songs, was the *generic* image of a Christian island falling to the
infidel Turks. Once the events in question were outside living memory, they
were gradually absorbed into a set of generalities. There is no reason to suppose that the same would not have happened to songs celebrating the minor
adventures of local brigands.

On the contrary, a recurrent feature of Greek naming symbolism suggests
that these songs are likely to have undergone the same process. Greek baptismal names are usually bestowed, especially on firstborn sons and daughters,
in commemoration (or "resurrection," as it is called) of the parents' own
parents or other close (especially prematurely deceased) kin. Only the order
of preference varies regionally. In all geographical areas, on the other hand,
this ostensibly commemorative act really results in a progressive forgetting of
the commemorated individuals' distinctive personalities. So many individuals
of the same name lie in a person's more distant ancestry that they have inevitably lost their distinct identities; only those who lie within a genealogical
distance of at most four or five generations from the present are remembered
as specific members of the community. When all this is borne in mind, it is
only to be expected that the brigands who operated at a genealogical distance
of more than five generations from the outbreak of war in 1821 should lack
identifiable, personal dimensions in the oral sources. After 1821, the situation changed radically; as literacy began to spread throughout the countryside, the last generation of prestatehood heroes was caught like insects in the
amber of official history.

This emergence from anonymity also coincides with the accelerated
growth of a national consciousness. Yet for us to treat the klefts as a discrete
analytical category, and thereby separate them both from their predecessors
and from the later brigands who defied the authority of Athens, is to violate
the indigenous usage of the term *kleftis* itself. Petropulos rightly observes
(1976a: 23) that the palpable existence of a national consciousness differ-
entiates the Greek uprising from any general model of "social banditry"
(Hobsbawm 1959), but he is careful not to claim that patriotic kleftism was
the only form that had ever existed; Vryonis, too, suggests that the acknowledged klefts who fought the Ottoman administration represent *social* continuity with the earlier, Byzantine phase (1976: 56). Once we thus escape the
narrow chronological limits which were formerly placed on the klefts' histori-

cal role, kleftism as a social institution—rather than the single, patriotically
motivated form of kleftism which the earlier writers selected for study—becomes more amenable to the treatment suggested by Hobsbawm's essay.
While "social banditry" is perhaps still too general, the more local model of
"kleftism" suggests a similar flexibility, a sense of a coherent value system
stretched across a fairly wide spectrum of specific kinds of historical situation
but seen within the peculiar context of Greek society.

Such a usage would correspond more closely to what can still be gleaned
of the rural use of the term *kleftis*. The island of Crete, particularly the
mountainous areas in the west, is one suggestive source of information.[6] Although the Cretans valiantly resisted the Turks, as they had resisted their
predecessors the Venetians, one does not find many references to the activities of "the klefts" on Crete. Yet the style of guerrilla warfare was not very
different from what was happening on the mainland. What is more, *kleftes*
are still found in western Crete; today they are, quite specifically, animal
thieves. Yet one aspect of this usage is extremely germane to the present inquiry. Those who are described as *kleftes* are not professionals, and they are
not described in general terms as *kleftes*, any more than they would usually
be described as habitual liars: both imputations constitute grave insults which
may lead to bloodshed among these frequently armed men. On the other
hand, just as one may lie in a particular context (such as the defense of family
interests) and be thought worthy for doing so, one may also steal sheep or
goats from neighboring villages under conventionally prescribed circumstances and in conformity with a set of procedural rules. Virtually all the
active shepherds of certain villages are *kleftes*, and *kala kleftes* ("good at
stealing")[7] at that, at certain times and in appropriate conditions. But, when
they are not out on a raid, they are not *kleftes*.

Conversely, moreover, the approach of sheep thieves may still bring the
warning cry, "The *kleftes* have come!" The definite article in this expression
does not, of course, mean that the entire category of named, professional
brigands has suddenly appeared; so, even if the historical conception of "the
klefts" has some basis in vernacular usage, it is still not necessary to argue
that the usage itself refers to an absolute, discrete category of people. *Kleftis*
is, rather, a category of *performative role*. It may be objected that one cannot
interpret a widespread historical phenomenon on the basis of so geographically restricted a datum. The objective here, however, is somewhat more modest.
First, we need only show that interpretations other than the conventional
historicist one are possible; the Cretan usage, which seems to have been classified out of the laographic record as "un-Greek," points in one possible direction, albeit a highly suggestive one.

Second, even standard Greek terminological usage raises doubts about the
literalist view of "the klefts." The Greek definite article is ambiguous in such

a context, since it can introduce both a finite category ("the klefts") and a generic description ("people of the type described as 'klefts'"); historical circumstances, especially the formation of the Hellenist ideology, favored the finite over the generic usage because, as will become apparent below, the independent Greek State could thereby dissociate itself conceptually from the successors of those men who had played so vital a role in its foundation. Something very similar happened in Sicily: as Blok (1974) has amply demonstrated, "the *mafia*" describes a range of social behaviors and values rather than a specific, bounded criminal organization. Even more apposite, perhaps, is the United States usage of "rebel," a term that "served as a touchstone to show the sympathies of the speaker" during and after the Civil War as well as during the earlier struggle for independence (Read 1978).[8]

The geographical, social, and historical limitations of the usual definition of "the klefts" are replicated in the folkloric category of "kleftic songs." Here, for example, is a song which would qualify as kleftic in any collection were it not Cretan:

> *At dawn I'll leave the foothills of the mountain*
> *and run to see the dawn, mountain mine, at your summit.*
> *I'll find a solid boulder and there sit down*
> *to fire off gunshots to gather some* kleftes *nigh:*
> *I'll put a* kleftis *in as a judge, and a* kleftis *as prosecutor,*
> *so that I won't hand out life sentences!*
>
> (Papagrigorakis 1956-57: 280, no. 493)

Kleftism is a broad behavioral continuum, and this song would sit well with several variants of the brigand's life. A burst of gunfire is still the (illegal) summons to a wedding procession in western Crete.

The chronological limits on the "kleftic song" category seem to be as selective as the social. There is in fact some evidence that guerrillas were commemorated in song long before the arrival of the Turks (cf. Morgan 1960: 26; Lambrinos 1947: 76). That such songs have disappeared or shed such personal references as they may have possessed does not mean that the guerrillas themselves never existed, and the evidence that encroaching anonymity is a common feature of oral transmission makes this particular *argumentum ex silentio* especially weak.

Another limitation of the category of "the klefts" is its restriction of a particular range of social behaviors to Greece. This is simplistic—Greek historians have recently discovered important evidence that Albanians and other non-Greek brigands participated in kleftic activities during the prerevolutionary phase (e.g., Vasdravellis 1975). The circumstances of the Greek Revolution were certainly very different from those of the subsequent uprisings in the neighboring countries, but this does not mean that treating kleftism as an exclusively Greek phenomenon does not impose an artificial sense of cultural demarcation. This, too, is reflected in the treatment of "kleftic songs," in which the conventional conception of the kleft as an individualist—the image which d'Istria had so assiduously fostered—could be contrasted with the Bulgarians' failure to make personalities of *their* guerrillas. This device is logically dependent on the literalist assumption that the names in the Greek songs represent specific, individuated klefts:

> . . . Bulgarian popular poetry cannot offer us a single historical or heroic poem: it can only take in certain Bacchic or amorous poems; or, indeed, *in the absence of any other sort of hero*, it exalts the *haidouts*, otherwise known as brigands, who have *absolutely no connection* with the Serbian *hajduks* or the Greek klefts. The latter are national heroes, *after a historical model*; the Bulgarian *haidouts* are common-law criminals, devoid of personality and lacking even the virile audacity of ordinary brigands.
>
> (Colocotronis 1918: 129; my emphasis)

Here is the legacy of d'Istria, transformed only in that the events of the First World War had ranged Greece and Serbia against Bulgaria, with the result that the Serbs, though Slavs, are now conceptually as well as politically closer to the Greeks. In comparison to the hated Bulgarians, even "ordinary brigands" display that "virile" character which d'Istria had declared to be the innate possession of the European peoples in general. Ideological boundaries are now erected across the existing linguistic ones (*haidout* and *hajduk* vs. *kleftis*, but cf. also Cretan *haïnis*). New cultural discontinuities are perceived where new political alignments have arisen. But the presumption of a Greek national character, exemplified by the behavior of "the klefts" and described in "their" songs, survives such ephemeral transformations.[9]

The Denial of Banditry

The ideal image of the Greek kleft was supported by the content of the published "kleftic songs." There was a certain amount of evidence in these songs, it is true, that the klefts had sometimes been indiscriminate brigands who raided Moslem and Christian alike (e.g., Baggally 1936: 73). Zambelios' suppression of the ransom story nevertheless suggests a pattern of bowdlerization which undoubtedly contributed to the usual picture of uniform patriotism which most of the folklore collections suggest. Songs in which *kleftes* behaved reprehensibly were classified into other categories; thus, a famous song in which a young merchant is ambushed and killed by a brigand (*kleftis*) who turns out to be his own brother is classified as a "ballad" (*paraloyi*; see Ioannou 1975: 97-99). Doubtless this could be justified on the grounds that

other, thematically and stylistically similar songs describing fatal family con-
flicts do not mention klefts at all, so that it is the narrative theme which
should determine the taxonomic placement. This, however, means that the
entire classification is contingent upon the accident of which songs have been
preserved in a sufficient number of variants for such resemblances to be evident. The terms in which the "kleftic" category has been constituted, moreover, are patriotic, historical, and descriptive. This song, however, narrates a
sorry tale of fratricide in which social warfare (by the brigands against the
wealthy) rather than defense of the homeland provides the setting and even,
to some extent, the theme. The category of "kleftic songs" supports a different view of history.

Brigandage against fellow Greeks was thus not subsumed under the Hellenist concept of *kleftouria*. The distinction between the patriot-klefts and the
latter-day brigands soon became a feature of the official vocabulary. *Kleptis*,
in Classical Greek, had meant "thief," and the Hellenists clearly hoped that
the ancient form would reappear in the language with that meaning and that
the obviously demotic *kleftis* might retain its newly patriotic sense (see Politis 1871: xxxvi). The latter form was given a set of *katharevousa* inflections,
so that a "new" word was actually added in this way to the neo-Classical
language—but one which was still recognizably Greek. At the same time, a
Classical term, *listis*, was reintroduced to denote "brigand"; all the *post-
revolutionary* brigands are so named in official writings. After a while, indeed,
the distinction between klefts and brigands became so widely accepted that
the negative term, *listis*, acquired a set of alternative demotic inflections; this
is the corollary of what happened to *kleftis* in the official tongue.

In 1870 there occurred an event which sharpened the definitional discrimi-
nation which had been created in the following manner. Four foreign travelers were murdered by a party of brigands whose extravagant demands for
ransom and amnesty had been turned down. Public opinion, both in Greece
and abroad, was outraged (see Jenkins 1961). The Hellenists, ever concerned
about the external image of Greece, were forced to confront a small epidemic
of anti-Greek feeling:

> If, however, one were carefully to go through the ancient and modern
> history of Greece, he would not find it difficult, if not to induce the
> West to alter its opinion entirely, then at least to persuade it that by
> using the word "brigandage" (*listia*) it frequently confuses the Greeks'
> inherent honor and patriotism—the so-called *pallikarismos*—with it.
>
> But, however eager the Hellene may be to become a kleft in order to
> exercise his *pallikarismos* at complete liberty in the mountains, to the
> same degree it is in his nature to reject brigandage (*listia*) . . .
>
> (Goudas n.d.: 1-2)

This is a much more precise statement of the distinction than one encounters in references of only ten or even five years earlier (e.g., Xenos 1865); after the Dilessi incident, kleftism and brigandage were irrevocably exclusive of each other. The more neutral Classical term *kleptis* has, in the course of these semantic shifts, been relegated to the meaning of "petty thief," while the form *kleftis* is generally used for the patriot-brigand of the national redemption (cf. Politis 1973: xii–xviii).

As a major consequence of this development, brigandage has now been defined as foreign to the Greek national character. In the aftermath of the Dilessi incident, this was of great concern to the naturally much embarrassed Greek élite. It has been described as the creation of an "ethnic truth" (Jenkins 1961: 99-117); this is a useful label provided that it is taken not as a concocted falsehood (e.g., Howarth 1976: 122) but as an internally consistent ideological statement. The Greeks did not try to pretend that there were no brigands in Greece at all, despite subsequent foreign claims to the contrary. Their concern was instead to demonstrate that brigandage was extrinsic to the pure Hellenic character, to that collective will which was still in the process of recovering from the foreign yoke. Within the set of definitions which such a perspective entailed, the klefts had been true Greeks; the surviving brigands were either of foreign blood (Albanians, Koutsovlachs) or the relics of Turkish oppression.

This argument had a Classical analogue, in that at least one ancient writer had similarly treated brigandage as something foreign to true Greek culture. Such a parallel lent redoubled force to the nineteenth-century Greek position:

> We are not unaware, moreover, of Thucydides' observation that "the Greeks in OLDEN times *were prone to brigandage*," but Thucydides himself, in the very same book, attributes this hateful deed to the Kares, whom Minos drove out (of Greece), setting up his own sons as leaders. . . . Besides, on the subject of the brigandage (*listia*) done by the Greeks, this same Thucydides says, "They are not ashamed of this deed (i.e., brigandage), but, rather, treat it as something glorious . . . and, until now, most of it, in Greece, is to be found according to the OLD style among the Locrians, the Ozolae, the Aetolians and the Acarnanians, and in Epirus" [I, iv-viii] . Here we must observe, first of all, that Thucydides does not attribute brigandage in Greece to the Hellenes but to the Kares, whom Minos drove out of Greece; and, second, that Thucydides is not writing about his own era but about OLDEN times . . . in his day, only the Locrians, the Ozolae, the Aetolians and the Acarnanians lived in an *old-style* polity, that, in other words, which obtained before the Kares were driven out of Greece.
>
> (Goudas n.d.: 4)

In Crete, villagers still attribute the incidence of animal rustling to the privations and bad moral conditions of the Turkocracy. The point of such a defense is obviously not to claim that banditry literally never occurs. While its endemic nature may not be so freely conceded, as British officials who tried to force the Greek authorities into giving satisfaction discovered, its persistence has to be explained in terms of existing ideological assumptions rather than unrealistically denied out of hand.[10]

Bandits to Nationalists: The Process of Transformation

The progressive canonization of the klefts is manifest in the treatment of songs which mention their activities. As the distinction between klefts and brigands hardened, its effects spread beyond the immediate confines of the "kleftic song" category to other texts in which klefts were mentioned. Since the view prevailed that, for every set of variant texts, one was most "correct" or closest to a putative *Urtext*, one criterion for preferring a particular variant was its apparent endorsement of the prevailing kleftic image.

An example is provided by this song:

> *Mount Olympus and Mount Kissavos are quarreling, the two of them . . .*
> *"Don't cross me, Kissavos, you Turk-trodden mountain . . .*
> *I'm old Olympus, famed throughout the world!"*

And Olympus goes on to boast that on him perches an eagle, holding a kleft's head in its talons. The eagle asks the kleft how he came to die, and the head responds with a tale of his exploits.

To Zambelios (1852: 605) and his followers (e.g., Ellinismos 1896: 92), the song conveyed (and was consequently entitled by them) "Hellenic freedom." Fauriel commented at an early date that the opening theme of the quarreling mountains had apparently been "borrowed" from other folk theme patterns in order to give dramatic emphasis to the heroic portrayal of the kleft (1824: 38-39; cf. Apostolakis 1950: 80). It is known as an independent theme in its own right, as in a similarly disputatious exchange between the three mighty mountains of Crete, although the progressive shortening of Cretan folksongs, which is well documented (cf. Morgan 1960: 50-51), may have deprived it of some comparable narrative conclusion. The theme belongs, however, to a pattern of songs in which the protagonists, who use similar formulaic expressions, may be birds (Kriaris 1920: 243) or flowers (Politis 1914: 235, no. 232); again, there is no attached kleftic tale. The common feature of all these texts is a motif of dissension rather than of specifically national unity.

Such national unity can be read into the text only if the epithet "Turk-trodden" is retained. Without suggesting that the line is in any way spurious,

however, we may legitimately question its historical priority. A version recorded by the German philhellene Theodor Kind has "kleft-trodden" addressed *by* Kissavos *to* Olympus (1833: 1-2). If it was sometimes insulting to
be called "kleft-trodden" before 1833, this is further evidence for a change in
the significance of *kleftis*. The sequence of textual changes, however, is less
easy to interpret, especially as Haxthausen records a still earlier rendering
with a form of "Turk-trampled" (1935: 48, no. 9).

But, what is perhaps most revealing of all, in the third edition of his collection Kind replaced his own original text with a "Turk-trodden" (*koniaropati-
mene*)[11] version taken from an anonymous Athenian disquisition, *On the
State* (Kind 1861: 24-27, 225). Again, this is not, in all probability, a case of
deliberate distortion; Kind does cite the source for his new rendering. But
what must have recommended the 1861 text to him was the fact that it made
far better sense than the 1833 variant in terms of the philhellenic-Hellenist
ideology. It represented the klefts as an unambiguously positive category, in
explicit opposition to a named, *national* enemy.

Regional Claims on National Character

The quarrel between Olympus and Kissavos, while perhaps sometimes interpreted as an expression of nationwide values, also reveals the intense localism
that often characterized relations among the various guerrilla groups and village communities involved in the fight for freedom. Such localism was likewise not uncommon among scholars and writers and became noticeably
stronger as amateur folklorists began to emerge from the ranks of the schoolteachers and other educated members of local communities. Even among the
professional scholars, the same phenomenon can be observed. It did not
necessarily conflict directly with the nationalist ideal, however, as local allegiances often took the form of claiming that the home region was the finest
repository of that ideal. Nor should the work of local folklorists be under-
estimated in assessing their contribution to the growth of national consciousness. Especially in Asia Minor (see Bryer 1976: 186-189), these enthusiasts
discovered and published the evidence of persistent and flourishing Greek
culture.

The province of Epirus remained under Turkish rule until the Greek in-
vasion of 1913. Many of the klefts who had aided in the liberation of the rest
of Greece were from Epirus, and sustained efforts were made to show that
these men and their exploits, the continued occupation of the province not-
withstanding, exemplified the heroic tradition of the Hellenes. In particular,
Epirote folklore proved a rich source of "kleftic songs," so much so that this
genre was soon said to be of Epirote origin in its entirety. Indeed, the extreme view was sometimes taken that *all* Greek folksong had originated in

Epirus (see especially Khristovasilis 1902). But the "kleftic songs" proved to be a particularly popular focus with local folklorists; the large number of texts actually recorded in Epirus itself is evidence of the collectors' enthusiasm as well as of, perhaps, the late demise of "legitimate" kleftism in the province. The quantity of accredited Epirote texts also benefited from the local folklorists' methodological assumptions:

> And if on the one hand it is true that amongst the above [texts] reckoned [by us as Epirote] there are some which are common in other rural districts of Greece, and thus not to be classified as purely Epirote, yet—since it is difficult to establish their homeland (*patris*), and they are to be encountered in general use in Epirus—we are justified in accounting them as such.   (Aravandinos 1880: ix)

Such reasoning is not always restricted to the single category of "kleftic songs":

> But, if Epirus is the homeland (*patridha*) of the kleftic songs, it is no less the home of the songs of exile. Naturally, other regions also have their songs of exile, but Epirus stands in the front rank. [This is] because the poverty-stricken populace of Epirus was given to emigration as far back as prehistoric times. . . . Out of the numbers of the expatriate Epirotes came the Great Benefactors of the nation (*ethnos*), making Epirus the intellectual center of Hellenism during the years of servitude. . . . Again, the funeral dirges (*miroloyia*), a pure product of the Epirote women's creativity, are among the most moving in the world *and may compete with the famous Maniat laments*: both sets originate in the ancient laments of the Hellenes.
> (Yangas n.d.: 25; my emphasis)

Note the explicit statement of competitive relations within the larger, national unity. Since the loyalties concerned are essentially concentric, rather than opposed to each other, the smaller allegiance could be justified in terms of the larger.

This balance between the two loyalties is especially well illustrated by the Epirote folklorists' treatment of the "kleftic songs." It was assumed that these songs would be found in their pristine form only in places where the klefts had been active; their presence was thus indicative of a region's devotion to the national cause. But they could also be used to point out the regional exemplification of true Hellenism in another way. Since these "kleftic songs" were commonly taken as the prototypical Greek folksongs par excellence, it was by attributing their origin to Epirus that local folklorists could argue that the province was the fount of all Greek folksong without exception (Aravandinos 1880: vii–ix; Yangas n.d.: 23–25). The success of their claim may be gauged from the alacrity with which the proponents of other localisms (e.g., Lanitis 1946 for Cyprus) accepted it, even while hymning the aesthetic qualities of their own local songs.

The Epirotes' argument depended on the successful blending of taxonomies. On the one hand, the historical and folkloristic "kleftic" categories were already immune to effective challenge within Greece. On the other hand, the classification of Greece by geographical regions had not yet settled down to its present exact disposition. The Epirus to which Aravandinos referred was larger than the modern province of the same name (Yangas n.d.: 23). Even aside from "Northern Epirus," which is today part of Albania, sections of the old Turkish Epirus are today incorporated into two other provinces of the Greek State. In short, there was some confusion over precisely what Epirus was. It was consequently possible to propound different cultural configurations on the basis of these differing definitions of the provincial borders, and Aravandinos' defense of the Epirote contribution to Hellenism was helped by his inclusion of a larger area and, therefore, of a greater demographic and cultural reservoir.

Aravandinos restricted his argument, however, to the comparatively modest claim that, if a song were known to Epirote singers, it could then be considered Epirote *in that sense* (1880: ix). His position was then extended to a more contentious view by Yangas. After first apparently endorsing Aravandinos' position, he showed that his conception of cultural origins was of a far more literal order: he complained of "hearing kleftic songs described on the radio as Peloponnesian, when they are nothing other than kleftic songs" (n.d.: 24). Since for Yangas kleftic songs were by definition Epirote, his position may be paraphrased: when songs are sung in Epirus they are Epirote; but, when they are sung in the Peloponnese, they are merely variants of Epirote songs.

Language and National Character: The Koutsovlach Case

The richness of the ethnographic record in Epirus thus served to illustrate the Hellenic heritage of the region. That same record, however, differently interpreted, could have posed a serious liability because of the province's several minority groups, which could and sometimes did offer neighboring countries the pretext for making territorial claims. The most consistently sensitive group of this kind was that of the Koutsovlachs; their language is closely akin to Romanian, and this has led Romanian scholars (e.g., Capidan n.d.) to advance ethnological arguments in support of their country's territorial interests. The Greek response has been largely philological, ranging from the "political philology" which derived *Koutsovlakhos* from Turkish roots to mean "only slightly Wallachian"[12] (Wace and Thompson 1914: 3) to a recent word count of the Koutsovlach language in which "the Turkish [words] have been counted among the modern Greek ones" (Papazisis 1976: 8), presumably on the assumption that they must have been channeled to Koutsovlach via Greek.

Such academic contortion was not an immediate political necessity, although it was doubtless intensified under the incessant pressures of Balkan realpolitik. To understand the Greeks' response in context, it is necessary to stress two fundamental points. First, they were not alone in using scholarly arguments for such purposes. Capidan's ethnological arguments for the Romanian case were matched by Bulgarian and Yugoslav attempts to claim parts of Greek Macedonia as their own. Second, while the Greeks might have rested their case with the simple argument that the Koutsovlachs were a numerical minority within a political nation-state, their own original claims to nationhood had been based on the concept of cultural resurgence; this imposed a certain pattern on their subsequent dealings with other newly formed Balkan states, at least in terms of scholarly and political rhetoric.

Folksongs, as linguistic evidence as well as the expression of *Volksgeist*, naturally fed these disputatious fires. The songs of the Koutsovlachs were of special interest to the Greek apologists, because some were in Greek rather than the Koutsovlachs' own language; of these, furthermore, many were "kleftic." Koutsovlachs, too, had made a signal contribution to the cause of Greek independence (see Papazisis 1976). Thus, although it is the Koutsovlachs' language which marks them as a distinctive group to this day (cf. Schein 1975), their performance of "kleftic" songs in Epirote Greek provides a potential basis for demonstrating their espousal of the Greek national consciousness. Local folklorists soon seized on this point.

Once again, the perception of ethnological relationships depends on the processes by which evidence is selected as relevant. It is true that the Koutsovlachs sing many songs in Greek, and the Koutsovlach community of Metsovo is bilingual. On the other hand, there are also many songs in the Koutsovlach language. These are often excluded from the published folklore, since few non-Koutsovlachs would be able to read them; in effect, then, they are excluded from "Hellenic laography" at large. The Greek-language songs, by contrast, are given primary significance. The Koutsovlachs, writes Aravandinos,

> though they do not use the Greek language at home, nevertheless compose [*sic*!] their songs in it. The reader will find many such songs in the present collection, mostly gathered in Metsovo, Grevena, and Malakasi—Vlach districts in part, certainly, but where one almost never hears a Vlach song. In their dances, at weddings, saint's day festivities, or at home when their women sing lullabies to their babies or keen dirges

over the dead, they always sing in Greek, even though occasionally some of them, *in their ignorance of the Greek language*, do not precisely understand the meaning of what they sing. Let this therefore stand as *yet one more proof of the almost complete assimilation of this race with that of the Hellenes.*   (1880: vii; my emphasis)

The author of these words, though undoubtedly eager to claim a special role for his much loved Epirus, was certainly no secessionist.[13] On the contrary, localism of this sort was but a more minutely focused expression of ideological Hellenism. The literature is full of essays in which a particular region is held up as the fullest realization of Greek culture.[14] Like the essays of more obviously national scope, moreover, these localist works looked to European models of propriety. Aravandinos, for example, cleaned up his klefts; "that dog" became "the bad man" (Apostolakis 1950: 77, n. 2). For, if the klefts embodied Greek heroism, they must also participate in "the virile habits of the Europeans." So, too, must all those members of minority groups whose destiny it is to enter the national consciousness of the Hellenes.

Such was the Hellenists' perspective. It is the perspective which we encounter when a Greek refers to "Europe" (*Evropi*) as including Greece. Yet there is an alternative usage, whereby "Europe" and "Greece" are treated as terms in a complementary opposition; and here the view expressed is the Romeic one, with its readier acceptance of Greece's more recent past. European observers in the nineteenth century were mostly inclined to favor the former interpretation. There was, however, one exponent, not so much of a "Romeic" as of a virulently anti-Greek culture theory. This was the *bête noire* already mentioned earlier, Jakob Philipp Fallmerayer. Now it is time to step back to the earliest years of Greek independence, to examine Fallmerayer's ideas in brief review, and to trace their galvanizing effect on the development of Greek folklore research.

Chapter 4
Attack and Reaction

". . . no Greek but a Slav . . ."

Fallmerayer against Hellas

The constitution of "the klefts" as a chronologically and ethnically bounded entity served three closely interconnected aims of the Hellenist ideology. It presented the modern Greeks as worthy descendants of the ancient heroes; it validated their claim, as true individualists, to a Hellenic and therefore also to a European cultural identity; and it provided a theme which would permit the conceptual assimilation of Christian ethnic minorities to that identity. These three goals were essential components of the philhellenic and nationalist search for a Greek "national consciousness." The kleftic theme has provided us with a specific context in which to examine in some detail how these goals were pursued. The creation of a kleftic history and folklore serves as a paradigm for the emergent methods of national culture history in mid nineteenth-century Greece.

We now return to the broader canvas. For the importance which Greek nationalists attributed to kleftism was by no means an isolated phenomenon, as must already be evident. More generally, indeed, the concern to establish a national history might never have generated such impressive results had it not been for the provocation offered by those foreigners who, unlike the more numerous philhellenes, had scant liking for the Greek cause. Chief among these was Jakob Philipp Fallmerayer (1790-1861), a pamphleteer, historian, and liberal pan-German nationalist of Tyrolean origin. The very name of Fallmerayer has been execrated in Greece from 1830 until our own time as the symbol and epitome of anti-Greek sentiment. That execration, however, was extraordinarily productive, for Fallmerayer flung down a challenge which the Greeks could ill afford to ignore; and they met it magnificently.[1]

Fallmerayer's crime consisted in denying the Greeks their claim to descent from the ancient Hellenes. Enough has already been said about that claim to show that he was, in effect, denying them their national raison d'être. In explicitly treating modern Greece as conceptually outside "Europe," moreover,

Fallmerayer (1845, II: 259-260) expressed a perspective which conflicted terminologically, ideologically, and politically with the Greeks' national aspirations. Unlike Kind (1861: xxii-xxiii), who proposed a pan-European folklore concordance that would include all the Greek material, Fallmerayer rejected the very notion of the Greeks as Europeans. He not only regarded them as mere chattels of an oriental dominion but argued that their claims to Hellenic identity had completely misled the gullible intelligentsia of "true" Europe (1845, II: 261). He thus made political capital of the ambiguity of the term "Europe" in the Greek context. The Greeks, not to be outdone, contemptuously informed him that he was "no Greek but a Slav" (Fallmerayer 1845, II: 462). In this debate, nationality and ideology were fully conflated.

Fallmerayer was not the first foreigner to sneer at the claims of Greek nationalism, but his use of supposedly ethnographic evidence for that purpose was certainly something new. Other observers who felt that the Greeks were not yet ready for self-government nevertheless conceded their essential Greekness. The British aristocrat F. S. N. Douglas, a notable exponent of this more moderate attitude, was convinced that the Greeks of his day still spoke a language akin to Classical Greek, although he "called the present Greek language Romaic, the term by which the modern Greeks distinguish themselves on account of their titular character of Romans, in distinction to Hellenic, by which they designate their ancestors" (1813: 30). He listed numerous parallels between ancient and modern custom in ritual, marriage practices, feasting, symbolism, and religious attitudes. None of this prevented him from opposing Greek independence; any threat to Turkish power was an encouragement to Russian ambitions in the area, and these ran directly counter to British interests (e.g., 1813: 187-195). In particular, Douglas feared the possible consequences for British trade should Russia ever gain control of Constantinople. "These may be considered as only national and British arguments: but while the weight of ignorance and superstition continues to oppress the Greeks, in vain may you confer upon them nominal freedom [*sic*!]: they cannot feel the value of the gift you bestow." The logic is that of the purest nineteenth-century colonialism: "An infant may be more safely entrusted with a sword, than the ignorant and the bigotted with the sacred weapon of liberty and dominion" (1813: 197). In the end, however, "if the wild fancies of politicians and enthusiasts do not hurry them out of the course in which they are advancing with cautious but accelerated steps, another age may witness the glorious period when the torch of knowledge shall conduct the Greeks to the enjoyment of happiness and freedom" (1813: 198). Events did not await the pleasure of this British apologist, but they did not bring the Russians to Constantinople either. Nevertheless, the fear that this might happen was a very real one at the time.

It is in his fear of Russia, moreover, that Douglas anticipates Fallmerayer. He shared with the German writer the conviction that the modern Greeks were largely descended from Hellenized *barbaroi* (1813: 40), attributing to this the features which to his mind bespoke decadence and superstition. Unlike Fallmerayer, however, Douglas also accepted a substantial element of true Hellenism in the modern Greeks; thus, he argued, when they showed that they once again measured up to the standards of their illustrious ancestors—standards which only a true "European" could judge!—they might then be allowed to have their independence.

Fallmerayer, similarly motivated by the fear of Russian expansionism, nevertheless developed a far more sweeping attack on Greek national identity. He denied the very basis of that identity as conceived by philhellenes and Greek nationalists alike, arguing that the Classical Greeks' heritage could not possibly have survived successive Slav and Albanian invasions during the Byzantine era; as a result, he maintained, the present population of the country must be of entirely non-Greek "racial" origin. His evidence for these claims was historical and cultural rather than genetic. Like his detractors (and, indeed, most of his contemporaries), he made no distinction between these two aspects of the problem, the cultural and the "racial," using the evidence of the one in order to support claims related to the other; it was not until later (Wachsmuth 1864; Lawson 1910: 25-28) that this crucial refinement was brought to the debate. Both Fallmerayer and the Greek nationalists saw the modern Greeks' "racial" origins as the key issue and ethnographic and historical evidence as the means of resolving it. They differed, however, both in their conclusions and in the political principles which guided their researches. It was the political aspect, furthermore, which determined those principles of selection and ordering by which we may explain so radical a divergence in their respective conclusions.

Fallmerayer's political stance offers a study in internal contradiction. Although aggressively liberal in domestic matters, he was "an ardent supporter of the Ottoman Empire" (Hussey 1978: 83). This was not merely a case of double political standards, although the Ottoman sultans were regarded in European intellectual circles as the very incarnation of despotism. Rather, it should be seen in the context of Fallmerayer's commitment to German unification. A liberal, united Germany would not be able, he thought, to resist the territorial ambitions of a strong Russia; therefore, any obstacle to Russian power was welcome. The older Fallmerayer grew, the more he protested against what was seen as the increasingly probable dissolution of the Ottoman Empire. His view of the importance of Turkey, which was shared by some of his German contemporaries, was to become a key motivation in postunification German policy in the Balkans (see Couloumbis, Petropulos, and Psomiades 1976: 30-32; Taillandier 1862: 129-130). Fallmerayer's fierce convictions in this respect certainly explain his implacable opposition to Greek nationalism and, perhaps, help show why he was apparently more extreme in his published views on Greek racial origins than he was in private conversation (Hussey 1978: 83).

Fallmerayer was thus not merely an academic commentator; his views held enormous political significance both for himself and for the Greeks. Abroad, his theories threatened to erode support for the Greek cause, or so his opponents feared. Within Greece, dominated as it was by a foreign monarchy and bureaucracy, he represented a potentially serious danger. Even King Otto came increasingly to endorse his views and to refer to them in his dealings with diplomats and administrators (Hussey 1978: 80). The view expressed by a fellow German, K. B. Hase, that Fallmerayer's theories could be endorsed without danger to the nation-state was thus hardly a plausible one. Even Fallmerayer himself did not trouble to dissociate his ethnology from his anti-Russian feelings. It may even be that he was aware that some of the earliest collectors of Greek folklore, notably Mustoxidi and Papadopoulos-Vrettos, had been ardently pro-Russian.

The truth of the matter is, of course, that virtually any position on the question of Greek ethnicity would have been invested with political significance: given the circumstances under which Greece became a nation-state, there was quite simply no such thing as a neutral stance. Fallmerayer, bluffly insensitive to such matters, seems to have been genuinely amazed at the hostile reception he received on the occasion of his first visit to Greece in 1840 (cf. also Politis 1871: ii). Undoubtedly, there was some irritation at his having performed his armchair ethnology *before* visiting the land itself. An instructive contrast is provided by the Frenchman Edgar Quinet, who initially shared some of Fallmerayer's interest in the Slavic and Albanian heritage of the modern Greeks; but Quinet expressed his views *after* visiting the country and subsequently modified them in deference to the young nation's quest for recognition (Karatza 1970: 48). However one approached it, the problem of Hellenic authenticity could not be separated from ideology, and Fallmerayer's attitude represented a threatening extreme.

It was in 1830 that Fallmerayer first achieved notoriety in the annals of Greek cultural studies, with the publication of volume 1 of his ethnologically oriented history of the Peloponnese (Morea). In this work, Fallmerayer first expounded in detail the theory that so enraged the Greeks and their supporters: the original Hellenic population had been completely destroyed and replaced in the course of successive invasions during the Byzantine period. Although he had already begun to establish his academic standing with his historical work on Trebizond, his Peloponnesian history gave his views on modern Greek ethnicity their first wide exposure. The reaction, which was further exacerbated by his subsequent writings (1845, 1860), was furious and sustained. Not only Greeks but foreign scholars also leaped into the fray; prominent among the foreigners were two other Germans, Kurt Wachsmuth and Bernhard Schmidt. Greek ethnology was suddenly well on its way.

Whether judged by contemporary or present-day standards, Fallmerayer's scholarship is uneven at best and makes extensive use of special pleading and blank assertion. For example, he attributed the absence of an aspirate (/h/) in modern Greek to Slavic influence, on the grounds that the Cyrillic alphabet used a *g* for the aspirate of foreign words (e.g., "Gamburg"; see Fallmerayer 1830: 236). Such confusion of the phonetic with the alphabetic makes for a weak philological argument, especially since the closeness of modern to ancient Greek in general was already well established by Fallmerayer's time. In another attempt to demonstrate the Slavicization of the Greek language, Fallmerayer contended that the loss of the infinitive verb forms in Greek was similarly the result of foreign models. This view did not stand up to close inspection for very long; it was soon established that the dropping of the infinitive forms occurred earlier in Greek than in neighboring languages (Hesseling 1892: 43–44; Sandfeld 1930: 178; Joseph 1978).[2] As for Fallmerayer's complaint that the modern Athenians spoke Albanian, this impressed few observers as having any real significance since (as he himself recognized) the Athenians also spoke Greek. One of his earliest Greek critics, Anastasios Lefkias, offered the sensible rejoinder that, since bilingualism and trilingualism in Northern Europe were not always taken as indicating separate nationality, it was scarcely reasonable to insist on so interpreting them in Greece (1843: 52). Much the same kind of objection may be raised against Fallmerayer's use of toponyms. Slavic place-names have little more bearing on the inhabitants' ethnicity or ancestry than do their present-day Hellenized replacements. They are an indication, certainly, of some sort of political or cultural event, but they do not justify claims of massive demographic change.

While some of these objections are more easily made with the help of concepts and materials that were not available to Fallmerayer's contemporaries, there is no doubt that they were uncomfortable with his polemical mode of argument. Many of them were nevertheless tempted into much the same intemperate style when responding to him, often at the expense of scholarship in those early years (but cf. Politis 1871). Even Lefkias, for all his perceptiveness on the subject of bilingualism, was not above hyperbole, as the title of his crusading treatise against Fallmerayerism shows: *Overthrow of What Has Been Claimed . . .* The fact of the matter is that the entire scholarly establishment of Greece was both dismayed and profoundly offended by Fallmerayer's activities.

The most remarkable outcome of the Greek reaction was the sudden flowering of folklore studies. While it would be absurd to suggest that folklore would never have attracted scholarly interest without the stimulus pro-

vided by Fallmerayer, it is certainly true that much of the best work done by
the first Greek folklorists represents a conscious response to the German
scholar's theories—and the political implications of these theories insured
folklore a role in Greek national life that was much more than purely academic. Most, if not all, of the volumes of "national folklore" which appeared
in the years between Fallmerayer's *Geschichte* and the beginning of the twentieth century were directly inspired by the goal of proving "the German"
wrong. Not all the folklorists explicitly said that this was their intention;
Zambelios, for example, does not, although a reviewer praised his essay on
the word *traghoudho* as "demolishing the rotten edifice of the crazy historian
from Germany" (Anon. 1859-60: 495). The reviewer made it abundantly
clear, moreover, that the "patriotic or archaeological" import of Zambelios'
work was appreciated:

> . . . words signify objects, and objects have history. As the discovery of
> a stone bearing some phrase engraved upon it, a name or a date, often
> clarifies an obscure aspect of antiquity, so too the philosophical in-
> vestigation of the origins, rise, decline, and degeneration of a word
> sometimes suffices not only to correct or refute erroneous opinions
> about history but also, by Zeus! to bear witness to the identity of an
> entire nation (*ethnos*).

The national significance of Zambelios' argument was so unambiguous that
neither he nor his reviewer had to mention Fallmerayer by name. Papadopoulos-Vrettos had already noted of Zambelios' 1852 historical work that "the
study of the history of one's forefathers is rarely a purely theoretical study.
But for us this history has come to acquire a more practical significance than
is usual, since the time that this historical doctrine took hold and began to
spread, that the great turmoil of medieval times totally uprooted the hoary
tree of ancient Hellenism" (1852-53: 397). Readers of such words did not
need to be reminded that this was the critical issue for their national identity
or that Fallmerayer was the target.

In describing the effects of Fallmerayer's writings upon the growth of
Greek folklore studies generally, we shall depart somewhat from strict chronological order. The development of a nationalist discipline of folklore in
Greece was not a simple chain of cause and effect or a straightforwardly unilineal sequence of books and articles. The development of a taxonomic system which adequately reflected the concerns of the Greek folklorists and
historians was uneven, a process of trial and error involving a wide range of
personalities and interests. In order to discern what presuppositions guided
Fallmerayer's critics, we may begin not necessarily with the earliest but with
some of the most vitriolic and uncompromising of their responses. If some of

these seem absurd today, that is partly because time and place no longer give them meaning. In the context of the newly emergent Greek nation-state, however, what might otherwise pass for mere invective cries out instead as the voice of a passionate, threatened commitment. Some of the apparent absurdity, moreover, simply reflects the very different state of anthropological and linguistic method at that time, not only in Greece but throughout all of Europe.

We should also remember that, at a less overt level, the reaction was not directed at Fallmerayer alone, although he was no mere figurehead. In the early years of the Greek kingdom, anti-German sentiment was provoked by the high-handedness of King Otto and his advisers. Even after major popular unrest led, in 1844, to the nominal curtailment of the king's powers, the work of his earliest ministers in fashioning a "European" administration remained to plague their successors. The entire legal code, for example, was drawn up by the Bavarian Georg von Maurer. In 1853, when an ostensibly more "nativist" government commissioned L. Khrisanthopoulos to conduct a survey of traditional family and inheritance law in the provinces, the questions which this agent sent the local authorities were all predetermined by the "European" categories of von Maurer's code. The strains were never fully alleviated. Popular unrest flared repeatedly; Otto himself was finally deposed in 1862, only to be replaced the following year by yet another foreigner, a Danish prince who became King George I.

Up to that point, then, Greece was ruled by an unpopular foreign monarch who fell increasingly under Fallmerayer's influence and who was served by ministers who largely shared with him a set of values alien to the populace. The Greek intelligentsia, while sharing their commitment to the nation-state ideal at the most general level, did not necessarily join in their enthusiasm for the institution of monarchy. The Greeks also saw both that their national self-respect demanded their firm resistance to Fallmerayer's influence and that the justification for a Greek State would ultimately stand or fall on the ethnological question. At one level, the rest of this book is an account of the way in which they fought that battle.

Lelekos: A Poetic Response

One prominent participant was Michael Lelekos, who published works on folklore in 1852 (second edition, 1868) and 1888. Sure that his own elaborately doctored "folk" texts had furnished proof incontrovertible of the Greeks' Hellenic identity, he concluded his first essay with a triumphant ode in an extreme form of neo-Classical Greek addressed "to the German, Fallmerayer":

Croak now as thou wouldst, O raven,
  Now behold in thy covetous sight,
Thou black villain in armor black-bronzèd—
  Fallmerayer! O bitter, cruel wight!

Tho' antiently gripp'd in midwinter,
  Of the Hellenes that Olympiad—
After centuries, centuries fighting—
  Sings high odes as she formerly had.

Hail! airy daughter of Tantalus,
  Hail! bashful Muse, who singst fair.
The voices of envy's brave offspring
  Hast thou utterly silenced fore'er . . .

(1868: 224)

The collector-poet apparently saw no irony in this proud claim. The "high odes" to which he refers were nevertheless extensively rewritten (and sometimes entirely concocted) by Lelekos himself (see especially Vlakhoyannis 1935: 228–232), in order to supply Classical parallels whenever none could be wrung from the untouched originals of the folksong texts.

Some of his texts seem to be outright forgeries. Direct references to Sophocles (1868: 31) and to "the Persian dogs" (1868: 21; this refers to the Turks—a metaphorical association of the ancient and the recent) are surprising in any folk text at so early a date, before widespread education had wrought extensive changes in the language and imagery of folk poetry. Likewise, the characterization of the Albanian ruler of Yannina, Ali Pasha, as a *tyrannos* ("tyrant") sounds like a suspiciously Classical gloss for any of a whole range of equally trenchant demotic terms (1868: 52).[3] Sometimes, Lelekos gives what may perhaps be adjusted forms in mid text (e.g., *ton* for *tous* in 1868: 126, 1. 30). On occasion, the purpose of all this classicizing virtually declares itself:

Leonidas' sword—
Kolokotronis wears it;
as soon as a Turk sees it he falls wounded
and his blood runs ice-cold. . . .

(1868: 25, no. 5)

Such texts are clearly "offered to national philology," and the "protests which the mountain-dwelling priests of liberty sang in the mountains and caves at times of national adventure and tyrannical proscriptions of Hellenism" have in many instances been amplified or composed with that purpose in mind (Lelekos 1852: iii, v; cf. also Apostolakis 1929: 115, n. 1).

Many of Lelekos' footnoted parallels with the great Attic dramatists and other ancient authors seem especially contrived. When no obvious parallel with antiquity could be found, he supplied weighty paraphrases of the songs themselves in neo-Classical doggerel. As an exercise in projecting the "European" image, the latter device was entirely characteristic: although the words and grammatical forms were largely simplified Classical Greek, he also used rhyme—which was not Classical but had a long and respectable ancestry in more recent Western European poetry as well as in vernacular Greek. Unlike the forged folksong texts, all these neo-Classical renditions as well as a few specially composed celebratory verses (including the ode to Fallmerayer) bear Lelekos' own name or initials. In this way, he "foregrounded" his own assumed role as the interpreter of vernacular poetry to an educated posterity.

That the forgeries escaped attention for many decades is not as surprising as it may seem. For one thing, textual accuracy had not yet become quite as much of a fundamental doctrine as it is in modern folklore scholarship. Insofar as he thought about it consciously, Lelekos may even have felt entitled, as a Greek, to participate actively in both the vernacular and the scholarly traditions. Furthermore, it was well understood by his Greek contemporaries that the value of Lelekos' work lay not only in the preservation of a steadily disappearing heritage (the same reason that had prompted the periodical *Pandora* to publish folksongs sporadically from 1854 on) but also in the presentation of that heritage to the West. Lelekos himself seems to have formed a highly personal view of the latter goal, showing at every juncture that he hoped to convince even Fallmerayer that Greek folksongs preserved "both the language and poetry and the manners and customs of their [i.e., the Greeks'] fathers, pure and genuine" (1868: 224). Other Greek commentators, while praising Lelekos' efforts, took a broader view of their significance. A group of professors and headmasters, in recommending that the Ministry of Church Affairs and Public Education reward Lelekos' dedication financially, remarked—in a manner strikingly reminiscent of Zambelios—that "our nation's popular songs are so much admired by the Europeans that Mendelssohn, that historian of modern Greece, was not slow to say that no art poetry possesses such internal power or deep feeling"; the group went on to list the names of Fauriel, Kind, and Passow as other worthy saviors of this precious heritage (Lelekos 1888: 5). Even had they been aware of Lelekos' textual interventions, it is unlikely that these enthusiasts would have felt terribly put out.

On the contrary, Lelekos' additions and alterations were a means of strengthening the case for cultural continuity. Not only was textual accuracy still a relatively minor issue, but, in a manner of speaking, the reverse principle held sway: the *folk* had corrupted their heritage, so that it was the task of scholars to purify it anew. In Lelekos' later collection, his supporters declared, "one could recognize as in a crystal-clear mirror the physiognomy of the Hellenic nation as it was in the years when, living in servitude, it could demonstrate only the very slightest trace of its character in political and public life. For this reason we judge these [songs] , *given careful cleaning and accurate classification*, most worthy of publication as a national treasure, and the labors of Mr. Lelekos in collecting them both impeccable [*sic*] and deserving of reward by the honorable Government" (Lelekos 1888: 7-8; my emphasis). Finally, the committee members point out, Lelekos deserved praise from *both Greeks and foreigners* for his work.

Three interrelated aspects of this statement are central to our theme. First, there is the reiterated appeal to foreign observers, as well as the concern that Lelekos' work should reflect glory on his country in their eyes. This reproduces Lelekos' own earlier affirmation of pride in the interest which Greek folksongs had already elicited from "German, French, and Italian neo-Hellenists" (1852: v). Second, for such an international appeal to be properly effective, the historical and spiritual purity of the texts themselves had to be restored before they could be published. Lelekos was especially well qualified for this task, thought his admirers, because he had devoted many years to the necessary research and had already (1852) published a book on it. In any case, there is no sign of doubt as to the necessity or propriety of textual emendation. The attitude which lies behind this state of affairs both reinforced and was fed by the presupposition of cultural continuity: since folk poets were the heirs of the Classical tradition, that tradition would provide the appropriate criteria for textual criticism by appropriately qualified scholars.

The third aspect of the committee's statement, though not heavily stressed in the official letter, is crucially important. It concerns the question of "accurate classification." Explicit interest in taxonomy was relatively slow to appear in the writings of the Greek folklorists, although the presuppositions on which it came to be based are present from the beginning. The various references to a category of "kleftic songs" are the first signs of its emergence as a central issue. Even before these became systematic, however, something of the same concern can be seen in the titles which the earliest collectors gave their folksongs. Lelekos himself actually did little to advance classificatory principles, but his supporters' enthusiasm for this aspect of his work is all the more revealing for that reason: it shows that they, at least, sensed the implications of the song titles and even of the order in which the texts were ranged. These implications still awaited a scholar who would articulate them into a comprehensive scheme of classification. Nonetheless, they were gradually taking on a more palpable form.

One factor which contributed to this process was the sheer volume of the material collected. Clearly, as the collections grew in number and size, some sort of order would have to be introduced, and for this purpose selectional criteria had to be formulated. While the earlier writers like Zambelios and Lelekos do not seem, from a present-day perspective, to have achieved a great deal of taxonomic sophistication, their attempts to equip texts with titles indicate an emergent awareness of the problem. In heading a "kleftic song" with its hero's name, for example, they indicated their sense that the song had something in common with those of the "historical" category.

But there is another guiding principle in Lelekos' work which is no less taxonomic for rarely being recognized as such. This is the process of selection whereby texts either were accepted as suitably "Hellenic" or were Hellenized to a sufficient degree. Implicit in this operation is a set of assumptions, not merely about folksongs but about vernacular culture in general: certain things were *Greek*, others were not, and the validating criterion was a demonstrable link with antiquity. In other words, the ethnological division between Greek and non-Greek was translatable into a historical theory of origins. This was the encompassing principle of the entire emergent system of classification of Greek folklore.

Lelekos' espousal of this principle may seem exceptionally immoderate today. It is nevertheless of great interest, in that it highlights the selectional principle involved. That his work was acceptable to his academic peers is evident in their support for his venture and in his hopes—realized in the form of funding for his later book—of government recognition. It is easy today to see Lelekos as an insufferable pedant and a poor scholar, to criticize the rambling format of his writings. But in his own day what he did exemplified an entire tradition of nationalistic scholarship and, as such, is still of prime significance in understanding that tradition.

For Lelekos' writings established folk poetry as recognizably *Greek*. He was not the first to do this, of course, but his uncompromising commitment to the task he set himself put him in the front line of the anti-Fallmerayer crusade. As he wrote:

> The poetic spirit which characterizes these popular epics does not reflect adulation or imitation of foreign models, nor does the arrogant pomposity of braggartism and noise sully their excellence; but sometimes the phrasing of the epic pours down in a rushing, living stream, to refresh the aesthetic judgment of the reader, sometimes the striving of the kleftic soldier-poet against tyranny and subjugation crashes thunderously out, sometimes again ecstatic love beholds its very own language and gracefully phrased, delicate expression in the expressiveness [*sic*] of a single love couplet. (1852: iii)

In this passage, the connections with Classical literature are spelled out with explicit clarity, so that we can see how the methods of Classical philology established a virtual template for the study of the modern oral traditions of Greece. In particular, the peculiar taxonomic idiom of that scholarly tradition has taken firm hold. Songs of perhaps fifteen lines of verbal text are described as "epics," a term which recalls the ancient glories of a very different genre (cf. Bynum 1969). The poetic virtues are those not of a foreign elegance but of a homespun honesty and expressiveness. The message is the same as the one which we have already encountered in the writings of d'Istria and Zambelios: there is something untarnishably, uniquely Greek both in the material itself and in the deeds which it celebrates. To such material, only the methods of Classical scholarship can do sufficient honor.

Vivilakis: A Scholarly Response

Lelekos' works, although largely devoted to songs, contain a limited amount of other material, such as dialect forms, descriptions of customs, and proverbial phrases—a somewhat uneven miscellany. Here, too, a major classificatory problem lurked, as yet unformulated: how could the rapidly increasing laographic corpus be organized so that materials of different kinds might be separately recorded but efficiently cross-referenced? The scope of Lelekos' interests did not extend to tackling this issue. Others, however, had already begun to deal with it, on the basis of selectional criteria that had once again largely originated in the antiquarian scholarship of Western Europe.

The title of Douglas' *Essay on Certain Points of Resemblance between the Ancient and Modern Greeks* spells out the main organizing focus of this endeavor. His account, however, was not a systematic collection; it represents a rather haphazard search for ethnographic evidence, although the search for identifiable parallels certainly acted as a filter through which the experiences of Douglas and other travel-minded authors could be sifted.

In Germany, however, more thorough ethnological research soon began, notably the remarkable work of a Greek scholar. In 1840 in Berlin, Emmanuel Vivilakis (Bybilakis), a Cretan who had lived through the War of Independence in Greece, published a short but significant treatise on parallels between ancient and modern Greek life. His aim was explicit:

> . . . to make an accurate comparison of the manners and customs of ancient with those of modern Greece, and therein to provide irrefutable proof not only that ancient Hellas is as yet far from defunct but that, just as these customs dwelt in her millennia ago, so today they live on in her children's children; that the preservation of the same manners and customs would have been impossible had there taken place at any one time a complete interruption in the existence of this people (*Volk*); finally, that the assertions of certain individuals (their number is for-

tunately quite negligible) are quite as far from the truth as heaven from earth, when they publish its very opposite *hōs ek tripodos* ("as from the [oracular] tripod [of the ancients]"), "in order," as they say, "to rescue educated Europe from the erroneous views it has held heretofore concerning the descent of today's Hellenes from the ancient Greeks."

(1840: viii–ix)

This first real salvo from the Greek side both anticipates Lelekos' works chronologically and surpasses them in scholarly sophistication. The reference to Fallmerayer is quite unambiguous, and the irritation over his attempt to divide "Greece" from "Europe" stands out sharply.

Vivilakis' argument, clearly and simply described in a brief introductory passage, is worth quoting in full:

> The material for comparing the modern Greeks with those ancestors who inhabited the same places three millennia ago, in relation to their manners and customs, religious festivals, etc., offers itself to us in such rich abundance that it almost causes us embarrassment, not as to how but as to what material we shall begin to solve our task with.
>
> It would seem expedient to us to begin our descriptions with the birth of children and to continue in like vein, through all the stages of life, taking all the different circumstances of life into consideration, finally accompanying today's Greek in his withered old age right to the grave, and from there following him even beyond the grave to darkest Orcus [Hades]. One should therefore not meanwhile expect, in this brief treatise of ours, that we shall also depict life in all the aspects of its physical and moral development; that would take us away from our proper purpose. We thus consider it only insofar as it allows us to make a comparison with ancient Greece, for this alone is the task which we have set ourselves. (1840: 1-2)

This statement is remarkable both for what it proposes to do and for the care which its author takes to exclude unnecessary side issues. We are promised a description of the entire series of life-cycle rites. This is a very early instance of systematic interest in the subject, and, although it may have served as a model for some of the later Greek folklorists' work (e.g., Politis 1871, 1874; see chap. 5), the obscurity which has since enveloped it does scant justice to its sophisticated conception and careful scholarship. Its descriptive detail is outstanding for the time at which it was written. For example, its analysis of wedding feasts and dances goes far beyond Douglas' vague generalizations on the same subject; while Lefkias (1843: 20, 80) simply contented himself with citing Vivilakis rather than attempt an analysis of his own.

Throughout his book, Vivilakis describes modern customs and practices in considerable detail; ancient parallels are discussed in each section, with appropriate references to Classical sources. The greater thoroughness of his work may not lie solely in some difference of ability or training between him and Lelekos. Subject matter must also have had some effect; Lelekos' heavy emphasis on folk *poetry* constrained him to look for literary parallels, rather than for similarities in life-style or ritual practice. Unlike Lelekos, Vivilakis was concerned to avoid dealing with anything as nebulous as *spiritual* continuity and says so. By excluding the kind of speculations about "national character" to which Lelekos, Zambelios, Valvis, and many others were so prone, he kept his field to manageable proportions.

Like any artificial grid on a body of data, however, Vivilakis' schema did result in some curious omissions and distortions. Thus, for example, evil-eye beliefs and practices are discussed in the section on childhood, as is a range of amuletic practices and associated concepts. The logic of this is clear: these matters are primarily concerned with the protection of children. But Vivilakis does briefly describe the alleged effects of the evil eye on animals (and implicitly also on adult humans) in the same passage. One gets the impression that this material has had to be forced into the unilineal format of the book, although it probably does represent a preponderance of childhood-linked beliefs in the data at Vivilakis' disposal.

Such difficulties are minor. A work written so early should not be faulted for occasional distortions which arise from the very sophistication of its overall design. Vivilakis' response to Fallmerayer was both timely and scholarly. Its subsequent lapse into obscurity may have been caused partly by the importance of the work soon to be done by Nikolaos Politis, who was not ashamed to acknowledge his debt to Vivilakis in appropriate citations.

Scholarly Reaction Abroad

Vivilakis set a high scholarly standard which was not surpassed for over two decades. Several specialized collections of a single genre appeared (e.g., Venizelos 1846 for proverbs; von Hahn 1864 for folktales; and Passow 1860 for songs), and these provided a sound basis for detailed research of a philological nature. A few general attempts at synthesis appeared abroad (notably Voutier 1826; Quinet 1830; Sanders 1844), and both in Germany (see Spiridakis 1966: 482-484) and in Greece Fallmerayerism remained the focus of heated discussion. Relatively little of this work, however, was to have a deep influence on the future development of Greek folklore studies in an epistemological sense.[4]

In 1864, however, the German philologist Kurt Wachsmuth (1837-1905) published *Das alte Griechenland im neuen*, a work not unlike Vivilakis' in scope and purpose but with considerably more ethnographic detail and less

passionate rhetoric in defense of the Greeks' national origins. The book opens
with a plea for calm and reason and with the complete rejection of one-sided
polemics of the kind that Fallmerayer had both issued and provoked. Wachsmuth clarifies his own position immediately, however: he is going to show
that there is indeed considerable evidence for continuity from ancient times.
It would actually be unreasonable to expect anything else, he argues, since
the historical evidence alone does not bear out the notion of a complete
demographic change. Of course, he conceded, the sheer numbers of Albanians
who passed into Greece in the fourteenth and fifteenth centuries would have
resulted in some admixture through intermarriage; and one does indeed see,
"here and there, clear traces of the Slavic type" (1864: 9)—presumably left
over from those earlier invasions of which Fallmerayer had made such capital.
On the other hand, wherever "the ancient blood has demonstrably kept its
purity, in the Mani, the Cyclades, and especially in Asia Minor and among the
Phanariots, there one encounters everywhere the finest ancient figures and
heads of the true Classical pattern" (1864: 10).

This does not sound like a promising approach. Here are the familiar
pseudogenetic attributions, the same apparent inability to distinguish between physical type and cultural pattern. But at this very point the picture
changes, and we are suddenly transported into a different epistemology:

> Finally, moreover, the nationality of a people (*die Nationalität eines
> Volkes*) is never completely displaced by foreign elements. Or were we
> therefore not really German anymore, just because we have absorbed a
> goodly quantity of Slavic and Wendish blood? A nation's essence and
> character lie, I think, quite incomparably more in its language, its
> thought and sensibility, its whole style and civilization . . . (1864:10)

This is a substantive change from the "racial" style of argument.

The argument continues in the same reasonable, moderate tone. Wachsmuth argues that loanwords in modern Greek do not hold great significance
for the issue of origins. One can easily counter such evidence with the fact
that some outlying dialects preserve highly archaic morphological features.
This is a useful addition to Lefkias' comments about the limited significance
of bilingualism for establishing national identity.

Here, then, Wachsmuth has rejected the simplistic equation of "blood"
with "nationality" and, with it, the notion of "purity" in any sense. What is
important in his scheme is not physical descent (though even on this score
Fallmerayer's argument can be shown to have been unsound), not what
people call themselves (a concern of later scholarship), but, quite simply, the
observable facts of their culture. If these people continue traditions which we
can recognize in the ancient sources, then they do indeed exemplify "the
ancient Greece in the new." The positivistic character of this approach be-

trays its origins in an archaeological, or artifactual, view of culture; we shall return to this point shortly. Whatever its merits or weaknesses, this represents a commonsense view of the continuity issue, deliberately phrased in a cool and detached manner so as to contrast with what Hussey has called Fallmerayer's "hasty, often sarcastic, temperament" (1978: 83).

Wachsmuth dealt with many of the culture traits that were soon to become crucial to the arguments of Greek commentators also. His treatment of concepts of death and fate, while more thorough, recalled the similar work of Vivilakis and also certainly provided some points of reference for the work on these topics which the young Politis was shortly to undertake. He gave us the first really detailed analysis of the "swallow song" (1864: 35-37), again anticipating Politis (1871, 1876). Lefkias had already attempted a brief analysis but claimed—almost certainly without any basis in ethnographic fact—that the terminology of the "swallow song" remained in popular use even in modern times (1843: 24-25). Wachsmuth adopted the same assumption (*schwalbelt*, p. 36; cf. Herzfeld 1974) and also continued the practice of conjoining the ancient text, which was from Rhodes, with a modern one from quite somewhere else—in his case, Epirus or Macedonia. Despite these difficulties, however, his analysis was the most careful and detailed to date. In general, his work represents a considerable advance in the level of documentation brought to the study of parallel traits.

The work of yet another German scholar, Bernhard Schmidt (1837-1917), surpassed even Wachsmuth's study in its attention to fine detail, though his aim—similarly expressed with unambiguous clarity in the title of his 1871 study, *Das Volksleben der Neugriechen und das hellenische Alterthum*—was much the same. But, if the study of Classical survivals was now well launched in Germany, it was also beginning to accelerate in Greece itself. A distinctively Greek laography was on the point of emergence, fusing the techniques of Western European scholarship with the special interests and firsthand knowledge that went with being a Greek oneself.

Christianity and Paganism in Greek Identity

In the next chapter, we shall look at the full flowering of Greek survivalism in the work of Nikolaos Politis. Before doing so, however, we must consider the development of a related issue—one which has already been encountered in the work of Zambelios, d'Istria, and Valvis and which was about to become critical. The Greeks claimed descent from the ancient Hellenes, who were (as it were by definition) "pagan"; yet they officially espoused Orthodox Christianity. With the growth of a more scholarly discussion of the continuity question, the contrast between these two religious traditions posed increasingly serious difficulties.

For foreign scholars, especially for those—and they were numerous—who had little patience with the Orthodox church, the problem was of course less acute. Pashley, for example, devoted a lengthy chapter to the Classical and pan-European parallels of modern Greek vampirism and nereid stories, and he did not hesitate to discuss the involvement of the local clergy in these decidedly un-Christian belief systems. As an antiquarian traveler, moreover, he positively delighted in the evidence for pagan cosmology and ritual among the Cretans of his own time:

> It is quite certain that the observance of the great celestial luminary [the sun], adopted by the Christians, has at times degenerated into something little better than the Persian worship, of which Herodotus and other ancient authors speak. I myself once met an ignorant Greek, who told me that the great difference between Christianity and Mohammedanism consisted in this, that the Christian worships the sun, and the Mohammedan the moon: and we learn from the mouth of one of the successors of St. Peter, that this adoration of the bright orb of day was practised by many Christians of his time. They even turned their backs on the altar, in the most splendid temple which Christian piety has ever erected, that they might bow down in their pagan adoration of the rising sun. (1837, II: 36-37)

Presumably Pashley had encountered in his "ignorant Greek" the usual attempt to describe Christian and Moslem as polar opposites (cf. "as the cat and the dog": Herzfeld 1980b), perhaps reinforced by the Islamic crescent symbol. His account displays all the ingenuous glee of the archaeologist, untrammeled by any commitment to local dogmas, upon discovering the survival of relics of the pagan past.

Wachsmuth, as usual, demonstrates both greater caution and an extremely good grasp of the data (1864: 19-23). He carefully discusses the location of chapels dedicated to the prophet Elijah and located on mountaintops in relation to the ancient worship of the sun, notes the similarity of names (*Ilias*, "Elijah"; *ilios*, "sun"), and then (and only then) comments: "Thus, underneath the change of names, the basic significance of the greatly adored Being remains largely the same, and for a considerable time the people may, half unconsciously, have worshiped their old deities under their new names"—a modest claim, indeed, which was to remain relatively unchallenged and unaltered in subsequent folklore scholarship right up to the present.

Wachsmuth describes a fair range of similar evidence for the survival of the pagan belief system. In his discussion of concepts of death, astronomical mythology, and the mythology of fertility and rebirth, he laid a sure foundation on which later authors were able to build. Linguistic survivals are especially useful if they are accompanied by thematic links. Thus, for example, he

notes the transformation of Charon, the infernal boatman of the ancients, into the modern Charos, the personification of death; then, citing a song text
which describes Charos' wily seizure of all earthly souls, he remarks: "Thus
does Charon accompany the souls [of the dead] to Hades. For the modern
Greeks, too, this is still a dark, cold, and waterless dwelling beneath the earth;
it is a completely comfortless resting-place, since water and light are for the
Greeks the two things which are precious and indispensable to life. A stairway
leads down into this Hades; a gate closes it in; here sits the implacable watch-
man Charos, who lets no soul go back toward the light for which it yearns"
(1864: 21). This account is a conflation of materials, possibly recorded at
different times, from different parts of Greece; the assumption that Greece
was historically a single, homogeneous culture left little room for considering
regional variation in the overall system of belief. Wachsmuth also allows himself the antiquarian luxury of using the Classical form Charon to denote the
modern death figure. On the whole, however, his argument for the survival of
pagan ideas about the afterlife is well taken and restrained.

Wachsmuth is consistently cautious about asserting such continuity between pagan and folk Christian cosmology. He is especially careful to distinguish between the material proper and its ulterior implications. After a (dis-
appointingly brief) discussion of "astronomical myths," he remarks: "Plainly,
then, in these accounts there certainly lies no great abundance of the tradition of the ancient mythology today, but, under the covering of Christianity,
only lightly veiled, numerous traces of paganism reveal themselves" (1864:
22). In other words, we should not look for the literally unaltered mythology
of yesteryear. Instead, we should try to tear away the Christian veil in order
to reveal the essential elements of that same mythology. To some extent, this
is what Pashley and others had already been doing, though less systematically.
It should be distinguished from the characterology of d'Istria and Valvis, on
the other hand, since Wachsmuth was concerned strictly with observable culture traits. Like Vivilakis before him, he avoided discussing "spiritual" survivals save in the most general sense possible.

This more ethnographic focus, while relatively unproblematical for non-
Greeks, created a painful dilemma for local scholars, who had to integrate
cultural survivalism with at least a nominal profession of Christian faith. For
the earlier writers concerned with "national character," the dilemma was not
brought into particularly sharp focus, since general attitudes and "spirit" do
not necessarily require the detailed explication of underlying cosmological beliefs. To describe the klefts as heirs to the glorious heroic tradition of yore
did not entail an elaborate analysis of their beliefs or ritual practices; and,
since they had been categorically separated from the present, their supposedly pagan attitudes to life—which could, anyway, be blamed on the exigencies

of outlawry and subjugation under the Turks—caused little offense. The new style of antiquarian ethnography was much more dangerous. It brought the pagan past, detail by detail, into the Christian present and claimed to represent the true national heritage by so doing. To such an endeavor, needless to say, the religiously minded—especially the ecclesiastical establishment—were far from friendly. Although the Greek church had been made independent of the Patriarchate of Constantinople as early as 1837, primarily to free it from domination by an authority which was itself answerable to the Turkish government, the higher clergy remained suspicious of the Hellenizing notions of the secular nationalists; this strain is still occasionally felt. The antiquarian folklorists therefore had to work under the disapproving eye of a church which had scant tolerance for their ideas or their activities and which was itself a powerful force in the political and social life of the nation.

The folklorists seem to have been quite undaunted. While they did not particularly reiterate the anticlericalism of Zambelios and d'Istria, they openly pointed to the many pagan elements which had survived in the very forms of worship to which the folk still clung—even, not uncommonly, in rituals of the church itself. They had a powerful argument on their side, that of national interest, since a primary aim continued to be the refutation of Fallmerayer. Since political life in nineteenth-century Greece was always dominated by one form of irredentism or another, these antiquarian folklorists—the doyens of the Hellenist ideology—were able, and indeed encouraged, to pursue their investigations.

Before we turn to the work of the greatest Hellenist folklorist of all, Nikolaos Politis, we might usefully consider the contribution of a far less well known and geographically more restricted scholar, one who was nevertheless in the forefront of the same methodological development. In 1874, Georgios Loukas published a work with the self-explanatory title, *Philological Visits to the Monuments of the Ancients in the Life of the Modern Cypriots*. While Politis' partly contemporaneous *Modern Greek Mythology* has remained a classic of Greek folklore, Loukas' book has fallen into obscurity. The reasons for this are not entirely clear. It cannot be simply a matter of the comparatively limited geographical scope of Loukas' work—Sakellarios' monumental two-volume compendium of Cypriot lore and language, published from 1855 to 1868 and revised in 1890 and 1891, has kept its place far more successfully; the original edition was even reprinted as recently as 1955. Perhaps Sakellarios' work has eclipsed that of Loukas simply because of its more massive format and coverage. On the other hand, the striking resemblances between Loukas' and Politis' works suggest that Loukas' deserves more recognition, if only on historiographic grounds, than it has in fact received.

Loukas' preface is both a vision and a scientific statement of purpose:

On a visit to my homeland, Cyprus, in 1869, and resting in her
bosom for a short while, one day I suddenly found myself in a tempest
of various roiling emotions. . . . The entire recollection of my studies in
Athens stood clearly before me at that moment, and all the cares of my
life were thrust away like a cloud; fortunately, I was concealed in a
lonely house, so that nobody chanced to interrupt these initial stirrings
of my thoughts or break the chain of my ideas. There lay before me
some manuscript pages which I had written at intervals years before and
had completed shortly after my return. In these pages were some accounts of the language and life of the Cypriots, of which the detailed
comparison with the language and life of our ancestors reminded one in
lively fashion of the names of the blessed Teachers of the modern
Greeks—especially those of Koraes and Mavrophrydes, men who warm-
ly recommended the study of the modern language and life of Greeks
everywhere. While I lay thus motionless, my body relaxed, occupying
my mind with lively thoughts, there strangely struck my hearing certain
squeaks and thuds, such as occur when a vehicle is thrown on its side
and into a ditch by suddenly startled horses. And behold, suddenly
there before me, the very Teachers who were the subject of my reminis-
censes, dragging along with them a certain German heretic. . . . "Come
along," said both Teachers to him with [feigned] anxiety, "and show
us these Slavs dwelling in the heartlands of Asia!" At the conclusion of
those words the problem of the modern Greeks' authenticity leaped
agitatedly into my memory, I recognized the face of the German Fallmerayer, and I understood that the superficially anxious irony of
this invitation of the Teachers boded well for a significant national
discussion.   (1874: v-vi)

The political implications of this passage are thinly disguised. Cyprus, then
still under Turkish rule (until 1878, when it was ceded to Britain), might
superficially resemble an oriental land, even as Fallmerayer had insultingly
treated the Greek mainland as part of "the Orient." In this fanciful passage,
Fallmerayer even speaks of Cyprus as "Syria," a poetic synonym for the
lands of Islam. Yet if that were true, for the sake of argument, how then
could the inhabitants of Cyprus also be Slavs? Is not the solution that even
outlying Cyprus must in fact be considered wholly Greek?

In Loukas' vision, Fallmerayer is taught a lesson, although his skepticism is
initially hard to overcome. He is shown Cypriot boys playing ball games, the
names of which are known from antiquity. Fallmerayer is suspicious: perhaps
these boys were taught the names of their ball games by overly patriotic
schoolteachers? The reply was a proud one:

"Yes!" responded our grand old Koraes, "and indeed by the famous Lycurgus himself, the lawgiver of Sparta, as well as by other men of antiquity." "How is it," replied the German ironically, "that after so many centuries Lycurgus could be resurrected, and in this corner of Syria at that?" "Continue with your visit," replied the old man, "and you shall see him before you at every step."   (1874: vii)

Eventually, indeed, Fallmerayer is forced to admit to the Greekness of Cyprus. He is a grudging loser, however: what about the Greek mainland, where his own researches started the whole trouble? "'Just so,' Mavrophrydes took up the point. 'Those places also keep up Hellenic customs and to this very day live the life of their ancient forefathers. This doubt of yours ought to be subjected to another visit to those parts.'"

Fallmerayer finally gives in entirely:

Visiting the town and villages of the island with the Teachers . . . he found in them the purest customs and most Hellenic life-style in humble huts and in the ravines inhabited by shepherds and farmers. . . . From time to time, he would express to the Teachers his wonder at the fact that so many centuries had not managed to obliterate Greek customs from the lives of the Cypriots; for they are recognizably preserved, to the shame of the enemies of Hellenism and especially to the shame of that pseudocivilization which at that time had begun to rise up fanatically against these most holy relics of antiquity!   (1874: ix)

The vision thus ends in triumph: the participants all make for a village at the foot of (the Cypriot) Mount Olympus, where a wise priest makes them welcome—and Loukas suddenly finds himself alone again in his recluse's study by the Limassol seashore, the manuscript which had originally fired his imagination still in his hands, "while unhappily this philological vision had dissolved."

So wishful a dream speaks eloquently both of the ardor with which the Greeks longed to disprove Fallmerayer's views and of the personal idiom in which they responded to his challenge. Loukas surpasses even Evlambios and Zambelios in what he expects folklore to prove; Greece should not be *resurrected*, he declares in marked contrast to those authors' favorite metaphor, but *rediscovered*. "Yes! unaltered, the Hellas of Perikles lives!" (1874: xii). For Loukas, the academic issue of "survivalism" took second place to the question of national "survival": an uncompromising response to Fallmerayer's no less uncompromising provocation, one couched in not altogether dissimilar terms.

Loukas' treatment of his material makes no concession to ecclesiastical sensibilities over the question of latent paganism. Like Wachsmuth (and Politis), he presented the assimilation of pagan concepts to Christian iconography as a common and easily understood phenomenon:

> In general, whenever they mention or invoke Charon, they also have the
> Angel in mind, and whenever they shout and revile the Angel, they
> are reviling Charon too. What is the cause of the assimilation of these
> two characters? Is there any doubt that the cause is Christianity
> [itself]?   (1874: 38)

And a little later we are told:

> The Cypriots, strict adherents (as I have said) to the Hellenic customs
> ..., both discharged their ideas about Charon into [the figure of] the
> Angel and dressed this Hellenic idea in the cloak of Christianity, but as
> we observe, *faithful to Hellenism*, they once again demonstrate to this
> day in many ways the texture and brilliance of these hallowed relics,
> preserving both the concepts *and their national character*.
>   (1874: 44-45; my emphasis)

Clearly there were more kinds of faith than simply that demanded by the
church.

A major part of Loukas' book is devoted to "mythology." That word,
which he (again like Politis) preferred to the demotic cognate *paramithia*
("folktales"), gives some idea of his firm conviction that he was dealing with
living antiquity. The ancients had myths, rather than tales, and their descendants were logically assumed to follow suit. Mythology, moreover, was
associated with the doings of supernatural beings. Viewed in such terms, the
"cloak of Christianity" seemed a superficial disguise indeed.

Loukas was completely overshadowed by his fellow philologist and folklorist, Nikolaos Politis. Politis' *Modern Greek Mythology* appeared in two
sections—one in the year of Schmidt's *Volksleben* (1871), the other in that
of Loukas' *Philological Visits* (1874).[5] Politis, too, conjoined the notion of a
modern "mythology" with penetrating insights into the character of folk religion. He conducted his researches on an inestimably vaster scale than Loukas, however, and brought to them a more international breadth of scholarship, a keenly inquisitive and analytical attitude, and a fund of sheer energy
that was itself almost of mythological dimensions. He was the inventor of the
Greek term for folklore (*laografia*), the founder of the highly respected
scholarly journal of the same name, an active participant in several scholarly
institutions, a taxonomist extraordinary, and perhaps the most scholarly pro-
tagonist of the Greeks' claim to the name of Hellenes. In his work, we reach
the climactic point, historically and epistemologically, of Greek folklore
studies.

Chapter 5
The Creation of a Discipline

". . . a discipline whose object is the study of the people . . ."

Politis and the Constitution of Folklore

Since it was Nikolaos Politis' particular achievement to organize the whole ground plan of laography and give the subject its name, a chapter devoted to his work should start with a review of the state of the art at the beginning of his long and productive career. Politis did not so much revolutionize as *constitute* the discipline by organizing his predecessors' ideas and goals into a comprehensive taxonomic system. In consequence, his work can be read semiotically as a "text" (Winner and Winner 1976) of the Hellenists' view of Greek culture much more efficiently, and with more coherent results, than can the scattered efforts of earlier scholars. Yet Politis undoubtedly leaned quite heavily on the achievements of his predecessors—he freely and honestly acknowledged his material debt to them for a rich fund of data, drawn from all over the Greek-speaking world and consequently ideal for the purposes of comparative study. His ideological debt is hardly less important, however; and, although it was above all his talent for synthesis that finally translated the Hellenists' perspective into a unified study of Greek culture, many key concepts came into his hands already half-formed.

The fundamental notion of cultural continuity was already well established by Politis' day, of course, but there was as yet little interest in cross-cultural comparisons of a sort that would place Greek cultural history in a more international perspective. The earlier Hellenists did not even consider that to be a topic of interest; they knew perfectly well that Greece was the *fons et origo* of European civilization. A few attempts at comparative studies by foreigners, notably Pashley's ethnological disquisition on vampirism (1837, II: 195-234), received little attention among Greek scholars before Politis' time. Although the Greeks saw themselves as the quintessential Europeans, it was not the culture of non-Greek *peasants* that interested them; rather, as in the admittedly extreme case of Valvis, their interest in the peasantry was directed toward showing that their own country folk might equal even educated Western Europeans in wit and sensitivity. Politis was to change all that.

Politis was also to give a definitive answer to the problem of whether the study of vernacular culture should have an autonomous status, thereby distinguishing it from history, archaeology, and philology—all disciplines which had contributed a great deal to it. The data basis of ethnological studies was uncertain; no consensus had been achieved as to what it might legitimately include, so that a separate branch of scholarship had not yet come into being to deal with folk culture. Those who wrote extensively about such things did so under other titles—Zambelios as a historian, Manousos as an editor, Vivilakis and Lelekos as philologists, Valvis in his capacity as a doctor of law. Although terms like "folklore" and "ethnology" were now coming into use abroad, their initial impact on Greek scholarship was minimal. Nor was the development of an autonomous discipline encouraged by the midcentury foreign scholars who wrote about Greece. Among the German scholars, for example, Schmidt—who disliked the English word "folklore"—rejected the very notion of comparative mythology in favor of a strictly antiquarian approach (1877: 5). Politis rebelled passionately against this narrow and exclusive focus (Kiriakidis 1937: 20-21), even though he made good use of its results and undertook a great deal of "patriotic or archaeological" research himself. For him, the real challenge did not lie in choosing which of the sundry disciplines already in existence would furnish the ideal methodology. It lay instead in abstracting from each those principles which could most usefully contribute to a unified discipline of folklore. The laography of Politis and his followers retains the textual analysis of classical philology, the goal of historical reconstruction which it derived from archaeological and archival research, and a set of concepts partially derived from the emergent anthropology of Tylor and others. To all this, a continuing concern to rebut Fallmerayerism gave a certain circumstantial unity. To some extent, we can say that Politis inherited a methodological ragbag and made a quilt, but it was a quilt of remarkably harmonious design.

The choice of methods and concepts was far from fortuitous. Folklore studies in Greece were in large measure a response to Fallmerayer's assault, which was primarily a historical one. All the various epistemological elements which Politis now brought together consequently shared one dominant characteristic: a highly literalist sense of historical fact. We have already witnessed this trend in the steady hypostatization of "the klefts" as a discrete historical phenomenon. To this we should add the growing acceptance (e.g., Zambelios 1852; Passow 1860; Kind 1861) of certain song texts as "historical" as well as the attendant subjection of these texts to criteria of factual "accuracy." Here was a real danger of circularity: if a text did not fully justify being so labeled, it was assumed to be the text rather than the classification that was at fault.

Politis both inherited and in turn elaborated this brand of historical literalism, not only in the study of "obviously" historical song texts but, more generally, in the interpretation of all ethnological data.

While he never seems to have questioned this basic premise, he was constantly aware of the difficulties of interpretation into which it led him. In attempting to deal with these, he progressively elaborated his classificatory system, apparently thinking that the fault lay in the underdeveloped state of that system rather than in its articulating principles. In so doing, however, he also created a much stronger sense of epistemological cohesion than had hitherto existed. The result was the creation of a distinctive branch of folklore studies to which Politis, in 1884, finally gave the name of *laografia*, by which it has been known in Greece ever since.

Politis and the Mythology of the Modern Greeks

Nikolaos Politis was born in 1852, the year in which Zambelios published his monumental history and folksong collection. The son of a lawyer of rural origins, the young Politis seems to have shown academic inclinations at an early age. Indeed, he published his first articles in learned journals at the age of thirteen. A year later, he was publishing brief notes on linguistics and folklore in *Pandora*; from 1868 on he also published articles in *Efimeris ton Filomathon*, a journal whose involvement with philological folklore studies had originally been prompted by Zambelios' call to all Greek scholars to engage in active ethnological research. There can be no doubt that Politis knew, even as a child, of the intense debate which Fallmerayer had provoked (cf. Kiriakidis 1923: ix-xi) and that this was a major influence in his precocious attraction to the subject that was to dominate his entire career.

In 1867, *Pandora* announced a philological prize competition, sponsored by the wealthy Odessa philanthropist Th. P. Rhodokanakis. The second such contest, in 1871, had as its theme "the collection from as many Greek locations as possible of the Greek manners, customs, and practices and their comparison with what is recorded in the surviving [ancient] authors, so that their [respective] similarities and differences [with regard to the latter] may be made known" (quoted by Politis 1871: iii). The youthful Politis, then a university student, responded enthusiastically. He was the only candidate. Yet the work which he produced for the Rhodokanakis competition, the first major essay from his pen, represents a landmark in the development of Greek folklore scholarship.[1]

This is his *Modern Greek Mythology*, a compendium of cosmological tales and related materials with detailed notes on possible contemporary non-Greek as well as Classical Greek parallels. A primary motive is, as one would expect, to refute Fallmerayer—but, says Politis, this must be done scientifically, not in the confused and polemical way that had prevailed up to that point. Textual materials are not sufficient for the purpose by themselves; customs provide the most telling evidence, since they "are not taught by others, nor are they transplanted from external sources among foreign races, but are transmitted only by word of mouth from parent to child, from old to young" (1871: ix). The materials of folklore must therefore be taken from real-life situations in order to establish the true continuity of the Greek people.

Modern Greek Mythology introduces a systematic crosscultural perspective for the first time. The competition judges criticized this as going too far beyond the contest's antiquarian objectives. But in fact, as Politis retorted, the discussion of non-Greek parallels certainly did no harm to the basic aim of establishing historical continuity within Greece and added greatly to our understanding of the Greek material itself. This stance is in marked contrast to Schmidt's explicit rejection of comparativism. When Kiriakidis, a pupil of Politis, remarked in 1923 that his teacher had moved away from a strictly "archaeological" view of folklore, this in no way diminished the "patriotic" intentions of *Modern Greek Mythology*, nor did it prevent Politis in 1909 from defining "monuments of the word"—verbal archaeology, as it were—as one of the two principal concerns of folklore research. Politis' approach was virtually a form of "ethnoarchaeology": he never ceased to seek out the ancient derivations of present-day culture traits, but he simultaneously looked for parallel (and sometimes historically related) phenomena in other lands. Kiriakidis points out that although Politis did not go to Germany until 1876 (i.e., after the Rhodokanakis competition), and although the German ethnologist and Politis' teacher-to-be Albrecht Dieterich did not publish his exposition of comparative folklore until 1902, *Modern Greek Mythology* anticipates some of the methodological aspects of Dieterich's treatise. More to the point, however, Politis had already thoroughly familiarized himself with the work of the brothers Grimm, who were the real founders of German comparative ethnology. The Grimms were also unsympathetic to Christianity, and their determination to find pre-Christian ideologies beneath the veneer of Christian symbolism undoubtedly spoke directly to the antiquarian Hellenist in Politis.

One of the most astonishing features of *Modern Greek Mythology* is its almost fanatical concern with accurate, detailed scholarship. Politis, well aware that many of his predecessors had proved scholastically deficient by the standards of their own time, frankly says so (1871: i). Although still only a student at Athens University, he was not afraid to criticize established figures of the scholarly world, at least in general terms. He also responded in print, point by point, to the criticisms which the Rhodokanakis competition judges had addressed to his manuscript, "not," he said, "being motivated by an attitude of contrariness, since in any case we respect the opinion of such established teachers, but because, as we think, the judgments made on scholarly writings are not like those appropriate to the products of light literature— which are dependent for the most part on the peculiar tastes of the judges— but, in order to carry weight, should be accepted on the basis of discussion" (1871: iv).

One of the highlights of Politis' defense is his discussion of the term *kleftis* ("kleft"). The judges had objected to his use of this form (as opposed to the Classical *kleptis*) as a violation of good *katharevousa* style. Not at all, replied the undaunted scholar; the form *kleftis* and its derivatives, "hallowed by the brave bulwarks of Hellenic freedom, are no longer equivalent to *kleptis*, etc." (1871: xv-xxxvi). Writing as he was in the immediate aftermath of the Dilessi affair, Politis had spotted the semantic shift which we have already noted, although he failed to see its historical implications; his concern was to use the "right form," rather than to probe the reasons why usage had developed in this particular way. Indeed, it was Politis who, perhaps more than any other scholar, accorded the "kleftic songs" their autonomous status in the classification of Greek folklore. The care with which he tried to rebut the judges' criticism on this seemingly minor stylistic point was thus a patriotic gesture; he wanted to guarantee "the klefts" their place in history.

In general, as the opening remarks about Fallmerayer disclose, *Modern Greek Mythology* is truly a patriotic enterprise. Its aim is explicitly stated as being "to seek the kinship between our own manners and customs and those of the ancient Hellenes" and "our continuity with our ancestors" (1871: xxii, xxix). Continuity, however, does not necessarily mean identity, and (as Politis realized) it certainly does not preclude similarities to other cultures. Even kleftism can be assimilated to this new, comparativist perspective. The klefts' name was a fact of *modern* Greek culture which could nevertheless be brought into line with the neo-Classical language; the etymological root and the patriotic and heroic virtues with which it was associated were the relevant elements of continuity here. Again, in 1885 Politis explicitly accepts the Serbian *hajduk* and Bulgarian *haidout* as "klefts," although the Bulgarians' "kleftic" poetry "lacks that ineffable charm which the folk poetry of every nation breathes, even that of those mountain-dwelling brigands (*listai*) of the Taurus, the wild Kurds." His prejudices occasionally got the better of his detachment, as in this passage, but he still thought it worthwhile to compare the "klefts" of different Balkan lands, even if only to demonstrate the poverty of the Bulgarians' kleftic tradition. He would probably have rejected the extreme view that the Bulgarians had never had klefts at all (e.g., Colocotronis 1918). For Politis, it was sufficient that the traditions of modern Greece could be both intimately related to those of the ancient past and scientifically compared with those of the contemporary cultures of Europe and the Orient.

A Greek Version of Survivalism

In 1865, six years before the compilation of *Modern Greek Mythology*, Edward Burnett Tylor's *Researches into the Early History of Mankind and the Development of Civilization* had introduced the "doctrine of survivals" to the scholarly world, and the theme was taken up again in his two-volume *Primitive Culture* in 1871. By 1880 at the latest, Politis (who read Tylor's works in French translations) had tried to engage the British anthropologist's interest by sending him a signed reprint, dedicated with "Hommage respectueux de l'auteur à M. Edw. Tylor" and currently preserved in the Tylor Anthropological Library at Oxford; two more signed pamphlets followed in 1882. Of course, these tell us nothing about Tylor's attitude, if he had one, toward Politis, but they do suggest that the Greek folklorist was interested in establishing some kind of communication with him.

What exactly was the influence of the British founder of "anthropology" upon the Greek founder of "laography," and how faithful a reflection of Tylor's is Politis' "survivalism"? Again, there is no evidence that Tylor ever actively encouraged Politis; more probably, Politis developed his own ideas independently and then drew on Tylor's for elaboration. Thus, for example, the short passage on sun worship in *Modern Greek Mythology* (1871: 17-24), which is strictly a survey of Greek materials, makes no acknowledged use of Tylorean theory; by contrast, its successor, the essay "The Sun in Popular Myths," is much broader in its comparativism and also admits to some explicit knowledge of the British anthropologist's writings (e.g., 1882a: 12, n. 4).

Kiriakidis (1923: xxii; 1937: 23) describes Politis' early work as "purely archaeological" and suggests that the influence of Tylor and Dieterich really appears in his later *Proverbs* (1899-1902) and *Traditions* (1904). But the Tylor Library reprints, while later than *Modern Greek Mythology*, at least show that Politis was exposed to Tylor's influence at a relatively early date. Not all forms of survivalism necessarily originated with Tylor himself, however, and it is apparent that Politis' intellectual path was already set in this general direction well before he began citing Tylor in his own works. In consequence, Politis was able not only to quote Tylor in support of his Hellenist version of survivalism but to exclude those aspects of the Tylorean thesis which conflicted with Greek nationalism—especially the conception of survivals as essentially relics of a *primitive* past, which would not have suited the Hellenist argument at all.

We have already noted Politis' debt to the German tradition of philological antiquarianism. Certainly, too, there are traces in his early work of the "national character" rhetoric of Zambelios, especially where Politis borrows Zambelios' own material in order to demonstrate the tragic sensibilities of the Greeks in a cheerful song which nevertheless represents death—"a dancing song, full (so to speak) of cheerful melancholy, and withal a faithful portrait of the Hellenic character" (1874: 242). But, amidst all these borrowings from more familiar scholarly traditions, Politis also displays a more "anthropologically" oriented kind of survivalism.

First of all, there is the general title, *Study of the Life (vios) of the Modern Greeks*. Politis retained the notion of studying "life" in the general title of the series which encompassed the later *Proverbs* and *Traditions*; *epiviosis* ("survival") is cognate with this term. From the outset, it seems, he regarded his task as being to establish connections between modern and ancient *ways of life* (1871: viii). If he acknowledges his debt to Tylor more generously in later years, this is not necessarily because Tylor's influence on him was as great as he himself seems to have been disposed to believe; indeed, as Kiriakidis has noted, Politis never really accepted the doctrine of survivals in its entirety. We might go further still and suggest that Politis' increasing acknowledgment of Tylor may not represent much more than an ex post facto attempt to connect his work with international scholarship. More even than that, it seems likely that Politis either misunderstood or misrepresented the full import of Tylorean survivalism. (Since Tylor does not seem to have reciprocated Politis' interest at any time, the discrepancies were probably never directly confronted by the two scholars.) Politis appears to have done much the same as many of Tylor's admiring contemporaries: reading "survivalism" not as a theory of societal progression which encompassed the fossils of a primitive stage but as a static doctrine of cultural continuity.

This has to be put in a wider context. In her authoritative study of the doctrine of survivals, Margaret Hodgen (1936: 48, n. 1) has shown that many of Tylor's imitators made no effort "in the Tylorean tradition to arrive at origins or to uphold the presuppositions of developmentalism." Notable among the offenders is John Cuthbert Lawson, whose *Modern Greek Folklore and Ancient Greek Religion* (1910) drew heavily on Politis' publications—and may indeed have absorbed more of Politis' than of Tylor's presuppositional framework. Hodgen presents the concern in such writings with the persistence of paganism as a continuation of the Renaissance antiquarians' search for "the indications of pagan or popish past" in folk practices. Now while in England this essentially negative emphasis may have transferred easily from antipapist rhetoric in the seventeenth century to colonialist ideology and ethnocentrism in the nineteenth, there are two reasons why the same process could not have occurred in Greece. First, no serious folklore studies were done by Greeks before the Revolution of 1821; as we have seen, the growth of folklore studies there was a *retrospective* response to the acquisition of statehood.

The second reason follows from the first: since the ideological basis of the Greeks' antiquarian philology was the alleged *superiority* of the ancient Hellenes, the developmentalist thesis that survivals were the relics of a primitive past made no sense. The Greek version of survivalism could only be a static model. Furthermore, a strictly developmentalist model would have allowed "the Europeans" to claim cultural superiority over the ancient Greeks and perhaps also over their descendants. Indeed, even those European scholars who adopted the philhellenic position, while using Tylor's terminology, preferred to treat the Classical world as an unsurpassed exemplar. An extreme exponent of this school of thought was the Celtic scholar J. S. Stuart-Glennie, who used folklore materials to demonstrate the *lack* of change in Greek speech and culture and went on to argue that the Greeks represented a "race" which had been superior in both ancient and recent times; thus, Tylor's advocacy of the essential homogeneity of humankind could not be allowed to pass (cf. Garnett and Stuart-Glennie 1896: 3).

While Politis was not usually concerned with these wider issues (see Kiriakidou-Nestoros 1978: 151), he seems to have been comfortable with the assumption that Classical Greek culture represented a superior form of civilization and that the doctrine of survivals could be brought into line with this view. As he explained:

> [Tylor] includes among the survivals absolutely all remains of past civilizations, but we think it would be better to single out for inclusion in another category all those [traits] which are in no way unseemly but preserve their original rationale and meaning, and which can be regarded as the partial but unbroken continuation of an earlier life (*vios*).
>
> (1909a: 6)

In this way, Politis sought to bypass the contradictions inherent in using Tylorean survivalism for a culture whose antecedents supposedly marked the very antithesis of the primitive. His method was frankly selective: he preferred to establish a "partial" continuity which at least had the virtue of being "unbroken." The selectional basis of Greek folklore classification begins to emerge very clearly here, especially if we keep in mind that the notion of cultural continuity was itself a taxonomic device for defining the extent of Hellenism.

Politis' ability to so transform Tylorean survivalism was hardly unique at the time. The problem lay in the ambiguities of Tylor's own expository style— in particular, in his use of archaeological metaphors for nonmaterial culture. Tylor's critics, indeed, "deprecated an explanation of the persistence of nonmaterial culture elements which endowed them figuratively with the physical endurance of the material" (Hodgen 1936: 146). It seems, moreover, that

Tylor himself was reluctant to face the implications of this criticism. Of course, neither Tylor nor his imitators (including Politis) assumed that ancient cultural forms would be preserved completely intact, any more than were archaeological artifacts under normal conditions. In this sense, Politis' survivalism is no less "archaeological" than Tylor's. The difference is only that, whereas Tylor makes his archaeological appeal to the anonymous reaches of prehistory, Politis makes his to the very starting point of historical time in the European tradition–to ancient Hellas. Yet the implications of this difference are radical enough.[2]

The Hypothesis of Original Texts

In using Classical Greece as his point of reference, Politis was treading the same path as his predecessors in Greece. Yet, far more aware than they had been of the unplumbed time depth of prehistory, he often asserted that the Classical traditions rested in turn on still older strata of myth and custom. His acquaintance with the development of Indo-European scholarship manifests itself as early as *Modern Greek Mythology*. Some of the themes in that book seem to offer glimpses into the mysterious older traditions of pre-Classical times and were given more detailed treatment from this angle in subsequent articles. Two of the reprints which Politis sent Tylor are of this type: "Popular Meteorological Myths" and "The Sun in Popular Myths." Indeed, in the sun mythology essay, Politis mentions Tylor's view that the Perseus myth may represent the survival of pre-Classical elements.

In this piece, moreover, Politis demonstrated a striking breadth of scholarship. His ability to see the relevance of Sanskrit materials is especially novel in local Greek scholarship. The interpretive restraint which this piece reveals is all the more extraordinary given the ideological and methodological background to Politis' work. The introductory passage deserves to be quoted in full:

> When we look at the host of myths which are demonstrably based on the observation of solar phenomena, we will find it hard to explain why the sun holds a secondary place in the Greek pantheon. But expert study and analysis of solar myths convince us that these myths, the first seeds of which are an inheritance from the prehistoric Aryans, rapidly became identified and fused with the myths about other gods, especially those about Herakles and Apollo, and that later certain of the attributes of the Sun were shaped into mythological matrices of their own, such as those of Hyperion-Sun, Phoebus-Sun, Phaëthon-Sun. We observe something analogous in Roman mythology, too, where Apollo, Liber, Hercules, and Mercury took on many of the characteristics of the

Sun god (Sol), and in Vedic mythology (which in addition to Sûryâ, the principal personification of the sun, mentions others such as the gods Savitri, Mitra, Vishnu, Pûshan, Aditya). Because of this sharing out of the solar myths, the importance of the Sun as a self-contained deity was radically lessened; not only in Greek mythology but even in the Vedas themselves, the sun is relegated to an inferior position.

In Classical times, to put it generally, the worship of the Sun was not a habitual practice and was indeed extremely rare. The *hēlieia* ("sun shrines") and the altars and statues of Helios (the Sun) which existed in some places should perhaps be regarded as the relics of a more ancient cult which had held sway before the Sun became identified with other gods. Most of the extremely ancient myths which derived from this cult were attributed to Herakles and other solar heroes, as well as to Apollo. Those which referred to Apollo are the most concerned with ideals, since they gradually took on moral significance and a thoroughly proper character; those which referred to Herakles more faithfully retained their old uncouth, artless style—this doubtless being reinforced by comedy and satyrical drama and the art of humor, pleasantly intermingled with such subjects; but above all the preservation of those archetypical myths is due to the fact that they were easily understood by the masses, whose intellectual level they did not exceed. For this reason, it is easy to understand why most of the myths have survived the passage of many centuries among our people, having undergone a negligible amount of insignificant change.

The aim of the present essay is to assemble these myths of our people and, in general, all mythological representations and images of the sun. Of these, some must be considered the remnants of extremely ancient myths, of which not the slightest mention is made by the ancient authors; others may be explained or completed by reference to Hellenic mythology or to the mythology of related peoples. They are to be found scattered in traditions, especially in folksongs and tales (*paramithia*), but nevertheless in altered and obscure form. Some traces of them, moreover, are to be clearly discerned in popular speech but unconsciously preserved, since they have long ago lost their mythological meaning.   (1882a: 3-5)

This passage is characteristic. It not only demonstrates Politis' concern to establish ancient links with modern folklore but shows how far he was prepared to push that search beyond the chronological and geographical limits of Hellenism. He was the first Greek scholar to draw systematically on Sanskritic research in order to illuminate both ancient and modern traditions of his own country. Much of this Sanskrit material came from the publications of Max

Müller, but there is nothing to suggest that Politis absorbed with it all the theoretical trappings of Müller's "solarism." Politis never became embroiled in the debate over this theory of the solar origins of mythology; his interests, although more international in scope, were ultimately directed toward the elucidation of the Greek materials rather than toward the broader ethnological questions of the day. He studied solar and meteorological myths for their own intrinsic interest, instead of trying to prove that they were ancestral to *all* mythology.[3] Moreover, he was not seriously affected by Müller's admonition to Tylor that all ethnological comparativism should be kept within linguistic boundaries, since his principal focus never strayed, in the final analysis, from the linguistically homogeneous area of the Greek-speaking world. Tylor was in any case far from being a severe critic of Müller's theories (cf. Dorson 1968: 169, 187), and there is no reason to suppose that Politis felt very differently. In one important respect, however, Politis' essay on solar mythology reverses the flow of a classic Müller argument: rather than treating myth as a "disease of language," Politis chose to view metaphorical usage as the scattered and degenerate relics of myth (see especially 1882a: 28-42). This, again, is a logical outcome of a form of survivalism which takes the Classical period as its sole point of departure. It is also consistent with the literalism which was so characteristic of Politis' thinking but which was antithetical to Müller's view of language (cf. Crick 1976: 15-35).

Recourse to a *pre*-Classical past was new in Greek folklore studies at this time, despite obscure hints of its possible relevance in Zambelios' reference to the eastern origins of some Classical culture traits. In the long passage just quoted, Politis mentions myths "of which not the slightest mention is made by the ancient authors." This approach involves bringing in non-Hellenic materials, of course, but it also permits an *argumentum ex silentio* whereby continuity can be posited even in the total absence of evidence from ancient literature. The device became popular; it could also be convincing, as in Lawson's attempt to show that the figure of Charos represents a true survival even though not in its literary guise as the ferryman of the Styx (1910: 106).

The fragmentation of this extremely ancient mythological stratum is traced through successive stages. It begins with the personification of the sun and the distribution of the sun's attributes among various heroes and gods— this being perhaps a pale refraction of Müller's "disease of language" theory, in that it represents the progressive fragmentation of a single, unified, and named concept (cf. also Dorson 1968: 162). Later, the specialized myths themselves became fragmented. Some became songs, others tales; note that Politis treats folktales, *paramithia*, as incomplete mythological segments rather than as full-fledged myths in their own right. Modern Greece has its mythology, but this takes a variety of forms which, when examined singly, lack complete historical autonomy.

At a more microscopic level, too, the search for original forms deeply interested Politis. Throughout his career, he exhibited a conviction that all legends and songs began as specific, if hypothetical, *Urtext* forms. In this, he differed from Zambelios in two significant respects. First, he explicitly rejected the notion—Vician or otherwise—of collective composition; it conflicted too deeply with his literalist perspective. "On a priori grounds, however, we may proclaim as a dogma which admits of no doubt that the people (*laos*), qua people, as a collectivity (*sinolon*), is incapable of composing a poem. Collective poetry is an impossibility" (Politis 1916: 8). This flat rejection of collective composition does not preclude the existence of processes of textual change; on the contrary, these are extensively discussed in many of Politis' publications. But the point is that variant texts are precisely what they are supposed to be: departures in each case from an individually composed *Urtext*.

This was the approach which Politis brought even to songs of a patently social nature. A notable example is provided by the so-called swallow song (*khelidhonisma*). The very name of this textual type illustrates the use of the Classical period as the one reliable, fixed reference point: it was concocted from a verb (*khelidonizein*) which the Greco-Egyptian writer Athenaeus (2d-3d century A.D.) associated with an apparently complete song text (Ath. *Deipn.* viii, 360b-d = Page 1962: 450–451). The noun form is thus a nineteenth-century scholastic neologism which Politis, building on an initial review of the subject by Wachsmuth, used to bring the ancient text together with thirteen modern "variants" from scattered locations (Politis 1872). The term "swallow song" appears to be unknown in present-day rural Greece, and it is not clear whether all of Politis' "variants" came from analogous performative contexts (cf. Herzfeld 1974, 1977). Yet his classification, rooted as it is in the search for continuity, remains popular among folklorists of essentially Hellenist outlook despite the vast increase in the volume of the material that has to be dealt with (e.g., Spiridakis 1969, with 164 texts). The appeal of the *Urtext* hypothesis is still considerable, and its ideological implications were already present in such early studies of Politis as his paper on the "swallow song."

But Politis, whose acquaintance with Indo-European scholarship seems to have made him properly wary of reconstructed forms, never went so far as to attempt a critical edition of a folksong *Urtext*. Such an extreme of philological antiquarianism, which was attempted by at least one later scholar (Romaios 1966, 1966-67; but cf. Kiriakidou-Nestoros 1975: 178–190), could not be reconciled with Politis' characteristically restrained conclusion that, "if we except the historical songs, the chronological point of origin of folksongs is generally unstable and uncertain, so that the examination of this substantial fragment of Greek poetry by historical periods is not feasible, at least for the present" (1916: 4). That the historical songs constituted an exception in this respect was possible only through Politis' literalist assumption that each song was "composed for" the event which it celebrated. More generally, the concept of an *Urtext* meant that he could treat local variants as sources on which to base textual criticism, albeit with due care: "The choice of a variant of each [song text] was not sufficient, because even the most perfect variant presents lacunae, which may nonetheless be corrected with ease on the basis of other variants. . . . My work is like that of the editor of a literary text, who treats it on the basis of the manuscript versions, limiting himself exclusively to restoration (*recensio*) and not daring to attempt correction (*emendatio*)" (1914: 7). This was not a hypocritical position, even though Politis attacked other scholars' (e.g., Khristovasilis') textual alterations. What he disliked was *invented* textual material, rather than careful philological reconstructions; indeed, the latter were, in his view, a legitimate means of purifying an *Urtext* of its later accretions, both folk and learned.

The second major difference between Zambelios and Politis modifies this picture somewhat. For, whereas Zambelios treated the whole Classical period as, one might say, a grand *Urtext* for the general national regeneration that was to follow, Politis treated Classical antiquity as but one stage in the panoramic progression of Greek history. Zambelios had conceded the influence of eastern art and religious thought on the formation of Greek culture, but his view of Greece as the "cause" of all true civilization meant that he could still treat Classical Greece as the real point of origin. Not so Politis, who realized that a good deal of what was preserved in modern folklore might have bypassed the Classical literati entirely. For Politis, then, an *Urtext* was not necessarily the origin of the *ideas* which it contained, although he generally assumed that it was contemporaneous with any *facts* which it might convey. Rather, an *Urtext* fixed the ideas in a particular *form*, and to this—in theory, at least—a date might be attached. The ideas themselves were virtually timeless, but they were also distinctively and unarguably Greek in the way in which they were expressed.

Thus, from the very beginning of his scholarly career, Politis avoided equating the form of texts with their intellectual content. On the other hand, he never rejected the key assumption that textual forms were fixed in historical time and that their relevance was above all historical. He began *Modern Greek Mythology* with a version of this theme:

> The history of a nation (*ethnos*) does not consist solely in the narration of those events which have had some influence on its destiny; rather, the accurate and detailed knowledge of this nation's character and spirit (*pnevma*) is also needed in order to supplement that history and put it together more perfectly. [This is] because such knowledge, apart

from the fact that it contributes to the easier discovery and understanding of the causes and consequences of such events, not infrequent-
ly aids in the elucidation of obscure and problematical historical
questions.   (1871: i)

The concern with "national character" is mainly rhetorical here. The approach which Politis suggests might more justly be described as a compound
of ethnohistorical aims and philological methods. Although the passage just
quoted sounds like something Zambelios might have written, the intention
behind it is substantially different. Politis does not seek historical "laws" *in*
the material itself so much as explanations of the material which will *also*
serve as explanations of events in national history. That perspective remained
with him to the end and was to bear bittersweet fruit when he turned to the
folklore associated with the main irredentist objective, the recapture of Constantinople (see chap. 6). It is perhaps best explained by saying that, for
Politis, the "survivals" of culture meant in a very real sense the physical survival of the nation itself. If the nation did not remember its identity, it was
no nation. Thus, the *vios* ("life") of the nation depended on the recognition
and maintenance of its *epiviosis* ("survivals"). Conversely, the past and present "survival" of national identity could be understood only by studying the
nation's "life."

Laography: Definition and Organization

In 1884, Politis publicly coined the word *laografia* for the first time (Kiriakidis 1931: 12). For some time, he had been moving toward a unified theoretical perspective. A founding member of the Historical and Ethnological Society of Greece (1882), in whose journal he now introduced the new term,
he distrusted the wide coverage of terms like "ethnography" and "anthropology"; as he later remarked in the first issue of another major journal,
Laografia:

> The term "demography" was concocted in 1855 by the Frenchman
> Guillard; this was the name given to the statistically based study of
> human life. Older still is the term "ethnography," which denotes the
> science that examines man as a political animal, constituting groups or
> nations, being distinct from "anthropology," which examines human-
> kind as an animal genus, as an isolated individual, without regard to
> social or national grouping.   (1909a: 2)

This is a somewhat curious statement to come from an admirer of Tylor. It
represents a simplification of Tylor's view that "stages of culture may be
compared without taking into account how far tribes who use the same

implement, follow the same custom, or believe the same myth, may differ in their bodily configuration and the colour of their skin and hair" (1924: 7).

It was in 1909 that laography finally gained official status with the foundation, under Politis' direction, of the Hellenic Folklore Society (Elliniki Laografiki Eteria). This institution published a journal, *Laografia*, the first issue of which contained Politis' now classic definition of the discipline (see also app. A). It opens with a historical survey of the antecedents and equivalents of the term *laografia* itself:

> The word *laografia*, which we have been using for the last twenty-five years to denote studies of folk traditions, beliefs, customs, the unwritten literature of the folk, and every possible contribution to a more accurate knowledge of the people (*laos*), is found in ancient Greek from the last years of the Alexandrian period but used in an entirely different, special sense. *Laographia* was the name of the poll tax paid by a large proportion of the inhabitants of Egypt from fourteen to fifty years of age. It was the "per capita contribution," as Josephus calls it, or the "head tax," as it is named in some papyri. The imposition of this tax, from which the Jews had been exempt, is mentioned in the passage of the apocryphal book of the Maccabees in which are recorded the edicts of the Egyptian king Ptolemy Philopator which were so crushing to the Jews (208 B.C.) [*sic*: now usually dated ca. 217 B.C. but historically dubious]. Those who paid the head tax were called *laographoumenoi* to distinguish them from those who were exempted from this tax (*epikekrimenoi*); the latter, however, were required to serve in the army. *Laographoi* were village headmen responsible for organizing the *laographia*.
>
> Despite the different meaning which it had in Egypt, this word is most suitable as the name of a discipline whose object is the study of the people (*laos*). Otherwise, similar words have been introduced and taken by us into scholarly usage; they are compounds of synonyms for the words *laos* ("people") and *grafo* ("write") and are used to denote sciences not wholly unconnected with laography, such as "demography" and "ethnography."
>
> In many European languages, the word "folklore" is used; it means *laografia*. This term was invented by the Englishman William John Thoms, who, writing under a pseudonym, published an article in the London literary journal *Athenaeum* of 27 August 1846 (pp. 842-843), in which he suggested that a special term was needed for those studies which already then were certainly widespread but were not regarded as constituting a special and distinctive discipline. The term, which was composed of the English "folk" (*laos*) and "lore" (knowledge, teach-

ing) on the model of the German compounds *Volkslied*, *Volksepos*, *Volksfest*, etc., was in many cases more suitable than the circumlocutions then current in English usage, "popular antiquities" and "popular literature" [as Thoms had in fact pointed out; see Dorson 1968: 1]. From that point on, the term kept its place in English and was also introduced into other European languages. The Danes, who were acquainted with the English word and cirtually "misetymologized" it, called laography *"Folkeminder"* ("folk recollections").

But certain folklorists, even though the English term has been introduced into their languages, have preferred some other term taken from their own tongue, in the interests of easier comprehension. The Italians call *tradizioni popolari* and the French likewise *traditions populaires* virtually all the subject matter of folklore, thereby investing a one-sided term with more general meaning. From here, some proceeded to add the word *traditionnisme*. This, as the French folklorist Gaidoz observes, is not only vague but necessarily confusing, since it means two different things: first, a love of tradition and an inclination to preserve it, and second the study of tradition, which is not the same thing at all—it is possible for one who loves tradition not to study it, and for one who studies it not to love it.

Thus, the French will be compelled to have recourse to the English term, using [for it] the French *traditions populaires* when and if they want to be understood by ordinary people. Gaston Paris concocted the term *mythographie*, but in the narrower sense of the "study of tales" for which the English use "storiology."

The Germans, again, having accepted the English term, now seem to prefer another which has been concocted out of their own language, the term *Volkskunde* ("acquaintance with the folk, knowledge of the people"). But that term has the following disadvantage: taken in its principal meaning, it extends the field of laographic studies more widely than it ought.   (1909a: 1-3)

This lengthy passage has been quoted in full here because it looks both forward to the creation of a new discipline and backward to that discipline's antecedents. In fact, Politis' formulation exhibits a presuppositional framework which is fully consistent with the previous history of Greek folklore studies, even if it does go much further in explicating a systematic basis for the organization of those studies. First, the search for an "ancient" (actually Hellenistic) term is presented as essential to the success of the enterprise. Then, that term is defined more precisely in relation to Western European concepts and labels. Politis seems to imply that the English word "folklore" is the most exact equivalent to *laografia*. He nevertheless adds in a footnote that Bernhard Schmidt had written this to him: "The term *laografia*, which you first introduced, seems most aptly chosen to me and very suitable for naturalization in other languages too. I never approved of the entry of the English word 'folklore' into our usage but always avoided that word, as did my late friend Reinhold Köhler. But the term *Volkskunde*, the use of which is now predominant in Germany, also seems apt to me" (1909a: 3, n. 3). Thus, Politis was able to hint that, in the absence of any real consensus among European scholars on this question, they might like to consider the Greek *laografia*, with its clarity and appropriateness; indeed, he also mentions an Italian proposal to do just that (1909a: 2, n. 3). But the idea never took hold. The reasons lay less in the term itself—though certainly other languages had their homespun equivalents to Thoms' "good Saxon compound"—than in the parochial nature of Greek laography as a discipline. Greek folklorists rarely tried to answer questions that were not of direct relevance to specifically Greek concerns, and Politis was no exception. *Laografia* remained locked into its ideological commitment to a derivative neo-Classicism. Politis himself, as he grew increasingly liberal in his political convictions (Kiriakidou-Nestoros 1978: 154-157), directed his magnificent scorn against the excesses of the earlier and more polemical anti-Fallmerayerists; yet still the newly defined discipline could not escape its inherited, one-sided dependence upon "European" models and "European" approval. This was, after all, a fair reflection of the continuing political condition of the Greek State, and Politis—who had spent part of his student career in Germany—was thoroughly familiar with western scholarship.

Taxonomy and Ideology

Politis gave *laografia* its name. In addition, he undertook to give it its first really systematic taxonomy and thus also the pattern for its future development. The materials which he listed as appropriate to the discipline (see app. A) constitute an almost exhaustive list of what were then considered to be recognizable cultural artifacts. These are divided between two main headings, "monuments of the word" and "traditional activities or practices." His bipartite division reflects the special status which the Greek folklorists always accorded vernacular literature; this is further borne out by the rather miscellaneous character of the second group, which seems to lack a clear, central organizing principle. It is the literary material, too, which receives "monumental" status; the archaeological allusion is no accident. Again, the second category seems to cover the "ordinary" aspects of folklife, although there are some items which suggest "art" (e.g., sculpture). Whatever its peculiarities and biases, however, Politis' organization of the materials of folklore into this general schema was to exert a massive influence on all subsequent scholarship. Most later classifications (e.g., Mazarakis 1964; Spiridakis 1962) are little more than elaborations of his system (cf. chap. 1, n. 1).

Like any classificatory system, Politis' schema set an artificial grid on the material and so partly predetermined what would be collected. In that sense, it became something of a self-fulfilling prophecy—the process which we have already noted in the very earliest stages of Greek folklore research. At least, however, the clarity with which he set up his grand schema is such that its operative principles are relatively easy, from a present-day standpoint, to identify.

Taking the "monuments of the word" first, we find a remarkable range of degrees of elaboration in the various categories. Songs, which significantly head this list, are divided into numerous subcategories; this indicates the central position which they had held since the very beginning. The lists enclosed in parentheses represent a still finer order of classification: "e.g., carols, songs of Lazarus, Holy Week laments, swallow songs, songs performed in the course of certain games, songs of the *perperouna* and *klidhonas*, swing songs, wedding songs, funeral dirges."[4] Politis indicates that this particular sublisting is not exhaustive, but it suffices to define the next most inclusive level of the taxonomy. Order and selection are dictated by academic rather than folk principles—for example, in the dissociation of personal laments from those sung for the dead Christ during Holy Week. The "swallow song" appears as an autonomous subcategory, without further elaboration. Yet Politis' classification of songs does in fact move laography substantially away from its earlier obsession to present only "seemly" material: "Apart from the lyrical, epic, religious," and other forms of song already well represented in the published collections, certain less "literary" genres are now also to be included—a great advance on Evlambios, for example. Obscene songs, which would formally have come under the "satirical" heading, are absent, however, and do not appear in Politis' 1914 collection of folksongs either—whether because of his own self-censorship, for fear of possible trouble with the authorities, or because of lack of available material, we can only guess.

Politis' handling of narrative categories is eloquent witness to his special preoccupations. The belief that narratives of one sort are true (item no. 9) sets them apart from "myths" (no. 6), "humorous stories" (no. 7), and "legends or tales" (no. 8); they are essentially cosmological narratives of the kind which form so important a part of *Modern Greek Mythology*. What, then, are myths and legends, and how do they really differ from each other? Here the classification seems to have become somewhat entangled in its commitment to doing two things simultaneously: establishing cultural continuity between ancient myths and modern fables but, at the same time, keeping them conceptually separate so as to preserve the inviolability of myth as a category of Classical discourse. Politis' British contemporaries seem, for all their disagreements, to have accepted a unitary category of "myth" as the proper object of both folklore and anthropology (e.g., Lang 1885: 22-23). While they tended to use the word "tales" to denote the less exotic and more recent forms of mythology, they did not attempt to create a clear analytical distinction between the two categories *for the purpose of studying their own culture by itself.* Again, *foreign* observers in Greece tended to use "myth" for the ancient and "legend" or "tale" for the modern stories, even when an intrinsic connection between them was recognized (e.g., Lenormant 1864: 524). Politis, by contrast, was trapped between a static model of cultural continuity, on the one hand, and the desire to demonstrate the "European" character of Greek culture on the other. These two motivations, tugging in opposed directions, are represented by "myths" (no. 6) and "tales" (nos. 7-9) respectively. The distinction was never worked out in detail in the actual classification of material, and indeed it is difficult to see, in practical terms, how it could have been.

In his treatment of proverbs (no. 5), by contrast, Politis demonstrates a sense of the interpretive importance of context that is quite new in Greek folklore studies. Once again, there is a slight clash with other categories, this time through his insistence on recording "the myths in which [the proverbs] are sometimes mentioned." But in this case the slight inconvenience is potentially far outweighed by the gain. In fact, we see Politis' sense of the intrinsic connection between proverb and tale as early as *Modern Greek Mythology*, where he cites numerous examples. A more surprising omission is the lack of any reference to the *social* context of proverb use as a necessary datum—surprising if only because Politis does in fact often cite the real-life situations to which particular proverbs are appropriate. It may be that the literary nature of his interests here deflected his attention away from this aspect of paroemiology.

Sociological considerations really appear only in the second, more heterogeneous division of Politis' laography. "Customs" (nos. 6, 7), "social organization" (no. 4), "justice" (no. 9), and "worship" (no. 10) are scattered throughout this list. The categories of this incipient sociology are still governed by the old principles. Particularly noteworthy in this respect is the perpetuation of the "kleft-brigand" opposition (in no. 4). Politis was too careful an observer to overlook the fact that "brigands" had their own concepts and means of applying justice, but he still could not bring himself to *equate* them with "klefts" or to catalog their forms of law under the more formal (and implicitly statist) notion of "justice" in general. The items listed under "justice," moreover, all correspond directly to the categories of state law in some obvious way; they are principally concerned with property

ownership and transfer, and the reader is further directed to the works of
Khrisanthopoulos and von Maurer. The ideology of the nation-state thus
directs the organization of Politis' classification of such phenomena.

A rare exception to this domination of the methodology by the forms of
state law is seen in the search for traces of patrilineal organization in village
society (in no. 4). This, however, is easily explained, despite the fact that the
state kinship ideology follows the usual "European" format of the bilateral
kindred. The point is that the patrilineal *genos* of Classical times might legitimately be sought as a survival, and it is in fact recognized minimally under
state law through the requirement that a bride-to-be announce her mother's
genos (i.e., maiden name).

In matters religious, Politis is somewhat more adventurous, perhaps because his first loyalty was to the Hellenist ideal rather than to the Orthodox
church. Under "worship," he distinguishes between ecclesiastical and nonecclesiastical cult practices. Among the latter, he recognizes a category of
"orgiastic" cults, though this is an instance of neo-Classical hyperbole: both
of the cults listed under this heading are in some degree ecstatic, but their
Dionysiac origins—if such they be (Kakouri 1965; but cf. Danforth 1979)—
are at best muted in present-day performance. In general, Politis seems to
have had no hesitation in listing ostensibly Christian cults as pagan survivals.
Influenced by the Grimms and Wachsmuth in particular, he recognized the
syncretic character of many saints' cults; and, while he was not the first to
do this, he dealt with the material more thoroughly than any of his predecessors. In his early discussion of the cult of Saint Nicholas, for example, he
acknowledged the insights of d'Istria (1863) and Wachsmuth (1864) into its
origins in the worship of the maritime god Poseidon, but he proposes "to examine the connection between the sea god of the ancients with this saint, because the above-mentioned writers confined themselves to merely hinting at
the similarity between Poseidon and Saint Nicholas" (1871: 58). His discussion indicates some knowledge of the medieval literature as well as of the
more usual Classical and modern folk sources.

At the most general level, Politis' laographic taxonomy may be seen as an
amalgam of Classical and modern categories. The choice of each term seems
to have been largely contingent on whether the material in question already
formed part of the existing corpus of folklore or whether its existence in
modern Greek culture was simply presumed on the basis of Classical or ethnographic parallels. Such speculative projection undoubtedly did take place during the construction of the taxonomy. Politis lists divination by sieving, for
example, yet Lawson soon afterward reported that he had not in fact encountered any present-day instances of this Classical practice (1910: 331). In
numerous such ways the taxonomy was predisposed to register possible survivals, whether or not there was much evidence for their widespread existence,

whereas other traits might not be catered for in advance by this schema. This is yet another instance of the way in which the Hellenist model could be characterized as largely self-perpetuating.

Politis' grand taxonomy remained essentially unmodified throughout his subsequent writings. It captures for us many of the strains inherent in the Greek folklorists' peculiar form of survivalism. Possibly Politis himself viewed it as little more than a first approximation, although all the operative principles were well in place. Later work, such as his immensely popular *Selections from the Songs of the Greek People* (1914), elaborates the original schema without substantially affecting its overall orientation. Most of the secondary trimming and adding, moreover, arose from a steady increase in the availability of historical and ethnographic data, much of it a direct outcome of Politis' own efforts to organize the discipline into an efficient operation. The new material which this process generated was thus selected and ordered to confirm, not to challenge, the tenets of ideological Hellenism. That ideology was now openly and actively irredentist.

A Verbal Archaeology

Greek irredentism was an explicitly historical movement: past glories would be restored in the none too distant future. In this context, Politis' focus on the "monumental" aspects of verbal folklore is not simply an abstruse archaeological metaphor. He regarded songs and folktales both as relics and commemorations of the past and as prophecies of future redemption. His extreme historical literalism is particularly well exemplified by his espousal of the "*Urtext* hypothesis," that essentially stemmatic arrangement of oral texts on a philological *Stammbaum*; but it was also buttressed by the growing record of folk texts which mentioned significant places and personalities of history. The desire to commemorate individual deeds, the peculiarly Hellenic characteristic of which d'Istria had made so much, was equally necessary to Politis' view of culture history as a series of fixed points to guide the voyage of national self-discovery.

It is thus no accident that Politis begins his *Selections from the Songs of the Greek People* with the category of "historical" songs. These are verses which commemorate events known from documentary sources, starting with the sack of Adrianople (1361) and, significantly (as we shall shortly see), the Fall of Constantinople and the ravishing of its famed Hagia Sophia cathedral (1453). The latest event to be commemorated in the songs of this section, Greece's failure to wrest the major portion of Epirus from Turkey under the terms of the Treaty of Berlin, occurred in 1881. Note that, although "anti-establishment" and factional songs have commemorated *internal* political events (e.g., see Katsoulis 1975: 225 on the politico-military upheavals of

1897), these found no place in Politis' collection—least of all in the "historical" section, which was concerned with events of a strictly territorial and international nature.

The next section of the *Selections* consists of "kleftic songs." Given the
elaborate critical notes in which Politis addresses the historical background to
some of these texts, it may seem surprising that they have not been included
in the preceding category. It should be remembered, however, that the notion
of a distinctive genre of kleftic song was already established in the ethnological literature by the time he entered the scene. The songs in this section,
moreover, do not deal with single events which—and this is the significant
point—can be given specific dates. In addition, the activities of the klefts, although conventionally interpreted by Politis as contributions to the patriotic
cause, are both *sui generis* and comparatively small in scale; they do not take
the form of pitched battles or the capture of cities, alien ways of fighting to
the mountain guerrillas and brigands, but celebrate the klefts' rugged life-
style. For all these reasons, Politis found no cause to challenge the viability of
the "kleftic" category of folksongs.

The "historical" songs deal with events which occurred before the places
which they celebrate became parts of a free and independent Greece, and the
"kleftic songs" commemorate a historical phase within the same time con-
straint. After the "kleftic" category, however, comes another group which
seems suddenly to take us further *back* in time to the Byzantine period. This
consists of the so-called Akritic songs.

It had been recognized for some time that certain narrative songs apparently recalled names and events of an identifiably Byzantine character (e.g.,
Zambelios 1852; Büdinger 1866). In 1875, however, the philological world
was given details of the discovery, some five years earlier, of the first known
manuscript of the "Akritic epic"—a long poem dealing with those same personalities and events (Sathas and Legrand 1875; Ioannidis 1887; cf. Kalonaros
1970). The thematic resemblances were striking in the extreme, and the
philologist-historian K. Sathas immediately proclaimed the folksong texts to
be the constituents of an "Akritic cycle." On January 14, 1907, on the occasion of his installation as rector of the University of Athens, Nikolaos Politis proclaimed that the entire textual corpus represented "the national epic of
the modern Greeks"; he followed this two years later with the publication of
a set of "Akritic" folksong texts in the first volume of *Laografia* (Politis
1909a).

The scholars' excitement was understandable. Quite apart from the possible literary merit of these materials, the manuscript epic—of which other versions soon came to light—seemed to confirm Zambelios' confident assertion
that Byzantium had provided the link in the popular culture between ancient

and modern times; indeed, he had based that opinion in part on a folksong text, "Andronikos' Sons," which was now classified as "Akritic."

To Politis, the songs no less than the manuscript texts supported both the territorial and the historical claims of ideological Hellenism:

> From the edges of Cappadocia to the Ionian Islands, and from Macedonia and the western regions of the Black Sea down as far as Crete and Cyprus, songs are sung to this day that relate the feats and adventures of Digenes and his struggles against the Apelates and Saracens; and traditions are recounted by word of mouth which recall the places and objects which are associated with Digenes' name. In these, the imagination of the people embroidered myths [*sic*], most of which it took over and renewed out of the rich mythical [*sic*] heritage of antiquity, and constructed the ideal type of the hero—as youthful as Achilles, as strong as Herakles, and as glorious as Alexander. To put the matter in its appropriately proud context, in Digenes Akrites the desires and ideals of the Hellenic nation reach their peak, because in this man the long centuries of ceaseless struggle by the Hellenic against the Islamic world are symbolized. (1907: 11)

The antiquity of the heroic ideals is combined with the presumed historicity of the actual text to present an epic that is truly "national." The argument is entirely characteristic of Politis. The territorial extent of Hellenism is claimed, as it were, by the songs themselves, and the border is clearly marked as that which separates Hellenism (rather than Christianity) from Islam. This is the philological embodiment of the Great Idea (*Megali Idhea*), the doctrine of Greek irredentism whereby all the lands of Classical and Byzantine Hellenism should be reclaimed for the reborn nation.

Politis' political involvement in the irredentist movement had always been intense. Even as a schoolboy, he had attempted to enlist as a volunteer to fight in the 1866 uprising in Crete. He later ran undercover courier missions for nationalist groups in Constantinople; although he himself escaped detection, his brother was accidentally arrested in his place by the Turkish police. Now he had a means at his disposal for pursuing the national goal in an arena more suited to his academic talents. The Akritic songs, while found virtually everywhere in the Greek-speaking world, were reported in particularly large numbers from Asia Minor (especially Cappadocia), Crete, and Cyprus—all lands which were still under foreign rule. Since these songs seemed to combine a form of mythology with medieval prosopography, the latter reinforced by the discovery of the manuscript poems, they rapidly assumed great importance in the scholarly dimensions of the Great Idea.

The label "Akritic," however, created something of a paradox. It was

taken to refer to the borders (*akrai*) of the Byzantine Empire, which the
Akritai were expected to defend against the depredations of both brigandlike
Apelates and Arab marauders. But, in practice, the status of these border
regions seems to have been unstable. As border barons, the Akritai evidently
attended to their own interests at least as assiduously as they did to those of
their imperial masters. This emerges quite clearly in the epic and the folksongs, as well as from independent documentary sources.[5]

A related difficulty concerns the name Digenes. Conventionally translated
as "twy-born" (e.g., Mavrogordato 1956: xxvii), it has been taken as a reference to the hero's mixed ancestry. The epics have him as the son of an Arab
emir and a Greek woman; the songs, while preserving the basic element of
dual ancestry, vary the actual "ethnicities" involved. Politis nevertheless pre-
ᴣnted Digenes as the very epitome of the Hellenic virtues; after all, as more
cent scholars have pointed out (notably Veloudis 1968), Alexander the
eat was also of mixed parentage. But a small minority of Politis' contemporaries were uncomfortable with his conception of the Akritic hero. Karolidis (1906) was the first to point out that one might just as easily take the
name as symbolizing the "twy-born culture (*politismos*)" of the border regions and, thus, as something very far removed from a cultural exemplar for
Hellenism. While it is evident that Digenes' dual ancestry represents some sort
of social conflict, as it does in the songs, there is no reason to suppose that
this conflict was necessarily concerned with anything that we might call
ethnicity (cf. Lambrinos 1947; Herzfeld 1980b).

Politis, who had studied in Germany under the great Byzantinologist Karl
Krumbacher, nevertheless chose to interpret the "Akritic cycle" in the literalist terms of his ideology, according to which everything "Byzantine" was also
"Greek." He was of course aware that parallels could be found in other
periods and places. Nor did he ignore the similarity of some of the texts that
he classified as Akritic to songs placed in other categories (mainly "kleftic
songs" and "ballads"), as his detailed commentaries show. But Politis had
never been deaf to the possibility of non-Greek parallels in any area of Greek
folklore; for him, these did not detract in the least from the Greekness of the
local materials. To explain the relationship between Akritic and other songs,
he applied the concept of *simfirmos*—literally, "conflation," but carrying a
strong sense of "contamination" that fits well with his concern and that of
his successors to maintain clear-cut distinctions between "pure" types of
cultural artifact. As a result, the integrity of the "Akritic cycle" has never
been seriously challenged by Greek scholars; even those who have disagreed
with the irredentist interpretation of the songs (e.g., Apostolakis 1929; Lambrinos 1947) have accepted the basic premise of the classification itself. The
Hellenists stuck to their view that the Akritic manuscripts represented a
"national epic," while their critics objected to the "ethnic" implications of

that title. But that the Akritic texts represent a discrete phase in Greek cul-
ture-history, somewhat analogous to that of the klefts, has never been the
object of a sustained critique in Greece.

Politis' technique for dealing with cross-categorial similarities, especially
his use of "conflation" as an explanatory device, shows how and why the
taxonomy was able to remain a self-fulfilling prophecy for so long. The
notion of formulaic variation had not yet been developed in the context of
Greek folklore, and Politis evidently thought that texts moved around the
country as massive unities. Not only single texts but even the entire categories
of "kleftic" and "Akritic" texts were presented as invariant arrangements of
ideas and motifs. Thus, for example, in discussing the "Song of Mavrianos and
His Sister," Politis, unable to detect clear thematic links with the Akritic
poems or identifiable episodes from Byzantine history, wrote: "The song has
a certain similarity with the Akritic songs: the names of the characters, where
names are mentioned, are the well-known ones of the Akritic songs; in some
variants, indeed, Digenes is mentioned by name" (1914: 112).

It is indicative of the thinking which this passage illustrates that *sinafia*,
the word here translated as "similarity," can also mean "contact." There is
thus a strong hint of the kind of textual miscegenation conveyed by that
other Greek term, *simfirmos*. Formally, the line between the category of
"ballads" (which includes the song in question) and that of "Akritic songs" is
sharp and clear, even if the texts themselves do sometimes inconveniently
straddle it. The taxonomy, moreover, is a strictly academic one and does not
reflect ordinary vernacular usage. Although the term for "ballads," *paraloyes*,
may just conceivably have been taken from the folk idiom (Economides
1969), its folk use covers many of the texts classified by Politis as "Akritic"
(which is *not* a folk term). Given the premises on which the taxonomy was
initially constructed, one can easily understand how the folk category of
paraloyes could be artificially emasculated to allow the "Akritic songs" a
discrete (and sufficiently numerous) existence in the corpus.

The self-fulfilling character of the taxonomy should be evident by now.
The Greek folklorists' attempt to build up a sound classification of the national folklore, their static view of history, and the effect of the taxonomy
itself upon the kinds of data that were collected—all jointly contributed to a
rapid reinforcement of the most important among the original articles of
faith, those of cultural continuity with ancient Greece, the European character of the entire Greek people, and the territorial and chronological boundaries of Hellenism. There is no point in trying to prove that any of these tenets
was factually wrong. Rather, as we have stressed throughout this book, they
all represented a particular selection of cultural phenomena as significant. The
size and sophistication of Politis' schema simply amplified the effects of the
original selectional criteria. The self-reinforcement of the folklore taxonomy

became, in his hands, an affirmation of the eventual triumph of Hellenic culture. The prophecy was thus a political one. When it failed, in what the Greeks still call *the* Catastrophe of their defeat in Asia Minor in 1922, the active political role of irredentist folklore also effectively came to an end. Politis presided over the achievement of a unified discipline, and it was only shortly after his death in 1921 that events pushed that discipline away from the center of the ideological stage. It is to be hoped that what has been said thus far will now lend some meaning to the final burgeoning of hope and its total, destructive collapse, as we examine these developments in the next chapter.

Chapter 6
Expansion and Collapse

". . . ours once more . . ."

Seeds of Contradiction: Defining Hellenism

Although the irredentists based their goals on the premise of continuity with the Classical era, it was the Byzantine capital, Constantinople (İstanbul), that they hoped to turn into the capital of a totally liberated Greek nation-state. The historians and folklorists did much, as we have seen, to reinstate the Byzantine period as the essential link between high antiquity and the present. The ironic result was to make Constantinople, the New Rome, the *Hellenists'* goal rather than that of more "Romeic" thinkers and politicians. Of course, we should not insist on drawing a rigid line between the two ideological trends insofar as their attitudes to irredentism were concerned. But it is fair to say that it was the Hellenists who showed particular alacrity in the pursuit of the Great Idea.

The Greeks' claim to be the modern representatives of Hellas did sometimes raise complex questions about the exact nature of their collective identity. That there were many different forms of the Greek language was the least of the difficulties: some of the most outlying or (to an urban Greek) incomprehensible dialects could be shown to preserve particularly archaic forms (cf. Browning 1969), and there was no doubt about the closeness of their relationship to each other and to ancient Greek. Even the non-Greek languages spoken on Greek territory revealed extensive traces of Greek influence, though claims of "Homeric" derivation for lexical items in Koutsovlach (Papazisis 1976: 8) and Cypriot Greek (Kiprianou 1967: 51) should be treated with great circumspection.[1] Politically, the geographical extent of the Greek language and its widespread etymological connections with minority languages provided a powerful argument for those who insisted that political boundaries should recognize the full expanse of Hellenism. The presence of songs and narratives that could be linked to Classical or Byzantine themes further strengthened such language-based claims, especially when the folk traditions could be interpreted as themselves giving voice to some irredentist sentiment. This, as we shall shortly see, was not thought to be at all improbable.

One nagging question has never been satisfactorily resolved. It concerns the use of the word "Hellenes" as a term of collective self-designation. The ancient Greeks at least as far back as Homer, as Zambelios had proudly noted, shared some awareness of their common cultural traditions; this was hardly diminished by their failure to translate it into political unity or by their bitter recognition of that failure. Their categorical distinction between "Hellenes" and "barbarians" became part of the latter-day nationalist vocabulary. Indeed, the literary antiquarian Eustathius, bishop of Thessaloniki, had roundly declared as early as the twelfth century that humanity could be divided into the opposed categories of "Hellene" and "barbarian" (Migne *PG* 135: 708; Politis 1901: 11). Such self-conscious archaism was not uncommon among Byzantine writers. On the other hand, some ecclesiastical writers used "Hellenes" as a term of *exclusion*, to describe all those who clung to their ancestral religion and refused to become Christians. From there, it was not a difficult step to using the term for any religious outsiders at all; Theodoret of Cyrrhus even described the Old Testament priests of Baal as "priests of the Hellenes" (Politis 1901: 7)!

The literary sources make their terms of reference reasonably clear. What is not at all certain is the degree to which their usages correspond to those of the populace at large. Knowledge of the "idolatrous" implications of "Hellenes" prevailed among the ecclesiastically minded until (and beyond) the 1821 Revolution. Some evidence from the folklore suggests that the name itself was preserved in popular usage (see especially Kakridis 1967), though whether rural Greeks commonly used it of themselves before the nineteenth century is far from clear. It is also uncertain how uninterruptedly the term had remained in vernacular speech or whether it had enjoyed equal currency in all parts of the Greek-speaking world.

Defining Greeks: Hellenic or Romeic?

The alternative term was *Romii*. Of its popularity there can be no doubt whatsoever, and its cognate *romeika* was no less unquestionably the usual label for the spoken language. Thus it was entirely logical for the protagonists of linguistic demoticism to prefer the term to "Hellenes" (although this was not a rigid association) and to make an ideological issue out of its use. It is this terminological opposition which has given us the labels used in this study for the two main ideological currents in Greek culture history; "Hellenist" and "Romeicist" are more suitable for our present purposes than *katharev-ousianos* (or "purist") and "demoticist," since the cultural issue is much broader in scope than the latter pair of terms, with their linguistic referents, would imply.

Politis, predictably, declared himself in favor of the name "Hellenes." Just a year before the language question (*ghlossiko zitima*) erupted in serious rioting in Athens, he published a defense of the Hellenic name against the views of the more extreme demoticists. The poet Palamas had criticized another writer, Eftaliotis, for publishing a *History of the Hellenic Nation* rather than of *Romiossini*. Politis, ever mindful of the need to deal with both sides of an argument, responded that "there never was any need whatsoever for evidence to prove that the Hellenes called themselves *Romii* also; nobody ever doubted that. But [Palamas] . . . ought to have demonstrated, first, that the foundation of the Byzantine state cut every link connecting the Hellene of the old world with the subject of the Byzantine emperors and, then, that from the years of Justinian's rule until the 1821 Revolution the name of 'Hellene' had disappeared from the national consciousness" (1901: 4).

Politis' essay on this subject is of interest for two reasons. In the first place, it gives a good picture of his careful scholarship, especially of his conscientious avoidance of purely *ad hominem* vituperation, even when he was discussing a matter about which he held passionate convictions. The other reason is more general and is also more closely related to the articulating theme of this book: the essay illustrates how a scholar, fully in possession of the evidence for both points of view, could still decide unequivocally in favor of one over the other. In the end, of course, as Politis himself saw, the issue was not one of deciding who was factually right. Rather, it was a question of which term was more *appropriate*. Where, in other words, was the most significant (rather than the "real") starting point of Greek history, in Classical Greece or in Christian Byzantium? The entire history of laography is that of attempts to derive significance from the riotous variety of Greek culture.

Hellenes or *Romii*? In posing and then attempting to answer that question, Politis was acting principally as a philologist, not a sociologist. He was not investigating ethnicity as a view of the collective self. Instead, he tried to establish that the term "Hellenes" had been *in use* among the Greeks since ancient times. His goal was thus to establish a link that was above all artifactual, or archaeological, in accordance with the wider principles of his methodology.

Politis was fully aware of the reasons why "Hellenes" gave way to *Romii* in popular favor: ecclesiastical disapproval of "Hellenism," the maintenance of "Roman" law in the Byzantine Empire, and the post-1453 continuation of the patriarch's temporal power as head of the "Romans" (*Rum*) (Politis 1901: 6). He also had detailed knowledge of the mythical character of the "Hellenes" who appear in folktales. Yet his unwillingness to examine such usages in context seems to have prevented him from exploring the sense of exclusion, quite apparent in some of his own ethnographic materials, which the term conveyed.

A single example will illustrate the problem. At least as early as 1871, Politis had read Robert Pashley's colorful *Travels in Crete*, for he makes several references to that work in *Modern Greek Mythology*—even, in the 1874 section on "Hellenes" itself, to Pashley's discussion of the related phenomenon of "the forty-cubit giant's tomb" (*tou sarandapikhou to mnima*). But he does *not* discuss Pashley's fully explicit reference to the term "Hellenes." When we look at the relevant passage in Pashley, the reason for such a curious omission becomes a little clearer:

> I find the belief in the ancient site said to exist above Samaría, and to have been the last refuge of the ancient Hellenes, is entertained by the Samarióte peasant who undertakes to shew me the way to them, and by most of his fellow-villagers. . . .
>
> As to the Hellenic remains my ascent ended in disappointment. . . . On my throwing out some slight doubts about the vestiges which I saw being *very* ancient, and suggesting that they could hardly belong to the celebrated "Hellenes," my Samarióte guide exclaimed, in the tone of one half offended at my ignorance or incredulity: "*Here* was the end of them my good Sir!" as if the matter had been one in which his local information entitled him to pronounce with authority.

(1837, II: 267-269)

We need not necessarily suppose that Politis intentionally suppressed this passage. Given his assumption that the memory of the name "Hellenes" alone was sufficient evidence of continuity, he may simply have dismissed the local guide's comment ("*Here* was the end of them . . .") as simpleminded nonsense; in Politis' view, the man was a Hellene himself! Pashley's own rather dubious remarks about this informant can hardly have inspired much confidence.

Yet what Pashley records is an unequivocal statement by a local person to the effect that he did not regard himself as a "Hellene" or think of the "Hellenes" as still in existence. This does not mean that, as a Cretan still living under Turkish rule, he would necessarily not have called his mainland compatriots "Hellenes" in the contemporary political sense of the word; such variable usage is characteristic of rural Greek "ethnic" terminology to this day. In this context, however, Pashley's Samariote guide was clearly not using "Hellene" as a term of self-designation.

Politis never denied that folk tradition had the Hellenes as a race of mythical giants; those stories were his main source of evidence for the continued use of the term. It is thus hardly likely that he deliberately suppressed such evidence as Pashley's in favor of "chauvinistic follies" (Kordatos 1972: 22,

n. 1). His interest, quite simply, was directed elsewhere. He is very forthright about the archaeological style of his arguments:

> As to [the Hellenes'] strength, there exist many traditions, one of which we present here. In it, *the recollections of ancient Hellas are apparently linked to those of Byzantium, since the scene is set in Constantinople.* Heuzey heard this tradition among the inhabitants of the village of Khrisovitsi in Acarnania. "This happened," they recount, "in the time of our grandfathers' grandfathers. Certain people from our village went to Constantinople. There, learning that there was a certain old woman of the race of the Hellenes, they went to see her. She was of supernatural height but was blind with advanced age. She asked them about the place whence they came and, turning to one of them, said to him, 'Give me your hand.' He was frightened and did not dare do so, but snatched up a fire iron, one end of which was broadened out (as is usual in the East), and offered it to the old woman. She squeezed it between her fingers and crushed it! 'You're strong,' she said, 'but not as strong as we are.' She thought she was holding his hand."
>
> (1874: 503-504; my emphasis)

The very name "Hellenes" alone was an artifact that, for Politis, claimed all the territories in which it was found for the Greek nation.

Politis concludes this particular passage by citing a Danish parallel, and we may be tempted to wonder why this, at least, did not deter him from so literal an interpretation. Given his frame of reference, however, there is no reason why it should have done so. Artifactual parallels between different cultures no more dissolved the conceptual boundaries between them than cross-categorial textual similarities between songs undermined the taxonomy which had been set up to accommodate them.

Some of the fluctuations in the fortunes of the Hellenic name were a matter of historical record. As Politis observed, its relative popularity was somewhat contingent upon political events during the Byzantine era; after the Latin sack of Constantinople in 1204, for example, "Hellenes" seems to have become more popular for a while, since any "Roman" term carried unpleasant associations. Folksongs which mention the last Byzantine ruler as "the Hellene Constantine" apparently mirror late Byzantine literary usage, even that of ecclesiastical authors, and references to "Hellene dragons" as the defenders of the last Byzantine outposts may reflect popular usage (Politis 1901: 15; cf. Vacalopoulos 1970: 183-186, 230-232, 356, nn. 93-95). But it is difficult to be sure: given the reputation of the mythical Hellenes of the folk narratives for superhuman strength and size, some of these usages may be metaphorical in origin. Politis, naturally, thought not, if indeed the idea ever suggested itself to him. It may be significant that these "historical" references

come from the eastern parts of the Greek-speaking world, especially Cappadocia—relatively near to the source, that is—and may indeed represent the
survival of a true self-designation.

Even among the eastern Greeks, however, the generic *Romania* remained
in common use as a term for the Greek-speaking regions. Again, this did not
really affect Politis' argument, since he never tried (or needed) to establish
that the Greeks had never used the term of themselves. In fact, his argument
went in the opposite direction at this point, revealing his assumption that the
Greeks had prior rights to the choice of nomenclature (1901: 18). Pointing
out that the Wallachians and Moldavians called their combined territories
Romania and themselves *Romani*, he argued that, had the Greeks wanted to
use these names officially of themselves, they would have had to force the
"real" Romanians to choose something else! Even allowing for rhetorical exaggeration, we see here the ethnocentrism of the true irredentist, the assertion
of prior rights to ethnic self-determination over an expanding geographical
space.

Unity, Homogeneity, and the Irredentist Ideal

From the foregoing, we can see something of the historicist logic whereby
New Rome was to become the capital of the new Hellas. The exponents of
the Great Idea, the *meghaloïdheates*, were determined to restore Greek hege-
mony over the widest territorial expanse that Greek culture had ever experienced. That dream never died completely; even the last king of Greece,
Constantine II, preferred to count his name in the line of Byzantine emperors
as Constantine XIII. But far and away the greatest flowering of the Great Idea
came in the first two decades of the present century, and the folklorists, led
by Politis, were active in its scholarly defense.

That the recapture of Constantinople remained a constant theme in both
learned and popular discourse ever since the destruction of the Byzantine
Empire is beyond doubt. But it was not a theme which held identical appeal
for all. The higher clergy, especially, discovered that their temporal power
over the Christian subjects of the sultan was actually greater in some respects
than it had been under the Byzantine emperors. Many of them consequently
opposed the rise of nationalistic activity during the years immediately before
independence (see, e.g., Dakin 1973: 46, 58, 238–239, n. 1; Kordatos 1972:
71–72; Katsoulis 1975: 17–49; Anthimos of Jerusalem in Clogg 1976: 56–
66). They argued that it was the will of God that Christendom should suffer
for its sins through subjugation to the Turks. This explanation of an otherwise (to the religiously minded) inexplicable event is reproduced also in the
folksongs, according to which "it is the will of God (*thelima Theu*) that the

City [i.e., Constantinople] should turn Turk [i.e., Moslem]." The crucial question here is thus to what extent the recognition of divine intervention constitutes a form of fatalism, a resignation to disaster.

The Fall of the City had been predicted in numerous popular prophecies, although the inhabitants of Constantinople had continued to hope for the last-minute intervention of God on their side. When the City finally fell, "the last glimmer of hope disappeared" (Vacalopoulos 1970: 203). At first, the despondency of the Christians must have been enormous. Some of the prophecies of the City's recapture—notably the story of the fish which leaped from the frying pan only half-cooked when the Turks arrived and would jump back into the pan to finish frying when the City reverted to Christendom— sound almost like allegories of the impossible.[2] Others, drawing on the mysterious circumstances of the disappearance of the last emperor's body, offered more hope: the emperor—having meanwhile been temporarily transformed into marble—would return one day with sword in hand and chase the Turks all the way back to their legendary ancestral home, the "Red Apple-Tree."[3] Some of the prophecies, again, were more contrived. The so-called *Prophecies of Agathangelos* "were reputedly written in Sicily in 1279 and printed in Milan in 1555. In fact they were forgeries compiled by the archimandrite Theoklitos Polyeidis, a native of Edirne [Adrianople], towards the middle of the eighteenth century" (Clogg 1973: 21; cf. Politis 1918: 165-169). Whatever their origins, most such prophecies seem to have exercised a considerable influence upon the popular imagination, especially as the new national consciousness began to take hold. That they were interpreted as signs of hope and imminent redemption is not at issue. It is less clear whether they represent a continuous desire to achieve that redemption on the part of the masses ever since 1453.

Politis thought that they did. Not only did he consider them evidence of widespread national aspirations, but he saw their extensive distribution throughout the Greek-speaking world as proof of the Greeks' cultural homogeneity and shared sense of destiny. In an important article on popular beliefs concerning the reestablishment of the Hellenic nation, he explained his position:

> One of the most solid foundations of national consciousness resides in a community of manners and customs, of beliefs and traditions; in a uniform perception of the outside world; and, above all, in an identical display of feelings, of aspirations, and of hopes. These are the *homotropic* customs which, in their admirable definition of the idea of fatherland and national solidarity, consumed the Athenians (according to Herodotus) when on the eve of the Battle of Plataea they rejected Mardonius' tempting and advantageous blandishments and showed the

Lacedaemonians [i.e., Spartans] that they had a very explicit sense of
the bonds which united them to the rest of the Hellenes.

(1918: 151-152)[4]

Heterotropic customs are those which one finds among ethnically mixed pop-
ulations. Such people, when they form a nation-state, are simply committing
an act of political invention; their collective identity is a wholly artificial construct. The Greeks, by contrast, aimed at a political union which by its very
nature would be indissoluble; for Politis, there was nothing "constructed" or
"constituted" about Greek national identity. The Greeks' aspirations, the
product of a "homotropic" culture, were said to be summed up in the Great
Idea, which above all else called for the recapture of Constantinople and the
resumption of the liturgy in the great church of Hagia Sophia: "voilà le cou-
ronnement de l'idéal grec."

Politis realized that, in the immediate aftermath of the Fall, the Greeks
virtually abandoned hope (1918: 154). This state of affairs did not, however,
last for a long while. The Greeks were not "oriental fatalists," he argued, and
they soon began to look forward to the future with renewed optimism. Politis' observation is not without some ethnographic support; whether "fatalism" as such exists anywhere in the world is a moot point, but it is certainly
true that Greek villagers disapprove of those who simply refuse to struggle
against the odds (Sanders 1962; Herzfeld 1981b). More relevant to our present concerns, however, is Politis' view of the more optimistic attitude as characteristic of Greek culture, not merely in general terms but also in the form
of specific beliefs about national redemption. Here, the verbal artifacts in
question combine the quality of archaeological culture traits with that of
ideological statements in their own right.

Of these texts, the most famous is probably the so-called "Song of Hagia
Sophia." Its last line became a rallying cry, not merely for scholars and politicians but for all Greeks who looked forward to the new golden age of Hellenism. For all of them, the song was a text which signified the ultimate goal.
I use the words "text" and "signify" advisedly: the semiotic dimension of
laography, its construction as a political and cultural text, is nowhere more
palpable than in the prominence accorded this one song, with what was interpreted as a stirring promise that all would be "ours once more."

Redeeming the Fall of the City

Here follows the text in full, preceded by Politis' explanatory comment:

Among the numerous laments for the sack of Constantinople which
were composed right after that disaster, the folksongs have pride of
place because, with profound simplicity, they express a feeling of per-

severance throughout the great national travails and the enslaved
people's certain hope of being restored to its freedom and to its rightful
position. It is indeed a matter for wonder that these were generated at a
time when the nation seemed to have lost all, with the Fall of Constantinople [just past] and not a glimmer of hope anywhere in sight. But
the nation's great disaster comes exactly midway between fear and
hope, desperation and encouragement. For before this disaster the
prophecies of the future were pessimistic and predicted calamities and
disasters, whereas after the sack [of Constantinople] they spread a
completely different message, one which indicated a change in the
national attitude. For a long time before the sack of the state capital,
oracles predicted the imminent disaster, but immediately after the sack
positive hopes for the nation's future destiny were born, and the conviction took root among the Greek people that it would inevitably re-
gain by the sword the paternal heritage which the enemy had [likewise]
seized by the sword:

God sounds forth, the earth sounds forth, the heavens too sound forth,
*and the great church (*monastiri*) of Hagia Sophia sounds forth also,*
*with its four hundred sounding boards (*simandra*), sixty-two bells,*
where for every bell there's a priest, for every priest a deacon.
The king sings to the left, to the right the patriarch,
and the very columns shook from the sound of so much psalmody.
As they began the mass and the king came out
a voice came to them from heaven, from the mouth of an archangel:
"cease the mass, bring down the saints' [icons],
priests—take the holy objects; you, O candles, snuff out your light,
for it is the will of God that the City should turn Turk.
Only send word to the West that three ships should come—
one to take the crucifix, the next to take the Gospel,
and the third and last to take our holy altar
that these dogs may not seize them from us and desecrate them."
The Holy Virgin was seized with trembling, and the icons wept tears.
"Be silent, Lady and Mistress, do not weep so much:
again in years and times to come, all will be yours again."

(1914: 12-13)[5]

The text given by Politis has been challenged in copious detail (Apostolakis
1939; Kordatos 1972: 55-56; cf. also Dimaras 1972: 55; Romaios 1959:
119-138). Here, however, we shall simply focus on the last line, which differs
in one minute but enormously significant detail from the version quoted in
Politis' 1918 "Popular Beliefs": the possessive pronoun "yours" is used instead of "ours." "Yours" is what Politis' sources mostly give, and "yours" is

what every responsible reprinting of the complete text (including Politis' own) provides, but *"ours"* is commonly substituted whenever the two lines (or just the second one) appear on their own, out of context. While it is unlikely that this habit originated with Politis, it did find in him an early propagator.

We should not underestimate this seemingly minor alteration. Its importance does not lie merely in the extent to which it enables us to see how far Politis could tolerate contradiction between his accurate scholarship and the interpretation that he sought; that contradiction lies more in our own retrospective view than in his schema of interpretation. The import of the pronoun shift is of a vastly more general kind. In it lies a whole conception of the Hellenes' place in the world, of their identity as a people, and of the territorial implications of the Great Idea. It calls for a detailed analysis and provides a fitting climax to this account of the development of laography as an ideological text.

A Text for a New Age?

The final line of the "ours" version fits with Politis' view that the Greeks, after the initial shock in 1453, had soon come to regard the future with renewed optimism. This view directs his interpretation of oracles about the restoration of Constantinople generally, as an example will illustrate. Referring to a Trapezuntine song in which the Fall of the City is blamed on a traitor who had handed the keys to the Turks, he observes that "the key of Hagia Sophia will fall from heaven and, in order to open the basilica, a mason from heaven and a workman from the earth will be needed, which clearly means that Hagia Sophia will not be restored to its first masters except by the help of God and with the assistance of a hero" (1918: 155). Here is that individualistic Greek hero once again. For Politis, the prophecy seemed to be a genuine folk expression of what later became the Great Idea. The senior clergy were often far less convinced that such predictions were divine calls to action. They preferred a more passive interpretation, for what evidence was there that God intended to help the Greek nation at that particular time? Or, in the words of Anthimos of Jerusalem: "Who cannot take as an example in the present life this same God [i.e., Jesus], seeing him hunger and thirst, suffering tribulation, distress, persecution? This truly is the present existence, the life of the true Christian, if he wishes to be worthy of the heavenly kingdom" (Clogg 1976: 58). Prophecies of divine intervention are especially ambiguous symbols, liable to diverse interpretations according to the ideological convictions of the interpreter.

Politis saw the promise of redemption as addressed to the Greek *ethnos*, rather than to Christendom (1918: 154). Such was the assumption which he brought to the "Song of Hagia Sophia"—found, he asserted with (in this case) more enthusiasm than accuracy, wherever Greek was spoken, "and even among the Vlach-speaking people of Macedonia," who are thereby brought within the sway of the Greek national consciousness. The song, he remarks, "explains the endurance of the race"—a synonym for the Greek *ethnos*—"in the face of national calamities and the ineradicable optimism with which the enslaved nation envisages its liberation and reorganization" (1918: 155-156).

Politis' interpretation of the song as national rather than religious in its frame of reference hinges to some extent on that errant pronoun. A recent commentator, Kostas Romaios, thought Politis' version improbable, but on the strictly literalist grounds that "*ours* once more" makes no sense in the mouth of an archangel (1968: 169). Yet this will not do either: apart from the fact that it is far from clear that the famous final line is meant to be spoken by the archangel, it is impossible to be sure what criteria of "sense" are applicable to a song wrested from its social context and displayed in a verbal museum. Besides, the familiar version obviously made, and makes, perfectly good sense to all those many Greeks who still quote it as the quintessential motto of national sentiment. There are nevertheless good—but quite different—grounds for doubting that the final line promises "us," the people, the realization of our national hopes. At least two comparatively reliable texts from early collections (Fauriel 1824: 340; Manousos 1850: 179) have the form "yours" instead. The "you" of these earlier texts is clearly the Virgin Mary, possibly (when the plural form is given) accompanied by the saints whose icons had to be taken down along with hers.[6]

Why did Politis go along with the popular rewording? That he did so from dishonest motives is extremely unlikely, since he elsewhere cited and published versions with "yours." Ironically, he shares the "ours" version with Khristovasilis (1902: 15), a folksong collector whom he castigated for irresponsibly altering texts because "he wanted to present the popular songs, not as they are, but as they should have been—in *his* judgment, be it understood" (1903: 275). Drastic textual emendation was no part of Politis' methodology. We can therefore conclude only that his acceptance of the "ours" version for the purpose of quotation was an act of carelessness prompted, no doubt, by patriotic enthusiasm. It is a rare lapse. As an exception to Politis' long record of painstaking scholarship, it illustrates in an extreme form how the most conscientious scholar's perception may be affected by preconceived assumptions—in this case, that the "Song of Hagia Sophia" was both "national" and "historical."

In fact, its "historical" is scarcely less problematical than its "national" significance. That the known variants do lament the actual sacking of Constantinople in 1453 seems beyond question. But the purportedly prophetic conclusion—"it *will be* yours/ours *once more*"—is also usually presented in historicist terms; if such a prophecy is tautologous, this is because it projects past events into future time, promising that what *was* ours *will again* be ours. It is not at all certain, however, that the phrase which (following the spirit of the nationalist writers) we have translated here as "will be yours/ours once more" really meant anything of the sort.

The future verb "will be" (*tha 'ne*) is found only in later renderings of the text, again not including Politis' *Selections* version. The usual early rendering has the present tense; and, while this may not be conclusive, since a good deal of semantically insignificant tense switching does take place in many of the songs, it does at least suggest that we should not accept the historicist "translation" unquestioningly. There is, furthermore, no guarantee that *pali* must mean "again" in a temporal sense. It also commonly has the meaning of "still," in the sense of "whatever the case may be." If we regloss the line to remove the intimation of future, historically conceived time, it acquires a radically different cast: "And still, whatever the times may bring, it is *still* yours!" Under a church committed to Ottoman rule for the foreseeable future, and for a populace convinced that even under the most adverse circumstances Christianity represented the eternal verities, such an interpretation might make better sense than the conventional one. Of course we cannot be sure about this. The line may be capable of carrying a wide variety of meanings, among which the nationalist interpretation has certainly enjoyed extraordinarily wide currency in our own time. But here lies the rub. Today, following Politis' lead, scholars and politicians present it as *the* interpretation, the only one suitable for the united nation-state whose symbol of collective regeneration it has become. It is only by assuming that the folklorists were totally divorced from their society that we could argue that they were "right" or "wrong" in their interpretation. In the political context to which they had contributed so much themselves, their reading of the line is neither right nor wrong but ideologically appropriate.

It is also an organic part of that cultural and ideological text whose development we have now followed through nearly a century of scholarship. The historicist assumptions involved in giving the song its title ("of Hagia Sophia"), its date, and its position in the *Selections* are self-evident. Politis also seems to have assumed, in accordance with his methodology, that the song was derived from an *Urtext*, albeit probably an irrecoverable one. Such an *Urtext* would have been a strictly historical account of the tragic end of Constantinople: the number of priests (sixty-two), for example, is upheld as a possibly accurate figure (1914: 12, n.). In such a presuppositional context, it was both logical and consistent for Politis to represent that final, ambiguous line as a temporal prophecy rather than simply as an undying truth. It was this same framework, moreover, that enabled him to suggest how the apparent volte-face from pre-Fall fatalism to post-Fall optimism had come about. For him, it was not a reversal at all. The truly Hellenic character thrived on adversity without the slightest disrespect to the "will of God."

Expanding Horizons

Exactly when the "ours" version originated is a matter for conjecture. It certainly appeared early in the century in quotation form (e.g., Khristovasilis 1902: 18, where it is described as "our national lament"). Even the "yours" versions were susceptible of interpretation in nationalist terms, however, as became evident in a memorial speech in 1906. The speaker declared that no Greek

> forgets that the popular muse . . . turned the aftermath of the sack of Constantinople into an unshakable conviction that divine Providence would return the captured city to the Hellenes . . . as, falling in battle on its ramparts, and intoning his swan song, the immortal emperor of the Greeks thundered unto the generations to come:
> *Our Lady was seized with trembling, and the icons wept tears.*
> *"Be silent, Lady and Mistress; and you, icons, weep not.*
> *Again in years and times to come it will be yours once more."*
> (Filaretos 1906: 60)

Whether spoken by emperor or archangel, whether claiming the City as "yours" or "ours," the song serves well as an anthem for resurgent Hellenism. And in fact, perhaps because it was easier to identify with, the "ours" version has remained the one which everybody quotes to this day.

The theme of "ours once more" has enjoyed a considerable vogue in patriotic works of literature also (e.g., Viziinos 1949), not to mention some of the more popularizing pronouncements of scholars (e.g., Megas 1953; Zoras 1953: 116; Sperantsas 1949). As early as the 1860s, Aristotle Valaoritis has the revolutionary hero Athanasios (Thanassis) Diakos—the object of Valvis' especial praise—contemplate the eventual realization of the Great Idea, even as he was still fighting in the original War of Independence:

> *—Bow before the throne*
> *of the first king, the monument of our last one . . .*
> *What's this? You tremble, Diakos? Why do you weep?*
> *Thanassi . . . it is ours!*

This passage (Fourth Song, quoted in Apostolakis 1950: 64, n. 1) shows how well entrenched that final phrase had become long before Politis' scholarly endorsement of it.

It was also taken up by at least one non-Greek writer. The English philhellene Ronald Burrows was moved to compose a paean to the Hellenic

"race" of Europe, on the occasion of the Greeks' capture of Thessaloniki
from Turkey in 1912:

> *We too of the younger North*
> *Claim that Hellas brought us forth,*
> *Made us all we boast to be,*
> *In our islands of the free,*
> *We who are of Byron's kin,*
> *We who fought at Navarin.*
> *Saloníka! Saloníka!*
> *We do seek her! We do seek her!*
> *After centuries of wrong*
> *Cometh true the ancient song.*
> *Lady! Stay thee from thy moan!*
> *Once again she is our own!*

$$(1913: 92)^7$$

Burrows, who enthusiastically dedicated a copy of this poem to the Greek
scholar-diplomat John Gennadius,[8] evidently thought that the "ancient song"
referred to the fall of Thessaloniki around 1430. It mattered little; Burrows
believed that *all* the Greek-speaking territories still under foreign control
should be handed over to the Greek State forthwith. Arguing for the cession
of Cyprus (which the British had in fact offered Greece, vainly, in return for
a promise of neutrality during the First World War), he contended:

> The Greek race is not decadent, not on the down grade, but on the up
> grade—fertile, progressive, constantly expanding. It has at its head one
> of the great men of the century [Prime Minister Eleftherios Venizelos],
> a man who fulfills in his own person the ideals and aspirations of the
> race.   (1919: 158)

Venizelos had already demonstrated his sympathy for the Allied cause by the
time Burrows penned these words. Forced to resign by the pro-German King
Constantine in March 1915, in October of the following year he assumed the
leadership of an alternative government in Thessaloniki. In 1917, a series of
events forced the king to abdicate in favor of his second son, Alexander, and
Venizelos once again headed a united government in Athens. To a British
philhellene such as Burrows, Venizelos embodied all the appropriate qualities—
patriotism, leadership, military initiative, and strongly pro-Allies sentiments.
Burrows had already apostrophized Venizelos in his 1913 poem:

> *Strength thou hast to rule our [sic] race:*
> *Great in war and great in peace,*
> *Thou, our second Pericles!*

Venizelos, a Cretan who had first led the government of Greece as recently as 1910, seemed set fair to achieve the goals of the *meghaloïdheates*. The Balkan Wars of 1912 to 1913 gave Greece Macedonia and Epirus; the Treaty of London (1913) placed Venizelos' own homeland under full Greek suzerainty; and the Treaty of Bucharest (1913) placed much of western Thrace in Greek hands also. Several of the eastern Aegean Islands were likewise incorporated into the Greek State during this period. On Venizelos' return to full power in 1917, Greek sympathy for the Allies seemed to promise further territorial gains as a reward.

Thus we see, in Burrows' enthusiasm for Venizelos' leadership, a classic instance of the overlap between political ideology and philhellenic sentiment. The assumption that Hellas embodied the virtues of "the race" (i.e., of the Europeans) is conflated with—rather than made explicitly contingent upon— the identification of Greek with Allied or "European" political goals; this foreshadows the similar rejection of the "un-European" or "anti-Hellenic" traits later attributed to the "foreign dogmas" and "Slavic" ideals of communism.

Indeed, that identification of communism with Slavic culture was developing its own internal logic. D'Istria had written about the "somehow communistic influence" of the Slavs half a century earlier, and we have followed the growth of the contrasted "individualism" of the Hellenes in subsequent ethnological writings. Now, too, with Bulgaria on the side of Germany along with Turkey, a case could be made for dismissing Bulgarian culture as essentially antithetical to everything that the Greeks held most dear. In an article which carries Politis' 1885 critical review of Bulgarian "kleftic songs" to an extreme of sorts, Vassilis Colocotronis remarked:

> The most suggestive antithesis between the Greek soul and the Bulgarian soul rings out in the popular poetry developed in Greece and Bulgaria during the Turkish occupation. During this dark age, the popular muse of the Greeks, as that of the Serbs also, sang of the ancient glories and the exalted deeds of heroes who frequently turned against the Turkish tyrant; by contrast, Bulgarian popular poetry cannot offer us a single historical or heroic poem . . .   (1918: 129)

And, as we have already noted in another context, Colocotronis portrayed the Bulgarian *haidouts* as characterless "common-law criminals" in contrast to their Greek and Serbian counterparts. Here is ideological folklore at its most explicit, defending the northern flanks of Hellenism even as others are guarding the east. Note, however, that the Serbs, who had been allied with Venizelist Greece and harbored analogous suspicions of Bulgarian expansionism, are presented in a kindly light. While the Greeks' songs even express "chivalrous feelings" (Colocotronis 1918: 140-141), surely the most "European" of attitudes, even the songs of the Serbs are relatively "historical" and "individualized." Such favored treatment is a clear reflection of international relations in the Venizelist age.

The main quarrel continued to be with Turkey; indeed, Bulgaria had even been allied with Greece and Serbia against their former overlords during the Balkan Wars. The Greeks looked toward Constantinople with ever increasing fervor. There, in Politis' phrase, lay the goal whose successful achievement would "crown the Greek ideal."

Catastrophe

But that success never came. Politis himself died just before the Great Idea collapsed in total ruin. On January 12, 1921, he suffered a fatal heart attack, "intensified," as his friend, student, and academic successor Stilpon Kiriakidis has written, "by the labor which continued uninterrupted up to the last moment of his life" (1923: xxvi). By that time, Greece seemed to be on the verge of entering that promised land which Politis would not live to enjoy. The Treaty of Sèvres (1920) gave Greece most of Thrace, including Adrianople, the eastern Aegean Islands, and administrative control over Smyrna. With this territorial expansion, the population of the Greek State had by now more than doubled its 1912 figure of below three million. Constantinople was still in Turkish hands, but the border seemed to be moving inexorably closer as Greek forces continued to skirmish with the Turks in Asia Minor. Venizelos was internationally respected, while many Greeks saw him as the national savior who would make the City "theirs once more."

At the critical point, with the Treaty of Sèvres still unratified, King Alexander died suddenly of a bite from his pet monkey. There followed a major constitutional crisis which led, in November of 1920, to Venizelos' electoral defeat. He went into voluntary exile, and his old enemy Constantine returned to the throne. Greece rapidly lost the support of the Allies; in particular, the representatives of Britain, France, and Italy set to work on a revision of the Treaty of Sèvres that would be more favorable to Turkey. Far worse was yet to come. During the course of 1922, the Greek army suffered humiliating setbacks at the hands of the Turks, and in September the Turkish army occupied Smyrna. The burning of that city spelled the end of Greek political and military operations in Asia Minor. The sadly battered Greek forces were immediately demobilized, while hordes of refugees fled to the state which many of them had never seen but which called them its own. Instead of total redemption, Greece now faced total *Katastrofí*; the martial call of the Great Idea had become an ironic echo in a wasteland.

Thus, too, the scholars who had dedicated their lives to providing a firm factual foundation for the irredentist movement found themselves suddenly thrust outside the main current of events and ideas. Their own prophet and doyen, Nikolaos Politis, was already dead, and the discipline to which he had given a name and a system only a few years before now became a truly academic concern, largely removed from the exigencies that confronted the shocked, humiliated nation. That the researches of folklorists had contributed so greatly to the national sense of identity was now a matter of past history. Despite the excellence of much of the laographic research done after 1922, the further development of that sense of identity passed mostly into other hands.

Epilogue

It would not be true to say that the discipline itself never recovered. The institutions which Politis had done so much to set in motion continued their scholarly labors; the collection of folklore materials went on apace; and the refugees of the *Katastrofi*, uprooted from their homelands, made every effort to record and preserve their precious local heritage for posterity. In the general reaction against the more extreme manifestations of the Great Idea, moreover, those who espoused a "Romeic" view of the national culture began to be heard more extensively; and they were able to produce some fairly trenchant criticisms of such founding fathers as Zambelios and Politis himself (see especially Apostolakis 1929). New circumstances spawned new interpretations and perspectives and undermined the sanctity of the old.[1]

But folklore studies never quite regained their erstwhile political importance. That they continued to rest on ideological tenets of one sort or another is obvious; given the origins of the discipline, it is hard to see how *any* statement about folklore in Greece could be ideologically neutral. Most folklorists, though in varying degrees of conformity, continued to work within the broad framework established by Politis; some of this work was tempered by the influence of other methodologies, notably the German *Kulturkreis* theories (see especially Kiriakidis 1937; Kiriakidou-Nestoros 1975: 74-77). For those, however, who regarded an efficient taxonomy as the crowning achievement of *laografia*, all that Politis' work left them to do consisted of tactical refinements (especially Mazarakis 1964; Spiridakis 1962, 1969) and the collection of more and more material within the established categories: from Politis' original 13 "swallow songs" in 1872, for example, we move to Spiridakis' 164 in 1969, without any substantive change in method or result. Ideological conservatism, linguistic purism, and a reluctance to countenance radical innovation in scholarship—these were the marks of a school of thought which had been rudely thrust aside from the mainstream of practical politics. The extreme chauvinism of the military junta of 1967 to 1974 did little to rejuvenate Hellenist laography; the basic work had been done long ago, and the prophecies were too well known.

Nationalist laography did nevertheless enjoy one brief period of real resurgence. This was the time of and around the Civil War (1944-1949), when communism had taken over the role of pan-Slavism as the epitome of treacherous "foreign dogma." Old enmities with neighboring lands to the north flared anew, fueled now by ideological strife of worldwide implications. Some of the old hatreds were thinly disguised: *Greek* communists, for example, might be called "Bulgarians" (e.g., Llewellyn Smith 1965: 164), on the old principle—recall the taunting of Fallmerayer as a Slav—of equating nationality with ideology. Within the same internal logic, there emerged a clear symbolic opposition between "Hellenes" and "communists" as mutually exclusive categories. The old antipathy between Orthodoxy and Hellenism was conveniently resolved in the emergent concept, whose origins go back at least to Zambelios, of *ellinokhristianikos politismos*—"Hellenic-Christian civilization" (e.g., Alivisatos 1949). Perhaps its most sinister embodiment, and certainly one of its most recent, is seen in the credo of George Papadopoulos, a leading member of the military junta of 1967 to 1974: "Hellas of the Hellene-Christians!"[2] In the heyday of his power, this slogan met the eye all over the Greek countryside.

Partly as a reaction to this ideological pattern, the Romeic interpretation of folklore gained some ground. Already, Yannis Apostolakis' attacks on the Hellenists' "national self-regard" (*ethnikos eghoïsmos*) had provided a focus, while the Marxist historian Yanis Kordatos made considerable use of folklore materials in order to establish the social conditions under which the modern Greeks had emerged into nationhood. In the course of the Civil War, a Marxist (and sharply antiirredentist) treatise on Greek folklore was composed by "George Lambrinos" (1947; the name is a pseudonym). This work addressed the nationalists' use of folklore classification; it severely criticized the "national epic" interpretation of the Akritic materials and treated both the Akritic and the kleftic songs as manifestations of class conflict instead.

None of these writers, however, seriously attacked the organizing principles on which the classification itself rested (but cf. Kiriakidou-Nestoros 1975: 50). They continued to write about *the* Akritic songs and *the* klefts, thereby perpetuating categories that had been designed to carry rather different ideological messages. Meanwhile, the Hellenists strengthened the conventional uses of the classification by collecting and publishing vast amounts of material organized in its inflexible structure. Even Stilpon Kiriakidis, whose sense of ethnography was far more holistic than Politis', maintained the basic format and the assumptions on which it depended. Despite his shift away from Politis' concern with historical origins to a greater concern with

the synchronic and social dimensions of folklore, he preserved Politis' bipartite division of the corpus and transmitted it to other scholars in turn
(see Kiriakidou-Nestoros 1975: 63-85). His commitment to a fundamentally
Hellenist perspective seems never to have wavered, despite his growing liberal-
ism in other spheres (Kiriakidou-Nestoros 1978: 154); the international development of more rigorous approaches to the study of culture traits—a development of which he made extensive use—served to amplify rather than
challenge the intrinsic assumptions this entailed.

The Civil War gave new life to the Hellenist approach. Folklorists of this
persuasion once again saw their task as the scholarly defense of Greece's
borders, this time against an international menace. The communist movement
in Greece failed to achieve lasting power, and, when Tito closed off the Yugoslav border as a result of his quarrel with Stalin, it collapsed rapidly. Some
years after the Civil War, in an essay appropriately entitled *The Northern
Ethnological Boundaries of Hellenism*, Kiriakidis felt able to claim:

> . . . after the happy and victorious end of this long and cruel war, which
> was fought in the name of freedom against the powers of darkness, the
> Greek people is justified to ask for the rearrangement of his [*sic*] fron-
> tiers on the basis of the historical and of the present-day facts. This re-
> arrangement . . . will help the Greek nation not only to survive but also
> to continue its life of progress and civilization which meant so much to
> the history of the world.   (1955: 60)

Although the "powers of darkness" are the communists, their identification
with the Slav nations gives the desire to preserve and expand the northern
borders considerable historical depth; the use to which ethnology has been
put here does not represent much of a change from similar, earlier arguments.

Other weapons likewise appear to come from the same armory as before.
Megas, to cite another example, claimed:

> . . . the causes that induced the Bulgarian klefts, the *haidouts* as they
> are called in their language, to spurn social life and turn to the moun-
> tains [for refuge] were not (as in Greece and Serbia) the desire for free-
> dom or any noble sentiment of patriotism but the fear of punishment
> for crimes already committed—the same fear that makes brigands
> (*listai*), too, become enemies of society.   (1946: 3)

As a further contrast between Greek and Bulgarian klefts, we are told that the
Bulgarians (and, by implication, only the Bulgarians) made no distinction in
their pillaging between Turks and Christians "if the latter were well-to-do"
(1946: 4). Interestingly, even here the Serbs are treated with relative friendli-
ness; the ranking of national enemies and allies which had grown up over
decades of complex politics died hard.

Megas also maintained that the Bulgarians had no "national epic" of their own but only a poor, fragmentary imitation of the Greeks' Akritic poems (1946, 1950: 21-29). This position, which seems to be mainly derived from the related arguments of Politis and perhaps also of Colocotronis (1918), was part of a larger attempt by Megas to show that the entire "so-called Balkan civilization" was in fact the product of cultural diffusion from Greece. This would in turn entail denying the possibility that other Balkan cultures could independently give birth to genres, such as "epic," comparable to those of Greece. Even the ground plans of houses from various parts of the Balkan Peninsula were agglutinated to the overall scheme (Megas 1951).

The Civil War ended, as we have noted, with the defeat of the Communists and the repression of most overt forms of communist political activity until 1974.[3] Marxist interpretations of folklore received little currency within Greek academic circles, although there were some stirrings of interest among Greek scholars abroad (e.g., Zakhos 1966). The more conventional folklorists, on the other hand, continued much as before, their major archive being the one which Politis had been instrumental in creating, under the aegis of the Academy of Athens. A few adventurous scholars have broached hitherto un-tried (and potentially offensive) fields, such as the *rebetika* songs of the un-derworld and the urban slums (Damianakos 1976; Petropoulos 1968) or the adaptation of traditional lore to such things as football, election campaigns, advertising, and traffic signals (Loukatos 1963). Damianakos and Zakhos, again, have brought sociological perspectives to bear on the various traditions of song, rural and urban, so that the arbitrary banishment of "the folk" to the countryside begins to weaken. Others have adapted new models from social anthropology, textual structuralism, and the semiotics of ritual and social interaction (e.g., Kakouri 1965; Gizelis 1974, 1976; Kiriakidou-Nes-toros 1975, 1978; Kapsomenos 1978, 1979; Skouteri-Didaskalou 1980) to the special problems of Greek folklore, while the growth of a more reflexive historiography (Politis 1973; Kiriakidou-Nestoros 1978; see also Kondogiorgis 1979) puts folklore research itself in a new light. These writers, in their quite different ways, represent a strong urge to escape the isolating effects of an existing intellectual tradition: the critical research of Kiriakidou-Nestoros, in particular, brings a welcome (and hitherto largely absent) perspective on the historical and global context of Greek folklore epistemology.[4] Yet change is often difficult to achieve. Some, at least, of the old battles are still being fought. Thus, for example, Kiriakidou-Nestoros' pithy critique of Romaios' "critical editions" of folksongs, both recalls and—to a striking degree—actually reproduces Apostolakis' similar criticisms of Zambelios, Lelekos, and Politis.

A consistent set of ideological concerns has thus dominated Greek laogra-phy from its inception right up to the 1922 disaster and, to some extent, for the next half century after that. The study of the national culture was simultaneously itself part of that culture, in which it has indeed played a critical role. What are at one level collections and discussions of folklore are thus, at another level, a textual record of that dialectic. It is fashionable among anthropologists and others who have worked in Greece to scoff at the local scholarly traditions in folklore, on the grounds that they are geared to narrow ideological interests. In this study, it has been my primary aim to show that such concerns are precisely what make the history of laography worthy of serious attention and that indeed—since in a real sense laography helped *define* the national culture—no student of Greek society can afford not to take some account of it. The development of an indigenous folklore discipline was not a boastful mixture of cynical forgery and political opportunism. On the contrary, it was a sustained, often painful attempt to discern order in chaos, on the part of a people whose national identity was often threatened by the very nations which had appointed themselves as its guardians. It gave the Greeks a chance of applying one of their most celebrated ancient proverbs— "know thyself"—by providing a framework for discovery. In this sense, Greek folklore studies were an organic part of the making of modern Greece.

Appendix A
Politis' Folklore Taxonomy

The following is excerpted from Politis' classic statement on the definition and organization of laografia *(1909a: 6-10). Representing the first comprehensive attempt to list the materials appropriate to folkloric research in Greece, it remained the primary model for most later attempts at systematic classification. It is translated here in full; only a small number of Greek terms, mostly alternative or local forms, are omitted as being irrelevant in an English-language version, and this is indicated by ellipses. I have added brief explanatory notes where these seemed potentially helpful.*

From the foregoing it may be inferred that, since the psychic and social life of the people is manifested in two ways—viz., by word and by acts or deeds—the folklorists' task is double-stranded: it consists of *transcription* and *description*. For it both transcribes oral tradition, the monuments of the word, and describes traditional acts or deeds.

In the following synoptic diagram, we list the principal themes with which the Greek folklorist has to be concerned.

Monuments of the Word

1. Songs. Apart from the lyrical, epic, religious, satirical, and humorous or disrespectful songs, as well as those which are sung on prescribed days or occasions (e.g., carols, songs of Lazarus,[1] Holy Week laments, swallow songs, songs performed in the course of certain games, songs of the *perperouna* [a rain-making ritual] and *klidhonas* [a fortune-telling rite associated with Saint John's Day],[2] swing songs, wedding songs, funeral dirges), this category includes dramatic games, children's songs (sung or spoken by or to children), and work songs (such as those which accompany rowing, milling, etc.); these last serve the purpose of rhythmically regulating the worker's movements or simply of enabling him to relax through song as he works.

2. Refrains (exorcisms, spells . . .).

3. Riddles (. . .) and word games. Riddlelike stories. Playful or echolike responses. Tongue twisters (. . .).

4. Wishes, greetings, drinking toasts, curses, oaths, blasphemies, with a description of the acts or movements with which they are sometimes performed. (In this category also come religious curses [anathemas] and the heaping up of stones [i.e., in verbal magic].)

5. Proverbs, with their interpretation and the transcription of the myths in which they are sometimes mentioned.

6. Myths (*mithi*).

7. Humorous stories (in which we include those that mock [particular] villages).

8. Legends or tales (*paramithia*).

9. Traditions, or mythical stories, believed to be true, which mention places or persons, heavenly bodies, meteorological phenomena, Christ and the saints, demons, and other imaginary beings.

10. From the treasury of language, those words and phrases through which are revealed customs, beliefs, popular superstitions, and jobs and occupations of the people, or those words which recall historical events or certain situations derived from them. Examples: names (baptismal, family), nicknames, toponyms, names of seasons of the year, months, days; personal names of cats, dogs, horses, oxen, and other domestic animals; generalized nicknames for animals (e.g., Nikos or Mendios for the donkey, Sir Nikolos for the wolf, Madam Maria for the fox); personal names given to weapons, utensils, dwellings, ships, boats; euphemisms (circumlocutions or metonyms or name substitutes or phrases used in response to [the mention of] feared names); names of animals and plants which betray traditions or beliefs or superstitions. Names of instruments and tools and the special names for the parts of each. Professional terms appropriate to each craft or occupation. *Korakistika*—a secret code language, which uses newly fashioned words or changes the meanings of words or inserts meaningless syllables into the words. Names of costumes and of the parts of each separately. Exclamatory expressions (shepherds', plowmen's, muleteers' sounds used to direct animals). Imitations of animal sounds. Words connected with some particular situation (e.g., *moskhomangas*, "urchin, blackguard"; *tramboukos*, "taker of petty bribes"). Metaphors and other tropes demonstrating a mythopoeic perception of the external world, such as the personification of natural phenomena and generally of the inanimate.

Traditional Activities or Practices

1. The house. Parts of the house, mode of existence therein, utensils, and furnishings. Special kinds of habitation (shepherds' huts, stone huts,[3] lake dwellings).

2. Food. Common and special victuals of the Greeks. Prescribed foods for certain days (e.g., Christmas loaves, Easter cookies, red eggs [for Easter], foods specially associated with particular festivals). Abstention from particular eatables, whether absolute or imposed for fixed periods (other than

religious fasts) or for certain people (as in the prohibition which debars those with only one brother from eating the eye of an animal, etc.). Beliefs about the effects of foods on the eater (e.g., that the eating of certain parts of animals strengthens the corresponding parts of the eater—such as the notion that eating the tongue makes one eloquent or that [according to legendary accounts] the liver of a bird shows the one who tasted it to be a mind reader). Foods eaten to ward off evil.

3. Costumes, hairstyles, personal ornament.

4. Social organization. Customs related to the administration of the community or to the management of communal property. Customs indicating the former division of the village by patrilineages. Social relations (participation of outsiders in family festivals, visiting, social etiquette, feasts, guest-host reciprocity [*ksenia*]).[4] Life away from home. Women's position in the home. Special communities. Blood brotherhood. Klefts. Brigands' laws. Employer-laborer relations, servant-master relations.

5. The child. Customs, beliefs, and superstitions regarding pregnancy, birth, and the postnatal phase. Care and treatment of the newly born. Foundlings. Matters related to baptism. Matters concerning children's upbringing. School customs. Apprenticeship (apprentice masons, shipboys, etc.). Children's language—as an appendix, the reading of popular books could also be added here.

6. Wedding customs.

7. Customs concerned with death. Funeral, tomb, mourning, memorial services.

8. Life-styles (*vii*).[5] Farmer's life (customs during sowing, reaping, grape harvesting, etc.). Herding life (special customs of animal herders, especially nomads).[6] Life-styles of soldiers, sailors, fishermen, hunters. Industrial professions. Miners. Female tasks and professions.

9. Justice. Ideas of the people regarding justice and jural relations. Popular customs concerned with family and inheritance law. (Especially worthy of study are certain entirely specialized customs such as, for example, the occasional, localized rights of only sons [sing. *kanakaris*] and only daughters [sing. *kanakarissa*].) Adoption. Disinheriting. Customary ways of concluding and drawing up contractual agreements, archaic customs concerned with confirming a legal situation such as bankruptcy. Signs of ownership (e.g., incisions in herd animals' ears, tattooing of horses' buttocks [like the brands or seals of the ancients], color codes, etc.). Written certifications of contracts; marriage contracts (*prikosimfona*). Penalties (public shaming, shaving of the head, school punishments, *falangas* [sitting in a variety of stocks while the soles of the feet are whipped]). Popular courts (e.g., in Olympia or Chios, during carnival).

10. Worship. Popular beliefs about God and the saints and their intervention in human affairs. Invocations to them by the use of special names. Miraculous aid and cures. Icons. Incubation.[7] Blessing with holy water. Sacrifices and offerings (occasional offerings of flowers and fruits in church, on prescribed days). Firstfruits. Blessings and curses (*tamata* [ex-votos]). Pro-

cessions. Feast days. Saints' days (special saint's day customs, especially during the twelve days between Christmas and Epiphany, carnival, Easter). Feast days not appointed by the church (such as May Day) and customs appropriate to them. Festival of the summer solstice (Saint John *Liotropios*),[8] bonfires during these. Bonfires to celebrate other days (Epiphany, Easter [(the burning of) Judas (in effigy)], Cheese-eating Week,[9] Saint Elijah, the first days of August). "Unsleeping lamps" [left burning for forty days in the room where someone has died], renewal of flames. Orgiastic cults (*Anastenaria*, Thracian *Kaloyiri*). Purificatory rites.

11. Popular philosophy. Beliefs about the soul and the afterlife. Beliefs about nature. Practices consistent with such beliefs.

12. Popular medicine. Medical learning. Doctors and doctors' wives. Community doctors. The use of curative herbs and their modes of collection. Curative properties of animals' limbs, skin, hair, nails. Curative power of metals and rocks. Preparations of medicines. Therapy. Curing by the use of similarity or analogy. Curing according to the principle that "he who wounded shall also cure." Cure of nonexistent illnesses and injuries (wandering navel, rising kidneys, etc.). Dietetics. Surgery. Veterinary medicine.

13. Fortune-telling. Various forms of fortune-telling. Diagnosis of facial features. Palmistry. *Klidhonas*. Fortune-telling by the use of various aids: oracle bones (shoulder blades [of sheep or goats]), fire, lead, eggs, keys, sieves, etc. Fortune-telling on special days or occasions (New Year, Saint John's [*klidhonas*], carnival, Saint Andrew's, first day of Lent).

14. Astrology. The influence of heavenly bodies on human life. Unlucky days. Days of the month. *Dhrimes* [first days of March and August, associated with homonymous evil spirits]. Numerological beliefs. Meteorological beliefs.

15. Magic. Magicians male and female. Magical books, utensils, and instruments. Magical acts. Angels and demons in charge of days and of hours of the day and night. Exorcisms. Fortune-telling using a basin of water, the [palm of the] hand, cards. Philters, binding spells. Haunting of houses.

16. Magical and superstitious customs to ward off evil or obtain good fortune. Magical customs in time of drought (*perperouna*, rain litanies, etc.). Amulets. Kinds of protection against witchcraft. Symbolic burial and expulsion of sickness, patient's abandonment of sickness in a prescribed place. Superstitions of curing by analogy, or similarity, or difference, or opposition.

17. Children's games and athletic contests.

18. Dances and their music. Mimicry, gestures of head and hands, their meaning.

19. Music and musical instruments. The precise transcription of the melodies of folksongs—if possible, in regular sol-fa notation, otherwise in ecclesiastical—is of maximum value.

20. Fine arts. Sculpture (wood); graphics. Ornament (especially ornamentation of clothing, sculpted or inscribed decoration of furniture, instruments, dwellings). Aesthetics of color and form.

Appendix B
Basic Chronology

This table is intended to provide a handy means of situating the development of Greek folklore studies in a general chronological framework. To that end, it is divided into three columns: Greek political history, Greek folklore studies, and general European and related history (including folklore studies). There is necessarily some overlap between these three categories, and the choice of key events can never be anything but arbitrary. The chart is thus meant simply as a reference for the reader's convenience.

Greek Political History	Greek Folklore Studies	General European and Related History (Including Folklore Studies)
B.C.	**B.C.**	
	6th century: Probable date of earliest attempt to transcribe "swallow song"	
	484?–424?: Herodotus, "father of anthropology and history"	
461–429: Perikles in power in Athens		
447–438: Parthenon built		
338: Battle of Chaeronea brings Athens under Macedonian rule		
A.D.	**A.D.**	**A.D.**
		Ca. 100: *Germania* of Tacitus (ca. 55 to ca. 117) introduces rich ethnographic description
	2d–3d centuries: Athenaeus compiles *Deipnosophistae*; includes "swallow song" and other folk texts	
285: Diocletian divides Roman Empire in two		
313: Edict of Milan formally proscribes persecution of Christians		
330: Byzantium dedicated as New Rome, capital of Eastern Roman Empire		
391: Theodosius I declares Christianity official religion by formally abolishing paganism	**407:** Death of St. John Chrysostom, who had campaigned actively against pagan folk practices	
		7th century: Foundation of kingdom by Turkic-speaking Bulgars; through assimilation, become Slav-speaking by mid ninth century
		622: *Hejirah* (Mohammed's flight from Mecca)

746: Widespread plague reduces Greek population; followed by massive Slavic incursions and massacres. These continue intermittently and with varying intensity

961: Nicephoros Phocas captures Crete from Saracens, massacres population, and introduces "twelve noble families" (*Arkhontopouloi*) to repopulate island

Late 11th century: Eustathius of Thessaloniki's commentaries on Homer include much folklore

12th century?: Vallicellian manuscript F-73 contains early example of "swallow song"

1204: Venetians, probably for mercantile reasons, incite Fourth Crusade soldiers to conduct (Latin) sack of Constantinople; kingdom established at Trebizond by Alexios Commenos

1205 on: Doges of Venice style themselves "Lord of one-fourth and one-eighth of the Empire of Romania"—i.e., of the "Roman" world

1332-1406: Ibn-Khaldūn, historian-ethnologist of Arab society

1361: Sack of Adrianople

Ca. 1380: Turks occupy Macedonia

1393: Turks occupy Thessaly

1453: Sack of Constantinople

1461: Turks take Trebizond

1470: Ottoman Turks divide Greece proper into six *sanjak* (administrative districts)

1492: Discovery of New World; expulsion of Jews from Spain—many move to Thessaloniki

1520: Joannes Boemus, *Omnium Gentium Mores, Leges et Ritus* (ethnological medley)

1522: After unsuccessful first attempt (1480), Turks take Dodecanese (including Rhodes) from Knights of St. John of Jerusalem, who move to Malta

1571: Cyprus taken by Turks from Venice

1590-1645: Flowering of Cretan vernacular literature; incorporates many folk influences

17th century: In Iviron Monastery (Mt. Athos), early transcriptions of folksongs (words and music)

1534: Sebastian Franck's *Weltbuch oder Cosmographey* includes much German folklore

1619-20: Richard James records Russian historical songs

Ca. 1660-70: Samuel Collins records Russian folktales

1679: **J.-B. Thiers,** *Superstitions anciennes et modernes*—an attack on nonecclesiastical religious practices; cf. contemporary antipapist works in England

1645-69: Crete, in Venetian hands since 1204, falls to Turks. Many refugees go to the Ionian Islands, carrying with them a lively literary tradition

1725: Giambattista Vico (1668-1744), *Scienza nuova*

1730-88: J. G. Hamann, teacher of Herder

1744-1803: J. G. von Herder (1778-79: *Volkslieder*)

1750: Carmeli's *Storia di veri costumi . . .*

1770: Unsuccessful revolts in Crete (under Daskaloyannis) and the Peloponnese, incited by Russia in connection with war against Turkey

18th and 19th centuries: Greek writers begin to build a case for the essentially Hellenic nature of European civilization—especially Katartzis (d. 1807), Moisiodax (d. 1800), Voulgaris (d. 1806). In 1791, Katartzis "translates" own work from demotic to *katharevousa*. See Henderson 1970: 140

1776-78: H. G. Porthan, *Poësi Fennica*

1789: Outbreak of French Revolution

1802-74: Niccolò Tommaseo

1803: Koraes publishes memoir (in French) on cultural conditions in Greece

1807: G. W. F. Hegel (1770-1831), *Phänomenologie des Geistes*

1812-15: Grimms' *Kinder- und Hausmärchen*

1813: Douglas' *Essay* seeks the resemblances between ancient and modern Greek culture

1814: Inspired by Herder, Sjögren and Poppius solemnly swear to collect the folklore of their native Finland

1816-18: Grimms' *Deutsche Sagen*

1814: Foundation of Filiki Eteria ("Friendly Society")—a secret group of Greek nationalists actively engaged in propaganda, etc., in Odessa

1821: Outbreak of Greek War of Independence

1822: Constitution of Epidaurus declares Greece a nation-state under presidency of Alexander Mavrokordatos

1827: At Battle of Navarino, a French-British-Russian fleet defeats Turks and Egyptians	**1824–25:** Fauriel's *Chants*	
	1825: Papadopoulos-Vrettos publishes memoir (second edition) on "some ancient Greek customs still existing in the island of Lefkas"	
1833: Otto crowned in Nauplion; sets up government with mainly German senior officials, including von Maurer (jurist)	**1830:** Fallmerayer's *Geschichte*	
	1835: Kind's anthology of Greek folksongs, first edition	**1835:** Jacob Grimm's *Deutsche Mythologie* shows links between ancient and modern German lore
		1835–36: Elias Lönnrot's first edition of *Kalevala*, acclaimed as Finns' national epic
1837: Athens becomes national capital; Athens University founded; Greek church becomes independent of Patriarchate of Constantinople	**1840:** Fallmerayer, visiting Greece for first time, coldly received	**1841–1916:** Giuseppe Pitrè, major Sicilian folklorist with whose work Politis later became acquainted
	1842: Tommaseo's Greek volume	
	1843: Evlambios' collection published in St. Petersburg; Lefkias refutes Fallmerayer	**1846:** Thoms coins term "folklore"
1844: Greece becomes a constitutional monarchy; French party achieves dominance		**1848:** *Communist Manifesto*; liberal revolutions throughout Europe
	1850: Manousos publishes clearly Romeicist volume of folksongs	
	1852: Zambelios publishes folksong collection to reinforce his claim that Byzantine period is essential link between ancient and modern Greece	
1854–57: Anglo-French military force occupies Piraeus in order to discourage irredentist Greeks from taking advantage of Crimean War to gain more territory		**1855:** Guillard coins term *ethnologie*

1855–63: Afanas'ev publishes major collection of Russian folktales

1859: Bulgarian nationalist Rakovski claims that Bulgarians were of Sanskritic origin and that Delphic oracle and ancient Greek place-names were of Bulgarian origin

1865: Tylor's *Researches into the Early History of Mankind*

1871: Tylor's *Primitive Culture*

1871: Germany unified and proclaimed an empire under Wilhelm I

1875: Dozon publishes major collection of Bulgarian folksongs

1859: Zambelios advances theory of history-in-language to demonstrate continuity between Classical Greek tragedy and modern folksongs

1860: Polilas replies to Zambelios' essay in defense of Solomos

1867: D'Istria explores Greek folksongs for evidence of "nationality"

1871: Politis wins the Rhodokanakis competition with *Modern Greek Mythology*

1875: First publication of a manuscript of the "Akritic epic"

1896: Garnett and Stuart-Glennie, *Greek Folk Poesy*. This includes discussion of "survival of paganism" which was to influence Lawson (1910). Explicitly rejected Tylorean view of essential equality of humankind, claiming Greeks as superior in ancient *and* modern times

1862: Otto deposed in coup d'état

1863: George I, second son of king of Denmark, ascends Greek throne

1864: Britain cedes Ionian Islands to Greece

1866: Uprising in Crete provokes violent Turkish response

1870: Dilessi affair

1870: Under Russian pressure, Turkey constitutes Bulgarian exarchate (ecclesiastical authority) independent of Patriarchate of Constantinople; its cultural proselytism becomes source of conflict with Greeks

1896: Renewed troubles in Crete

1897: Disastrous thirty-day war with Turkey follows border skirmishes in Thessaly; Greece loses some territory in Thessaly, but Crete is now given autonomy within the Ottoman Empire

1908: Young Turk revolution

1909: Van Gennep, *Les Rites de passage*, a major work on the structure of ritual, influential in folklore and anthropology

1913: Bulgarian General Kirkoff claims Alexander the Great as "the most glorious of our countrymen"–i.e., this was a Bulgarian claim to Macedonia

1914: Outbreak of First World War

1917: Revolution in Russia; establishment of Soviet State

1918: Conclusion of First World War

1909: Volume 1 of *Laografia*

1910: Lawson, *Modern Greek Folklore and Ancient Greek Religion*

1914: First publication of Politis' *Selections from the Songs of the Greek People*

1918: Colocotronis publishes disquisition on Bulgarian and Greek "souls" as mirrored in folk poetry

1921: Death of Politis

1910: Venizelos becomes prime minister of Greece for first time

1912–13: Balkan Wars

1913: George I assassinated in Thessaloniki; Constantine I succeeds to throne; Crete finally incorporated into Greece

1915: Venizelos invites Anglo-French landing at Thessaloniki in response to Bulgarian alliance with Germany

1916: Venizelos, in opposition to the king, sets up alternative government in Thessaloniki

1917: Entente Powers force Constantine to abdicate in favor of his son Alexander

1920: Treaty of Sèvres

1922: *Katastrofi* in Asia Minor

Notes

1. Past Glories, Present Politics

1. Cf. Geertz' observation that nationalist revolutions are commonly epistemological as well as political (1973: 239). He also rightly criticizes the negative valuation of "ideology" as counterproductive (1973: 199), although, as he clearly recognizes, it is necessary for analysis to take the selectivity of ideological "truth" into account (e.g., Mannheim 1936: 20; cf. also Jenkins 1961: 99-117 for his formulation of Greek "ethnic truth"). On the tendency of the scholars' arguments to become cumulatively self-reinforcing, a theme repeatedly sounded throughout this book, cf. Burke's observation that "the instruments of precision and thought by which we made our examinations were themselves shaped by the same point of view" (1954: 258).

The selectional basis of ideological codes is treated analytically by Eco (1976: 139-142, 289-290), whose definition of ideology is extremely pertinent here: ". . . a message which starts with a factual description, and then tries to justify it theoretically, gradually being accepted through a process of overcoding" (1976: 290). Since I am here discussing culture historians as ideologically motivated, I also lean heavily on Goldstein's (1976) lucid treatment of the "construction" of history by its practitioners. Crick's critique of anthropological literalism is also germane (1976: 154-159).

Henderson raises the related possibility of alternative interpretations as to whether or not there was continuity in Greek thought after the Fall of Constantinople in 1453 (1970: 1-2). It should also be noted that the admiration of Classical culture abroad had ideological and political implications that did not necessarily have anything to do with the modern Greek cause at all; see especially Jenkyns 1980: 4, 84.

2. It should be noted, however, that the Old Testament provided an alternative "origin myth" for Christian Europe, perhaps most notably in Ireland; traces of the notion that the Greeks are somehow "descended" from the Old Testament Jews may even be found today among rural Greeks (cf. Herzfeld 1980c). In addition, various northern European scholars attempted to find more localized origins in recorded mythology, especially in Germany and Scandinavia.

3. Cf. Geertz on the problem, often faced by emergent nation-states, of reconciling "epochalism" with "essentialism" (1973: 240–249).

4. This is a paraphrase of the programmatic dimension of Hallowell 1965.

5. To these references we might usefully add the ethnological information contained in the writings of Crusius (1526–1607), a professor of Greek at the University of Tübingen, as well as the subsequent works of such observers as La Guilletière (1676), Stephanopoli (1800), Pouqueville (1805), and Leake (especially 1814); Bondelmonti (fl. 1420; see Sinner 1824) is a useful early source for historical demography. The information provided by these and other outside observers before independence, though generally no more systematic than that of local sources, adds up to a fairly substantial corpus of data. See especially Simopoulos 1972, 1973, and 1975, for an exhaustive account of foreign travelers in Greece, and Spiridakis 1966: 477–481; cf. also Loukatos 1978.

Folklore studies were similarly initiated by foreigners in Russia (the Englishmen James and Collins; see Oinas 1961 and Sokolov 1950: 44). Ecclesiastical fear of a pagan revival clearly motivated some of the early local-level opposition to the study of folklore in various parts of Europe, although this does not seem to have been a major factor in the relatively late development of folklore research in Greece.

6. The term *Altneuland* was coined by Theodor Herzl to denote the projected Jewish national home. Political Hellenism shared with political Zionism a preoccupation with the physical site of the nation's history and cultural evolution, and both faced the paradox (cf. also n. 3, above) which Herzl's phrase so concisely suggests. Note the title of Wachsmuth's 1864 *Das alte Griechenland im neuen* and others like it.

7. The Greeks are sometimes referred to in formal discourse as *i Fili* ("the Race"); cf. demotic *ratsa*, not often used on its own in this way but often combined with a specifying qualifier (possessive pronoun or adjective) to denote a particular "race" (Herzfeld 1980c). In general, the Greek vernacular terminology of "ethnicity" is extremely context-sensitive; even such apparently precise terms as "Vlach" or "Hellene" may refer to more than one level of group inclusiveness. Politicians usually use such terms in more fixed senses to denote a set of absolute demographic or geopolitical entities. The phenomenon, which is widely characteristic of emergent national identities, makes it very difficult to speak confidently of "*the* people of a given ethnic group" (cf. especially Ardener 1972).

8. It is less clear whether they explicitly perceived the semantic shift in the term "politics"—Classical Greek *politikē*, "matters relating to the city-state (*polis*)"; cf. Kitto 1957: 75–79. On the persistence of this model of the Greek role in cultural evolution, and its pervasive effects in educational practice, see Bialor 1973: 476–477 and Frangoudaki 1978. Cf. also Chapman's (1978: 197–198) application of Ardener's concept of an "englobing" self-view, to explain Scottish perceptions of the position of Gaelic culture in Britain as a whole: economic and political subordination is not necessarily reflected in the Scots' view of their *cultural* role, any more than the Greeks

found it absurd to claim intellectual primacy over a politically dominant West.

9. In the "old" (i.e., Julian) calendar, then still in use in Greece. With the introduction of the "new" (Gregorian) calendar, the date of March 25 has been retained for the celebration of Independence Day (and of the Feast of the Annunciation). For convenience, I have retained the dates 1821 to 1833 for the War of Independence, although in practical terms the Greek cause was secure after the Battle of Navarino and the first Treaty of London in 1827.

2. Extroversion and Introspection

1. Tipaldo and Mustoxidi were Heptanesian Greeks, Tommaseo a Dalmatian. Their main language of intellectual discourse was nevertheless Italian.

2. The French collector Marcellus also, from 1816 to 1820, obtained folksongs from the Greek poet Christopoulos. The latter was clearly aware of the political potentialities of "these cries of the national muse, which resound unheard but yet unextinguished from Trebizond to Cyprus" (Christopoulos in Marcellus 1860: vii). An account of Tommaseo's life and work is provided by Ciampini 1945.

3. E.g., *leo* ("I say") can take *traghoudhia* ("songs") as well as *miroloyia* ("dirges, laments") as its object. Zambelios (1859), too, implicitly treats *miroloyia* as a subset of *traghoudhia*, with consequent difficulties for his own argument; cf. Menardos 1921 and the extended treatment in Herzfeld 1981.

3. National Character, National Consciousness

1. Classical Greek *sun* ("syn") and *oida* ("know").

2. This name means "Bulgarian" but has no "ethnic" significance for its bearer, since it may have originated as a *paratsoukli* (hypocoristic name) with one of his ancestors.

3. George Castriota Skanderbeg (1403?–1468) was a national hero of the Albanians; he led a successful revolt against the Turks in 1443. With intermittent help from Venice, Naples, and the papacy, he succeeded in keeping the Turks at bay until his death, after which Albania—with the exception of a few districts controlled by Venice—reverted to the Ottomans.

4. See especially the detailed study by Campbell (1964) of these values as they are found among the transhumant Sarakatsani of northern Greece.

Zannetos (1883: 3) explicitly attempts to demonstrate the continuity of "manliness" (*andria*) from the Homeric heroes to the klefts, using folksongs as a principal source.

5. *Paratsouklia*, sometimes translated as "nicknames," are often handed down in the male line; in highland western Crete, they frequently become the collective names of lineage segments.

6. The data from western Crete are taken from my own fieldwork there, conducted intermittently from 1974 to 1978. See Herzfeld 1980a.

7. *Kala kleftis* will strike the reader with a knowledge of standard demotic Greek as an unusual form (adverb and noun). In western Crete, however, the combination of the adverbial *kala* ("well") with a noun suggesting a "heroic role" is not uncommon: *kala eghoïstis*, "a man who is good at demonstrating his aggressive self-regard"; *kala 'ndras*, "one whose manliness has been proved beyond doubt." Cf. also *etsa dhoulies*, "goings-on like that" (lit., "thus works").

8. I am extremely grateful to Allen Walker Read for permission to cite his unpublished paper. Its thorough documentation indicates a wide range of similarities in the respective ranges of implication of "rebel" and *"kleftis."*

9. Even in the popular press, the "kleftic song" category became widely used in defense of the Hellenist argument. One recent newspaper article (Motsias 1977) mined these songs in order to demonstrate that the klefts had revived the athletic contests which had disappeared with the abolition of the Olympic games in 393. References to jousting and rock hurling, which recall medieval at least as much as ancient accounts, are overlooked, and the legendary ability of the kleft leader Tasoulas to leap from one mountain peak to another is cited without any reference to the similar exploits of the "Byzantine" hero Digenes; thus, the "Akritic songs" (cf. chap. 5) are kept apart from the "kleftic," confirming the established taxonomy, and the "kleftic songs" serve to provide a conceptual link with Classical antiquity. While Motsias' is a popular, journalistic essay, it usefully reminds us of the broad appeal of such arguments and their capacity for bridging the gap between academic and lay modes of discourse.

10. For a comparable taxonomy applied to Yugoslav Macedonian materials, cf. Trærup: "There are among the *hajduks* robbers (*hajduk* or *aramija*), whose deeds are so frightful that even their own mothers on their deathbed condemn them" (1970: 21); the songs about both types of outlaw are distinguished from "historical" songs. Baggally deals with the problem of an obviously "brigandlike" kleft by allowing that the term *kleftis* might occur in a particular song "in the wider sense of a robber" (1936: 28). Cf. further Baggally 1936: 6-8, on the earlier history of the term. Iatridis provides good early examples of the "translation" of *kleftes* into *listai* in the "titles" of songs whose heroes were clearly brigands (1859: 22, 42, 57). Quinet treats klefts as revolutionary soldiers (1859: 258, 290, 541). For a contemporary account of post-1821 kleftism, see Soteropoulos 1868.

11. Lit., "trampled by [Turks] from Konya." Quinet, on the other hand, may have been more deliberately serving the Greek position when he changed "Albanian songs" to "modern folksongs" and "Albanian Corinth" to "Christian Corinth" (Karatza 1970: 57, noting Quinet 1830: 294, 275, 1859: 215, 202).

12. From a confusion of Greek *koutsos* ("lame") with Turkish *küçük* ("small, little"): "Political philology has shown that Koutsovlach means 'little Vlach' and that 'a little Vlach' means one who is mostly a Hellene" (Wace and Thompson 1914: 9).

13. See also his *Monograph on the Koutsovlachs* (Aravandinos 1905). A

similar view is expressed by an anonymous writer in the journal *Pandora*: "This race . . . since it has been accustomed for centuries to regard the Hellenes as brothers and has mixed Greek into its own language, in a short time will of course erase from its speech (lit., mouth) the last remnants of foreign ancestry and will speak that pure Greek language which alone has the incomparable right to be heard under such a sky and in the midst of such recollections, i.e., the ancient monuments" (1852-53: 283).

14. This is particularly true of certain outlying areas which were not part of the original Greek State. See especially Lanitis 1946 (Cyprus); Vlastos 1909 and Lambithianaki-Papadaki 1972 (Crete); and the cited works on Epirus.

4. Attack and Reaction

1. Further references to the (nonfolkloric) scholars' reactions to Fallmerayer are given in Xydis 1968: 4, especially nn. 9 and 10. For a current Greek view of the demographic aspects of the problem, see Zakythinos 1975: 4-6.

2. I am indebted to Brian Joseph for directing my attention to pertinent information on this problem.

3. Ali Pasha (1741-1822) was a semiindependent Albanian governor whose rule, based on Yannina, extended over much of Epirus and Thessaly. He entertained ambitions of creating his own independent state, and Sultan Mahmud II had him deposed and assassinated. His opposition to the Porte earned him the retrospective admiration of many Greeks, although he is also commemorated in a much quoted Greek folksong ("Kira Frossini") for having a wealthy Greek merchant's wife and her attendants drowned when she refused to yield to his advances.

4. Marcellus, though a collector of folksongs, seems to have had little interest in the analytical study of cultural continuity. Rather, he sought through his Greek travels the kind of inspiration that would help him understand the Classical authors: "Thus, I am persuaded that, having seen the Naxian girls washing their brothers' *foustanelles* [pleated skirts] at the beautiful springs by the sea, then showing astonishment at my foreign dress and smiling at the imperfection of my [Greek] speech, I am better prepared for [the task of] reproducing the games of Nausicaa's companions as they washed Alcinoous' tunics and fled at the sight of Ulysses" (1861: 2). Earlier, Voutier (1826: 40, 42) had sought reflections of ancient speech and even of historical events in the modern folklore; but this, too, was the scarcely systematic hobby of an observant soldier.

5. And of Schmidt's collection of folksongs and tales.

5. The Creation of a Discipline

1. *Pandora* 22 (1871-72) carried the original report from the judges and a description of the announcement of the result (p. 83), as well as a review

praising Politis' work but criticizing his youthful presumption in attempting to rebut the judges' critical remarks (pp. 471–472).

2. Politis' survivalism is the version which continues to guide Greek folklore research: "Laography as the science of 'survivals' (the English ethnologist Tylor's *survivals in culture*) has been served in but a single manner by the Cypriots. The Cypriot folklorists worked according to the mainland Greek procedural model under the influence of that great figure N. Politis, the father of Greek laography" (Kiprianou 1967: 7). The reprints Politis sent Tylor are filed in the Tylor Library as "Neo-Hellenic, Polites, etc.," cat. ref. O 5/7.

3. In this Politis was a good deal more restrained than some non-Greek commentators (e.g., Geldart 1884: vi, who treated German tales as less solar and therefore as more recent than their Greek counterparts). The connection between Müller's theory of the "disease of language" and the notion of textual "corruption" is much more fully developed in the work of the Russian folklorist A. N. Afanes'ev (see Sokolov 1950: 50–52). On the pre- and post-Classical "borrowing" of cultural traits, within a general Indo-European context, Fauriel (whose interest in Sanskrit was considerable) had already anticipated Politis' approach in terms of historical linguistics (1854: 58–61). Kind (1861: xiv) provides an early instance of comparison between modern Greek and German myths, drawing on Jacob Grimm for the latter.

4. Explanations and further references are given in the notes to appendix A.

5. See Herzfeld 1980b for a discussion of the taxonomic issue.

6. Expansion and Collapse

1. E.g., the attempt to derive *ois* ("sheep") in both languages from a Homeric form, even though a Latin derivation (*ovis*) would seem at least as plausible (particularly for Koutsovlach).

2. For these legends in detail, see Politis 1904: 21–22, 656–674. The *adynaton* (e.g., "when the crow turns white and becomes a dove") is a long-established figure of speech in Greek tradition; see Tuffin 1972–73 and Petropoulos 1954: 96–103.

3. The significance and origin of this image are uncertain.

4. The Battle of Plataea, at which the Persian general Mardonius met defeat at the hands of a combined Greek force, took place in 479 B.C. The Athenians had threatened to fight the Persians unaided, until the Spartans were goaded into cooperating. See Herodotus, *Hist.* viii: 143–144; ix: 6–11.

5. In lines 1 and 2 the verb is *simeno*, "toll," but also "mean, signify"—hence perhaps having connotations, in the present context, of "marking" an especially "significant" event; cf. *simandro*, "sounding board," an instrument used to summon people to church for worship.

6. It is also possible that the plural form is the result of "polite" editing, although this is perhaps less likely.

7. At the Battle of Navarino (October 20, 1827), a British, French, and Russian naval force under the British Admiral Codrington defeated a combined Turkish-Egyptian fleet and thereby effectively confirmed the victory of the Greek cause. Codrington, who had originally been meant not to engage in active battle but merely to make the Turks accept a truce to which the Greeks had already agreed, was apparently goaded into making an attack when a British officer bearing a message from him to the Turkish admiral was killed.

8. The copy is preserved in the Gennadius Library, Athens, which is based on Gennadius' own collection.

Epilogue

1. On Apostolakis' life, see Koukhtsoglou 1947 and, in general, the special issue of *Nea Estia* devoted to him. For a more critical view, see especially Kiriakidou-Nestoros 1978: 155.

2. Clogg (1972) gives an excellent critical account of the colonels' "ethnic" and "religious" ideology.

3. In 1974, with the restoration of democracy, communist parties were legalized. Before the military dictatorship of 1967 to 1974, the only legal party of Marxist ideology had been the United Democratic Left (EDA).

4. Kakouri (1965), however, is still concerned with the problem of establishing cultural continuity. Papadopoullos (1970) provides an account of the development of folklore and anthropology internationally in relation to Greek (including Cypriot) scholarly concerns.

Appendix A. Politis' Folklore Taxonomy

1. A carol performed on Lazarus Saturday, which precedes Holy (i.e., Easter) Week.

2. The *perperouna* is performed by a naked child festooned with leaves, grass, and flowers (Lawson 1910: 23-25). The *klidhonas* (cf. Homeric and Classical *klidōn*) is a form of divination performed on the feast day of Saint John the Baptist at midsummer (see Lawson 1910: 304-305). A boy (preferably the firstborn son of living parents) is sent to fetch the "speechless water," so called because he may not speak to anyone on his way. Unmarried girls throw some object, usually an apple, into the water; as each of these objects is recovered the next morning—by the boy or by the girls themselves in rotation—a verse is recited or improvised, and this is held to indicate the marriage prospects of the girl whose contribution the recovered object is then discovered to be.

3. E.g., the so-called *mitata*, built by Cretan shepherds in their upland summer pasturage.

4. *Xenia* is a Classical term for the reciprocity between those who stood as *xenoi* (reciprocal hosts) to each other. Today, *kseni* are "outsiders" (i.e., to

any reference group); reciprocal host relationships (e.g., between *yarenidhes* on Rhodes) subsisted in some areas at least until recently.

5. *Vios*, "life, way of life"; cf. the titles of Politis 1871, 1874, 1899-1902, and 1904.

6. E.g., the Sarakatsani—who are, strictly speaking, transhumant rather than nomadic; see Campbell 1964.

7. Incubation: sleeping overnight in a church, in order to be cured or to receive guidance through the medium of a dream on the right way to find a cure.

8. From *ilios* ("sun") and *tropi* ("turning").

9. The last week before the Lenten fast.

Bibliography

Note. *Works in Greek are given translated titles and marked with an asterisk.*

Alexiou, Margaret B. 1973. *The Ritual Lament in Greek Tradition*. Cambridge, Eng.: Cambridge University Press.

Alivisatos, Hamilcar S. [1949.] *Marriage and Divorce in Accordance with the Canons of the Orthodox Church*. London: Faith Press.

Anonymous. 1852-53. "Vlach Men and Women." *(Nea) Pandora* 3: 282-283.*

————. 1859-60. Review of Zambelios 1859. *Pandora* 10: 495-499.*

————. 1860-61. "Dora d'Istria." *Pandora* 11: 113-114.*

————. 1871-72. Bibliography. Includes review of Politis 1871. *Pandora* 22: 470-472.*

Apostolakis, Yannis M. 1929. *Folksongs: The Collections*. Pt. 1 (no other published). Athens: Kondomaris.*

————. 1939. *The Song of Hagia Sophia*. Thessaloniki.*

————. 1950. *The Kleftic Song: Its Spirit and Art*. Athens: Estia.*

Aravandinos, P. 1880. *Collection of Folksongs of Epirus*. Athens: Petros Perris.*

————. 1905. *Monograph on the Koutsovlachs*. Athens: S. Kousoulinos.*

Ardener, E. W. 1972. "Language, Ethnicity and Population." *Journal of the Anthropological Society of Oxford* 3: 125-132. Reprinted in J. H. M. Beattie and R. G. Lienhardt, eds., *Studies in Social Anthropology: Essays in Memory of E. E. Evans-Pritchard by His Former Oxford Colleagues*, pp. 343-353. Oxford: Clarendon Press, 1975.

Austin, J. L. 1975. *How to Do Things with Words*. 2d ed. Ed. Marina Sbisà and J. O. Urmson. Cambridge, Mass.: Harvard University Press.

Babiniotis, G. 1979. "A Linguistic Approach to the 'Language Question' in Greece." *Byzantine and Modern Greek Studies* 5: 1-16.

Baggally, John W. 1936. *The Klephtic Ballads in Relation to Greek History (1715-1821)*. Oxford: Basil Blackwell.

Beaton, Roderick. 1980. *Folk Poetry of Modern Greece*. Cambridge, Eng.: Cambridge University Press.

Bees (Veis), Nikos A. 1956. "Claude-Charles Fauriel and Greek Folksongs." Editor's note in Fauriel 1956: i–xiv.*

Berlin, Isaiah. 1977. *Vico and Herder: Two Studies in the History of Ideas.* New York: Vintage. Also London: Hogarth, 1976.

Bialor, Perry A. 1973. "A Century and a Half of Change: Transformations of a Greek Farming Community in the Northwestern Peloponessos, Greece." Ph.D. dissertation, Department of Anthropology, University of Chicago.

Blok, Anton. 1974. *The Mafia of a Sicilian Village, 1860–1960: A Study of Violent Peasant Entrepreneurs.* New York: Harper & Row.

Blum, Richard, and Eva Blum. 1970. *The Dangerous Hour: The Lore of Crisis and Mystery in Rural Greece.* London: Chatto & Windus.

Bouvier, Bertrand. 1960. *Folksongs from a Manuscript in the Iviron Monastery.* Athens: Institut Français d'Athènes.*

Browning, Robert. 1969. *Medieval and Modern Greek.* London: Hutchinson University Library.

Bryer, Anthony A. M. 1976. "The Pontic Revival and the New Greece." In Diamandouros et al. 1976: 171–190.

Büdinger, Max. 1866. *Mittelgriechisches Volksepos: Ein Versuch.* Leipzig: B. G. Teubner.

Burke, Kenneth. 1954. *Permanence and Change.* 2d ed. Palo Alto: Bobbs-Merrill.

Burrows, Ronald. 1913. "Song of the Hellenes to Venizelos, the Cretan." *Manchester University Magazine* 9 (3): 92.

————. 1919. "The Unity of the Greek Race." *Contemporary Review* 115: 153–164.

Bybilakis, Emmanuel. See Vivilakis, Emmanuel.

Bynum, David E. 1969. "The Generic Nature of Oral Epic Poetry." *Genre* 2 (3): 236–258.

Campbell, J. K. 1964. *Honour, Family, and Patronage: A Study of Institutions and Moral Values in a Greek Mountain Community.* Oxford: Clarendon Press.

————. 1976. "Regionalism and Local Community." In Muriel Dimen and Ernestine Friedl, eds., *Regional Variation in Modern Greece and Cyprus: Toward a Perspective on the Ethnography of Greece*, pp. 18–27. Annals of the New York Academy of Sciences 268.

Capidan, Théodore. N.d. *Les Macédo-Roumains.* Académie Roumaine: Connaissance de la Terre et de la Pensée Roumaine 5. Paris: Ernest Leroux.

Cecchetti, Bartolomeo. 1868. *Di alcune opere della principessa Dora d'Istria.* Venice.

————. 1873. *Bibliografia della principessa Dora d'Istria.* 5th ed. Florence: Rivista Europea.

Chapman, John Jay. 1915. *Greek Genius and Other Essays.* New York: Moffat, Tard.

Chapman, Malcolm. 1978. *The Gaelic Vision in Scottish Culture*. London: Croom Helm.

Ciampini, Raffaele. 1945. *Vita di Niccolò Tommaseo*. Florence: G. C. Sansoni.

Clogg, Richard. 1972. "The Ideology of the 'Revolution of 21 April 1967.'" In Richard Clogg and George Yannopoulos, eds., *Greece under Military Rule*, pp. 36–58. London: Secker & Warburg/New York: Basic Books.

————, ed. 1973. *The Struggle for Greek Independence: Essays to Mark the 150th Anniversary of the Greek War of Independence*. Hamden, Conn.: Anchor Press.

————, ed. 1976. *The Movement for Greek Independence, 1770–1821: A Collection of Documents*. New York: Barnes & Noble.

Cocchiara, Giuseppe. 1952. *Storia del folklore in Europa*. Turin: Edizioni Scientifiche Einaudi—Collezione di studi religiosi, etnologici e psicologici 20.

————. N.d. *Storia degli studi delle tradizioni popolari in Italia*. Palermo: G. B. Palumbo.

Colocotronis, Vassilis. 1918. "L'Ame bulgare et l'âme grecque d'après la poésie populaire." *Revue de Grèce* 1 (1): 129–143.

Colquhoun, Archibald. 1954. *Manzoni and His Times*. London: J. M. Dent.

Couloumbis, T. A., John A. Petropulos, and H. J. Psomiades. 1976. *Foreign Interference in Greek Politics: An Historical Perspective*. New York: Pella.

Crick, Malcolm. 1976. *Explorations in Language and Meaning: Towards a Semantic Anthropology*. New York: John Wiley.

Croce, Benedetto, and Fausto Nicolini (editor and additional author). 1947 (vol. 1), 1948 (vol. 2). *Bibliografia Vichiana*. Naples: Ricciardi.

Dakin, Douglas. 1973. *The Greek Struggle for Independence, 1821–1833*. London: Batsford.

Damianakos, Stathis. 1976. *Sociology of the "Rebetiko."* [Athens]: Ermia.*

Danforth, Loring M. 1979. "The Role of Dance in the Ritual Therapy of the Anastenaria." *Byzantine and Modern Greek Studies* 5: 141–163.

Dawkins, R. M. 1916. *Modern Greek in Asia Minor: A Study of the Dialects of Sílli, Cappadocia and Phárasa, with Grammar, Texts, Translations and Commentary*. Cambridge, Eng.: Cambridge University Press.

Diamandouros, Nikiforos P., John P. Anton, John A. Petropulos, and Peter Topping, eds. 1976. *Hellenism and the First Greek War of Liberation (1821–1830): Continuity and Change*. Thessaloniki: Institute for Balkan Studies 156.

Dimaras, C. Th. 1972. *A History of Modern Greek Literature*. Translated by Mary P. Gianos from the fourth Greek edition (Athens: Ikaros, 1948). Albany: State University of New York Press.

Dimou, Nikos. N.d. [1975 or later.] *The Misery of Being Greek*. 5th ed. Athens: Ikaria.*

d'Istria, Dora. 1863. *Excursions en Rumélie et en Morée*. 2 vols. Zurich: Meyer & Zeller.

―――. 1865. "La Nationalité serbe d'après les chants populaires." *Revue des Deux Mondes* 55: 315-360.

―――. 1866. "La Nationalité albanaise d'après les chants populaires." *Revue des Deux Mondes* 63: 382-418.

―――. 1867. "La Nationalité hellénique d'après les chants populaires." *Revue des Deux Mondes* 70: 584-627.

Dorson, Richard M., ed. 1961. *Folklore Research around the World: A North American Point of View*. Indiana University Folklore Series 16. Bloomington: Indiana University Press.

―――. 1966. "The Question of Folklore in a New Nation." *Journal of the Folklore Institute* 3: 277-298.

―――. 1968. *The British Folklorists: A History*. Chicago: University of Chicago Press.

Douglas, F. S. N. 1813. *An Essay on Certain Points of Resemblance between the Ancient and Modern Greeks*. 3d ed. London: John Murray.

Dozon, Auguste. 1875. *Chansons populaires bulgares*. Paris: Maisonneuve.

Eco, Umberto. 1976. *A Theory of Semiotics*. Bloomington: Indiana University Press.

Economides, Dimitr. V. 1969. "The Folk Terminology of Greek Popular Song." *Epet. Kentr. Erevnis Ellin. Laografias* 20-21 (1967-68, published 1969): 126-150.*

Ellinismos. 1896. *National Songs of Greece, 1453-1821*. Athens.*

Evlambios, George. 1843. *The Amaranth: The Roses of Hellas Reborn: Folk Poems of the Modern Greeks*. In Greek and Russian. St. Petersburg: Academy of Sciences. Reprinted in Greek edition, Athens: Notis Karavias, 1973.*

Fallmerayer, Jakob Philipp. 1827. *Geschichte des Kaiserthums von Trapezunt*. Munich: Weber.

―――. 1830 (vol. 1), 1836 (vol. 2). *Geschichte der Halbinsel Morea während des Mittelalters*. Stuttgart & Tübingen: J. G. Cotta.

―――. 1845. *Fragmente aus dem Orient*. 2 vols. Stuttgart & Tübingen: J. G. Cotta.

―――. 1860. "Das Albanesische Element in Griechenland." *Abhandlungen der Historischen Classe der Koeniglich Bayerischen Akademie* 8: 419-487. Munich: Verlag der K. Akademie.

Fauriel, Claude. 1824 (vol. 1), 1825 (vol. 2). *Chants populaires de la Grèce moderne*. Paris: Dondey-Dupré. Further renditions were published in German (by W. Müller in 1825), English (by C. B. Sheridan in 1825), French (by L. J. N. Lemercier in 1824), and Italian (by P. Aporti in 1881).

―――. 1854. *Dante et les origines de la langue et de la littérature italienne*. Vol. 2. Paris: Auguste Durand.

―――. 1956. *Greek Folksongs*. Greek edition of Fauriel 1824 and 1825, rendered with an introduction by Nikos A. Bees (Veis). Athens: Nikos D. Nikas.*

Filaretos, George N. 1906. *The 28th May 1453: Speech Delivered during the Civil Memorial for Constantine Palaeologos (on May 28, 1906).* Athens: To Kratos Press.*

Finnegan, Ruth. 1977. *Oral Poetry: Its Nature, Significance and Social Context.* Cambridge, Eng.: Cambridge University Press.

Frangoudaki, Anna. 1978. *The Reading Books of Grade School: Ideological Coercion and Pedagogical Violence.* Athens: Themelio.*

Garnett, Lucy M. J., and J. S. Stuart-Glennie. 1896. *New Folklore Researches: Greek Folk Poesy: Annotated Translations, from the Whole Cycle of Romaic Folk-verse and Folk-prose.* Includes Stuart-Glennie's essays on "the science of folklore, Greek folkspeech, and the survival of paganism." Guildford, Eng.: privately published (printers Billing & Son).

Geanakoplos, Deno John. 1962. *Greek Scholars in Venice: Studies in the Dissemination of Greek Learning from Byzantium to Western Europe.* Cambridge, Mass.: Harvard University Press.

————. 1966. *Byzantine East and Latin West: Two Worlds of Christendom in Middle Ages and Renaissance.* New York: Barnes & Noble.

Geertz, Clifford. 1973. *The Interpretation of Cultures.* New York: Basic Books.

Geldart, E. M. 1884. *Folk-Lore of Modern Greece: The Tales of the People.* London: W. Swan Sonnenschein.

Gizelis, Gregory Kh. 1974. *Narrative Rhetorical Devices of Persuasion: Folklore Communication in a Greek-American Community.* Athens: National Center of Social Research.

————. 1976. "Modern Analytical Approaches to Artistic Narrative Communication: A Case Study." *Spira:* 408–429.*

Goldstein, K. 1967. "Bowdlerization and Expurgation: Academic and Folk." *Journal of American Folklore* 80: 374–386.

Goldstein, Leon J. 1976. *Historical Knowing.* Austin: University of Texas Press.

Goodfield, June, and Stephen Edelston Toulmin. 1965. *The Discovery of Time.* New York: Harper & Row.

[Goudas, A.] N.d. [1870?] *Fourth Memorandum: On the Nature of Brigandage in Greece, on the Causes of Its Genesis and Existence, and on the Means of Its Extirpation.* [Athens?] *

Hahn, Johann Georg von. 1864. *Griechische und Albanesische Märchen.* 2 vols. Leipzig: W. Engelmann.

Hallowell, A. I. 1965. "The History of Anthropology as an Anthropological Problem." *Journal of the History of the Behavioral Sciences* 1: 24–38.

Hammel, Eugene A. 1972. *The Myth of Structural Analysis: Lévi-Strauss and the Three Bears.* Modules in Anthropology 25, pp. 1–29. Reading, Mass.: Addison-Wesley.

Haxthausen, Werner von. 1935. *Neugriechische Volkslieder*. Ed. Karl Schulte
    Kemminghausen and Gustav Sonter. Münster i.W.: Aschendorffsche
    Verlagsbuchhandlung, Veröffentlichungen der Annette von Droste-
    Gesellschaft, no. 4.
Henderson, G. P. 1970. *The Revival of Greek Thought, 1620-1830*. Albany:
    State University of New York Press.
Herzfeld, Michael. 1969. "The Song of the Siege of Rhodes and Its Variants."
    Kritika Khronika 21: 494-498.*
————. 1973. "'The Siege of Rhodes' and the Ethnography of Greek Oral
    Tradition." *Kritika Khronika* 25: 413-440.
————. 1974. "Oral Tradition and Cultural Continuity in the Spring Rituals
    of Southern Rhodian Villages." *Dodekanisiaka Khronika* 2: 270-289.*
————. 1977. "Ritual and Textual Structures: The Advent of Spring in
    Rural Greece." In Ravindra K. Jain, ed. *Text and Context: The Social
    Anthropology of Tradition*, pp. 29-50. A.S.A. Essays 2. Philadelphia:
    Institute for the Study of Human Issues.
————. 1979. "Exploring a Metaphor of Exposure." *Journal of American
    Folklore* 92: 285-301.
————. 1980a. "Honour and Shame: Problems in the Comparative Analysis
    of Moral Systems." *Man*, n.s. 15: 339-351.
————. 1980b. "Social Borderers: Themes of Ambiguity and Conflict in
    Greek Folk-Song." *Byzantine and Modern Greek Studies* 6: 61-80.
————. 1980c. "On the Ethnography of 'Prejudice' in an Exclusive Com-
    munity." *Ethnic Groups* 2: 283-305.
————. 1981a. "Performative Categories and Symbols of Passage in Rural
    Greece." *Journal of American Folklore* 94: 44-57.
————. 1981b. "Meaning and Morality: A Semiotic Approach to Evil Eye
    Accusations in a Greek Village." *American Ethnologist* 8: 560-574.
————. 1981c. "An Indigenous Theory of Meaning and Its Elicitation in
    Performative Context." *Semiotica* 34.
Hesseling, D. 1892. "Essai historique sur l'Infinitif Grec." In J. Psichari, ed.,
    Etudes de philologie néo-grecque, pp. 1-44. Paris: Emile Bouillon, Ecole
    Pratique des Hautes Etudes: Bibliothèque: Sciences Historiques et Phi-
    lologiques 92.
Hobsbawm, Eric. 1959. *Primitive Rebels: Studies in Archaic Forms of Social
    Movement in the 19th and 20th Centuries*. Manchester: Manchester
    University Press.
Hodgen, Margaret T. 1936. *The Doctrine of Survivals: A Chapter in the His-
    tory of Scientific Method in the Study of Man*. London: Allenson.
Holden, David. 1972. *Greece without Columns: The Making of the Modern
    Greeks*. London: Faber & Faber.
Howarth, David. 1976. *The Greek Adventure: Lord Byron and Other Ec-
    centrics in the War of Independence*. New York: Atheneum.
Hussey, J. M. 1978. "Jakob Philipp Fallmerayer and George Finlay." *Byzan-
    tine and Modern Greek Studies* 4: 78-87.

Iatridis, A. 1859. *Collection of Old and New Folksongs, with Various Illustrations.* Athens: D. Ath. Mavrommatis.*

Ibrovac, Miodrag. 1966. *Claude Fauriel et la fortune européenne des poésies populaires grecques et serbes: Etude d'histoire romantique, suivie du cours de Fauriel professé en Sorbonne (1831-1832).* Paris: Marcel Didier.

Ioannidis, S. 1887. *A Medieval Epic from the Trebizond Manuscript: Basil Digenes Akrites the Cappadocian.* Constantinople.*

Ioannou, G. 1975. *Folksong: Ballads.* Athens: Ermis New Greek Library.*

Jenkins, Romilly. 1940. *Dionysios Solomos.* Cambridge, Eng.: Cambridge University Press.

————. 1961. *The Dilessi Murders.* London: Longmans.

Jenkyns, Richard. 1980. *The Victorians and Ancient Greece.* Cambridge, Mass.: Harvard University Press.

Jireček, C. 1891. *Das Fürstentum Bulgarien: Seine Bodengestaltung, Natur, Bevölkerung, Wirtschaftlische Zustände, Geistige Cultur, Staatsverfassung, Staatsverwaltung, und neueste Geschichte.* Wien: F. Tempsky.

Jones, Maldwyn Allen. 1960. *American Immigration.* Chicago: University of Chicago Press.

Joseph, Brian Daniel. 1978. *Morphology and Universals in Syntactic Change: Evidence from Medieval and Modern Greek.* Bloomington: Indiana University Linguistics Club.

Kakouri, Katerina. 1965. *Dionysiaka: Aspects of the Popular Thracian Religion of To-day.* Athens: G. C. Eleftheroudakis. Greek edition, 1963, same publisher and location.*

Kakridis, Johannes Theoph. 1967. *Die alten Hellenen im Neugriechischen Volksglauben.* Munich: Heimeran.

Kalonaros, Petros P. 1970. *Basil Digenes Akritas: The Verse Texts.* Athens: Papadimas.* Reprint of the 1941 edition.

Kambanis, Aristos. 1920. *Kalligas and Zambelios: Lectures on Greek Narrative Writers.* Lectures of the Parnassos Philological Society 4. Athens: Michael S. Zimakis.*

Kapsomenos, Eratosthenis G. 1978. *Greek Folk Song: Its Aesthetics, Myth, and Ideology.* Rethinno: privately published.*

————. 1979. *The Modern Cretan Historical Song: Its Structure and Ideology.* Athens: Themelio.*

Karatza, Eleni. 1970. *Edgar Quinet and Modern Greece.* Athens.*

Karolidis, P. 1906. "Critical, Historical, and Topographical Notes on the Medieval Greek Epic *Akritas.*" *Epistimoniki Epetiris* of the National University of Athens for 1905-1906: 188-246.*

Katsoulis, George D. 1975. *The Establishment in Modern Greek History.* Athens: Nea Sinora.*

Kemminghausen, Karl Schulte, and Gustav Sonter. 1935. "Einleitung." In Haxthausen 1935.

Khrisanthopoulos, L. 1853. *Collection of the Local Customs of Greece, from Official Responses of the Local Authorities to the Greek Government.* Athens: K. Garpolas.*

Khristovasilis, Kh. 1902. *National Songs, 1453-1821.* 2d ed. Athens: Ellinismos.*

Kind, Theodor. 1827. *Eunomia.* Vol. 3. Grimma: Carl Friedrich Göschen Beyer.

————. 1833. *Neugriechische Poesien.* Vol. 1. Leipzig: in der Deutschen Buchhandlung.

————. 1838. *Geschichte der Griechischen Revolution vom Jahre 1821 bis zur Thronbesteigung des Koenigs Otto I.* Leipzig: Literarisches Museum (Schiller und Robitzsch).

————. 1861. *Anthologie neugriechischer Volkslieder.* 3d ed. of King 1827; 2d ed., 1849. Leipzig: Veit.

Kiprianou, Khrisanthos S. 1967. *The Pan-Cypriot Gymnasium and Folklore.* Vol. 1. Nicosia.*

Kiriakidis, Stilpon P. 1923. "N. G. Politis." *Laografia* 7: ix-li.*

————. 1931. "Gli studi folkloristici in Grecia." *Lares* 2 (2): 11-15.

————. 1934. *The Historical Beginnings of Modern Greek Popular Poetry.* Rector's speech. Thessaloniki: University of Thessaloniki.*

————. 1937. *What Is Laography and What Ends Can the Study of It Serve?* Thessaloniki.*

————. 1955. *The Northern Ethnological Boundaries of Hellenism.* Thessaloniki: Institute for Balkan Studies 5.

Kiriakidou-Nestoros, Alki. 1975. *Folklore Studies.* Athens: Olkos.*

————. 1978. *The Theory of Greek Folklore.* Athens: Moraitis School.*

Kitto, H. D. F. 1957. *The Greeks.* Harmondsworth, Eng.: Penguin.

Kofos, Evangelos. 1964. *Nationalism and Communism in Macedonia.* Thessaloniki: Institute for Balkan Studies 70.

Kondogiorgis, George D. 1979. *Helladic Folk Ideology.* Athens: Nea Sinora.*

Koraes, Adamantios. [1803.] *Mémoire de l'état actuel de la civilisation dans la Grèce, lu à la Société des Observateurs de l'Homme le 16 nivôse, en XI (6 janvier 1803).*

————. 1805. Letter, February 2. In A. Koraes, *Correspondence,* 2 (1799-1809): 230-234. Athens: Estia/Society for the Study of the Hellenic Enlightenment.*

Kordatos, Yanis. 1972. *The Social Significance of the Greek Revolution of 1821.* Athens: Ekd. Diethnous Epikerotitos.* 5th ed. Edited with an introduction by Than. Kh. Papadopoulos.

Koukhtsoglou, Yannis. 1947. "The Man Apostolakis." *Nea Estia* 42 (491): 204-209.*

Koukoules, Phaidon I. 1950. *The Folkloristic Materials of Eustathius of Thessaloniki.* 2 vols. Athens: Society for Macedonian Studies, Scientific Treatises, Philological and Theological Series 5-6.*

Kriaris, Aristidis. 1920. *Complete Collection of Cretan Folksongs.* 2d ed. Athens: Frantzeskakis & Kaitatzis.*

La Guilletière, Sieur de [Guillet, André Georges]. 1676. *Lacédémone ancienne et nouvelle, où l'on voit les mœurs et les coutûmes des grecs modernes, des mahométans, & des juifs du pays*. Paris: Jean Ribou.

Lambithianaki-Papadaki, Evangelia. 1972. *The Passion of the Young Brave: Marriage Brokerage, Engagement, and the Wedding in a Village of Crete*. Iraklion.*

Lambrinos, George. 1947. *Folksong*. Historical Library 8. Athens: Ta Nea Vivlia.*

Lang, Andrew. 1885. *Custom and Myth*. 2d ed. London: Longmans, Green. Reprinted 1970 by Oosterhout N. B., Anthropological Publications.

Lanitis, Nik. Kl. 1946. *The Soul of Cyprus*. Athens: Aetos.*

Lascaris, M. 1934. "N. Tommaseo ed A. Mustoxidi." *Società Dalmata di Storia Patria, Atti e Memorie* 3: 5–39.

Lawson, John Cuthbert. 1910. *Modern Greek Folklore and Ancient Greek Religion: A Study in Survivals*. Cambridge, Eng.: Cambridge University Press. Reprinted 1964, with a foreword by Al. N. Oikonomides, New Hyde Park, N.Y.: University Books.

Leake, William Martin. 1814. *Researches in Greece*. London: Booth.

———. 1835. *Travels in Northern Greece*. Vol. 1. London: Rodwell.

Lee, Dorothy. 1953. "Greece." Anon. article in Margaret Mead, ed., *Cultural Patterns and Technical Change*. Paris: UNESCO. Reprinted in Dorothy Lee, *Freedom and Culture*, Englewood Cliffs, N.J.: Prentice-Hall/Spectrum, 1959.

Lefkias, Anastasios Georgiadis. 1843. *Overthrow of What Has Been Claimed, Written, and Broadcast in the Press, That None of Those Now Living in Greece Is a Descendant of the Ancient Greeks*. Athens.* With Latin translation.

Legrand, Emile. 1870. *Collection de monuments pour servir à l'étude de la langue néo-hellénique*. Vol. 12. Paris: Maisonneuve.

———. 1876. *Chansons populaires grecques*. Paris: Maisonneuve.

Leigh Fermor, Patrick. 1966. *Roumeli: Travels in Northern Greece*. New York: Harper & Row.

Lelekos, Michael S. 1852. *Demotic Anthology*. Athens: P. Angelidis.*

———. 1868 (vol. 1), 1869 (vol. 2). *Demotic Anthology*. Athens: Nikolaos Rousopoulos.*

———. 1888. *Dessert*. 2 vols. Athens: A. Papageorgiou.*

Lenormant, François. 1864. *Monographie de la voie sacrée éleusinienne, de ses monuments et de ses souvenirs*. Vol. 1 (no other published). Paris: L. Hachette.

Lipset, Seymour Martin. 1963. *The First New Nation: The United States in Historical and Comparative Perspective*. New York: Basic Books. Republished 1967, Garden City, N.Y.: Doubleday.

Llewellyn Smith, Michael. 1965. *The Great Island: A Study of Crete*. London: Longmans.

Loomis, Louise Ropes. 1906. *Medieval Hellenism*. Lancaster, Pa.: Wickersham Press.

Lord, Albert B. 1960. *The Singer of Tales*. Harvard Studies in Comparative Literature 24. Cambridge, Mass.: Harvard University Press.

Loukas, Georgios. 1874. *Philological Visits to the Monuments of the Ancients in the Life of the Modern Cypriots*. Vol. 1 (no other published). Athens: Nikolaos Rousopoulos.*

Loukatos, Dim. S. 1963. *Folklorica contemporanea*. Athens.*

————. 1978. *Introduction to Greek Folklore*. Athens: National Bank of Greece.* 2d ed.

Luciani, Vincent. 1967. *A Brief History of Italian Literature*. New York: S. F. Vanni.

Mandouvalou, Maria. 1969. *Unknown Correspondence between Dora d'Istria and D. Voulgaris*. Athens: Texts and Studies in Modern Greek Philology 61.*

Manesis, N. V. 1860–61. "Andrea Mustoxidi." *Pandora* 11: 249–252.*

Mannheim, Karl. 1936. *Ideology and Utopia: An Introduction to the Sociology of Knowledge*. New York (1966 reedition): Harcourt, Brace & World.

Manousos, Andonios. 1850. *National Songs*. Vol. 1 (no other published). Corfu: Ermis.*

Marcellus, M. L. J. A. C. D. du T., Comte de. 1851. *Chants du peuple en Grèce*. Paris: J. Lecoffre.

————. 1860. *Chants populaires de la Grèce moderne*. Paris: Michel Lévy frères.

————. 1861. *Les Grecs anciens et les Grecs modernes*. Paris: Michel Lévy frères.

Marinoni, Ernesto, ed. 1926. *Prose e poesie di Ugo Foscolo*. 2d ed. Milan: Ulrico Hoepli.

Martellotti, Guido. See Tommaseo 1943.

Mavrogordato, John. 1956. *Digenes Akrites*. Oxford: Clarendon Press.

Mazarakis, E. D. 1964. *Folklore Research and Its Systematic Organization*. Athens.*

Megas, George A. 1946. *Do the Bulgarians Have a National Epic?* Athens: Society for the Propagation of Hellenic Letters.*

————. 1950. "La Civilisation dite balkanique: La Poésie populaire des pays des Balkans." *L'Hellénisme Contemporain*: 8–30.

————. 1951. *The Greek House: Its Evolution and Its Relation to the Houses of the Other Balkan Peoples*. Athens: Ministry of Reconstruction 37. Greek edition, 1949.*

————. 1953. "The Sack of Constantinople in the Songs and Traditions of the People." In *1453–1953: The Quinquecentenary of the Sack of Constantinople: Commemorative Volume*. Athens: *L'Hellénisme Contemporain*, May 29, pp. 244–255.*

Menardos, Simos. 1921. "History of the Words *Tragōdō* and *Tragōdia*." Pamphlet. [Athens?] *

Migne, Jacques Paul. *Patrologiæ cursus completus. Series græca.*

Morgan, Gareth. 1960. *Cretan Poetry: Sources and Inspiration*. Iraklion: A. Kalokerinos. Originally published in *Kritika Khronika* 14 (1960): 7-68, 203-270, 379-434.

Motsias, Khristos. 1977. "In the Kleftic Refuges Athletics Flourished Anew." *Ta Nea*, April 7, p. 7.*

Mure, G. R. G. 1965. *The Philosophy of Hegel*. London: Oxford University Press.

Mustoxidi, Andrea. 1821. *Prose varie del Cavaliere Andrea Mustoxidi Corcirese, con aggiunta di alcuni versi*. Milan: Bettoni.

————. 1860. See Tripaldo 1860.

Nea Estia. 1947. Special issue devoted to Yannis Apostolakis. 42 (491): 188-212.*

Nisbet, Robert A. 1969. *Social Change and History: Aspects of the Western Theory of Development*. London & New York: Oxford University Press.

Oinas, Felix J. 1961. "Folklore Activities in Russia." In Dorson 1961: 76-84.

Orlandos, Anast. 1969. "The Work of the Greek Folklore Research Center in the Fifty Years since Its Foundation (1918-1968)." *Epet. Kentr. Erevnis Ellin. Laografias* 20-21: 5-14.*

Page, D. L., ed. 1962. *Poetae Melici Graeci*. Oxford: Clarendon Press.

Paleologos, P. 1977. *"That's* What Greece Is All About." *To Vima*, March 23, p. 1.*

Papadopoullos, Theodhoros. 1970. "The Field and Content of Folklore According to Its Definition." *Epet. Kentr. Epist. Erevnon* 3: 1-62.*

Papadopoulos-Vrettos, Andreas. 1825. *Memoria su di alcuni costumi degli antichi Greci tuttora esistenti nell'Isola di Leucade*. 2d ed. Naples.

————. 1837. *Mémoires biographiques-historiques sur le président de la Grèce, le Comte Jean Capodistrias*. Paris: Firmin Didot.

————. 1852-53. Bibliography. Review of Zambelios 1852. *Pandora* 3: 397-406.*

————. 1860. See Tipaldo 1860.

Papagrigorakis, Idomenefs I. 1956-57. *The Cretan "Rizitiká" Songs*. Vol. 1 (no other published): *For the Feast and the Road*. Chania.*

Papazisis, Dimitrios Tr. 1976. *Vlachs (Koutsovlachs)*. Athens.*

Pashley, Robert. 1837. *Travels in Crete*. 2 vols. London: John Murray.

Passow, Arnold. 1860. *Carmina popularia Graeciae recentioris*. Leipzig: B. G. Teubner.

Petropoulos, D. 1954. *La Comparaison dans la chanson populaire grecque*. Athens: Institut Français d'Athènes (coll. 86).

Petropoulos, Ilias. 1968. *"Rebetika" Songs*. Athens.*

Petropulos, John. 1968. *Politics and Statecraft in the Kingdom of Greece, 1833-1843*. Princeton, N.J.: Princeton University Press.

————. 1976a. Introduction. In Diamandouros et al. 1976: 19-41.

————. 1976b. "Forms of Collaboration with the Enemy during the First Greek War of Liberation." In Diamandouros et al. 1976: 131-143.

Polilas, Iakovos. See Valetas 1950.

Politis, Alexis. 1973. *Folksong: Kleftic*. Athens: Ermis New Greek Library.*

Politis, Nikolaos G. 1871 (pt. 1, to p. 204), 1874 (pt. 2). *Study of the Life of the Modern Greeks*. Vol. 1 (no other issued in this series): *Modern Greek Mythology*. Athens: Karl Wilberg & N. A. Nakis.*

————. 1872. "Swallow Song [*Khelidhonisma*] ." *Neoellinika Analekta* 1: 354-368.*

————. 1876. "The First of March." *Estia* 1: 142-143.*

————. 1880. "Popular Meteorological Myths." Athens: Parnassos. Originally published in *Parnassos* 4.*

————. 1882a. "The Sun in Popular Myths." Athens: Enosis.*

————. 1882b. "Introductory Lecture for the Class in Hellenic Mythology." Athens: Aion. Originally published in *Aion*, December 7-9.*

————. 1885. "Bulgarian Klefts According to Popular Bulgarian Songs." *Estia* 19: 754-758.*

————. 1899-1902. *Studies of the Life and Language of the Greek People: Proverbs*. Vol. 1. Athens: Marasli.*

————. 1901. "Hellenes or *Romii*?" Athens: Agon Press.*

————. 1903. "The Mistranscription of the National Songs." Athens: *Athinai* (June 10, 11, 12, 16) and *Agon* (August 1, 8, 15).*

————. 1904. *Studies of the Life and Language of the Greek People: Traditions*. Athens: Marasli.*

————. 1907. *On the National Epic of the Modern Greeks*. Rector's speech, delivered in 1906. Athens: University of Athens.*

————. 1909a. "Laography." *Laografia* 1: 3-18.* See appendix A.

————. 1909b. "Akritic Songs: The Death of Digenes." *Laografia* 1: 169-272.*

————. 1914. *Selections from the Songs of the Greek People*. Athens: Estia.*

————. 1916. *Known Poets of Folksongs*. Athens: Lectures of the Parnassos Philological Society 1.*

————. 1918. "Croyances populaires sur le rétablissement de la nation hellénique." *Revue de Grèce* 1 (1): 151-170.

Pommier, Armand. 1863. *Mme. La Comtesse Dora d'Istria*. In the series Profils contemporains. Paris: Lecrivain & Tonbon.

Pouqueville, F. C. H. L. 1805. *Voyage en Morée, à Constantinople, en Albanie, et dans plusieurs autres parties de l'Empire Othoman . . .* Paris: Gabon.

Quinet, Edgar. 1830. *De la Grèce moderne et des rapports avec l'antiquité*. Paris & Strasbourg: F. G. Levrault.

————. 1859. *Oeuvres complètes*. Vol. 5, pp. 173-598. Paris: Pagnerre.

Read, Allen Walker. 1978. "The Persistence of Verbal Symbols of Emotion in Charged Contexts." Paper delivered at the annual meeting of the Semiotic Society of America in Providence, R.I., cited by kind permission of the author.

Romaios, Kostas A. 1959. *Close to the Roots: Research on the Psychic World of the Greek People*. Athens.*

————. 1966. "*Ksandinon the Far-Famed*: A New Methodological Beginning for a Critical Edition of the Texts of Folksongs." *Arkhion Pondou* 27: 150-206.*

————. 1966-67. "The Poet and the Betrayed Fortress." *Arkhion Pondou* 28: 197-212.*

————. 1968. *The Poetry of a People.* Athens: Folklore Institute of the Greek Travelers' Club 1.*

St. Clair, William. 1972. *That Greece Might Still Be Free: The Philhellenes in the War of Independence.* London: Oxford University Press.

Sainte-Beuve, C.-A. 1870, *Portraits contemporains.* Vol. 4. Paris: Michel Lévy frères. Fauriel is presented on pp. 125-268.

Sakellarios, Athanasios A. 1891. *Kypriaka.* Vol. 2: *Language in Cyprus.* Athens: P. D. Sakellarios.*

Sanders, D. 1844. *Das Volksleben der Neugriechen, dargestellt und erklärt aus Liedern, Sprichworten, Kunstgedichten, nebst einem Anhange von Musikbeilagen und zwei kritischen Abhandlungen.* Mannheim: F. Bassermann.

Sanders, Irwin T. 1962. *Rainbow in the Rock: The People of Rural Greece.* Cambridge, Mass.: Harvard University Press.

Sandfeld, K. 1930. *Linguistique balkanique: Problèmes et résultats.* Collection de la Société Linguistique de Paris 31. Paris: H. Champion.

Sathas, K., and Emile Legrand. 1875. *Les Exploits de Basile Digénis Acritas: Epopée byzantine du dixième siècle . . .* Paris: Maisonneuve/Athens: Coromilas.

Schein, Muriel Dimen. 1975. "When Is an Ethnic Group? Ecology and Class Structure in Northern Greece." *Ethnology* 14: 83-97.

Schmidt, Bernhard. 1871. *Das Volksleben der Neugriechen und das hellenische Alterthum,* Leipzig: B. G. Teubner.

————. 1877. *Griechische Märchen, Sagen und Volkslieder.* Leipzig: B. G. Teubner.

Simopoulos, Kiriakos. 1972 (vol. 1, 2d ed.: 333-1700), 1973 (vol. 2: 1700-1800), 1975 (vol. 3, pt. 1: 1800-1810; pt. 2: 1810-1821). *Foreign Travelers in Greece.* Athens.*

Sinner, G. R. L. de. 1824. *Christoph. Bondelmonti, Florentini, Librum Archipelagi.* Leipzig & Berlin: G. Reimer.

Skouteri-Didaskalou, N. 1980. "For an Ideological Reproduction of Inter-Sexual Discriminations: The Sign-Providing Function of the 'Ritual of Marriage.'" In Karin Boklund-Lagopoulou, ed., *Semiotics and Society.* Athens: Odhisseas.

Sokolov, Y. M. 1950. *Russian Folklore.* Trans. Catherine Ruth Smith. New York: Macmillan.

Soteropoulos, S. 1868. *The Brigands of the Morea: A Narrative of the Captivity of Mr. S. Soteropoulos.* 2 vols. Tran. J. O. Bagdon. London: Saunders, Otley.

Sotiropoulos, Dimitri. 1977. "Diglossia and the National Language Question in Modern Greece." *Linguistics* 197: 5-31.

Spectator, The. Review of G. F. Abbott, *Songs of Modern Greece.* November 3, 1900.

Sperantsas, Stelios. 1949. "'Ours Once More . . .'" *Elliniki Dhimiouryia* 3 (32): 884-886.*

Spiridakis, George K. 1962. *Directions for the Collection of Folklore Material.* Athens: Academy of Athens.*

————. 1966. "The Scientific Foundation of Folklore Studies in Greece." Reprinted from *Epet. Filosofikis Skholis,* Athens University, 1965-66.*

————. 1969. "The Song of the Swallow (*Khelidhonisma*) on the First of March." *Epet. Kentr. Erevnis Ellin. Laografias* 20-21: 15-54.*

Stephanopoli, Dimo. 1800. *Voyage de Dimo et Nicolo Stephanopoli en Grèce pendant les années 1797 et 1798, d'après deux missions . . .* London.

Stuart-Glennie, J. S. See Garnett and Stuart-Glennie 1896.

Taillandier, Saint-René (R. G. E.). 1862. "Publicistes modernes de l'Allemagne: Jacques Philippe Fallmerayer." *Revue des Deux Mondes* 42: 119-154.

Tipaldo, Emilio de. 1860. *Biografia del Cavaliere Andrea Mustoxidi.* Ed. A. Mustoxidi and (subsequently) A. Papadopoulos-Vrettos. Athens: P. A. Sakellarios.

Tommaseo, Niccolò. 1841 (vols. 1, 2), 1842 (vols. 3, 4). *Canti Popolari Toscani, Corsi, Illirici, Greci.* Venice: Girolamo Tasso.

————. 1904. *Il Primo esilio di Nicolò [sic] Tommaseo, 1834-1839: Lettere da lui a Cesare Cantù.* Ed. Ettore Verga. Milan: L. F. Cogliati.

————. 1929. *Colloqui col Manzoni.* Ed. Teresa Lodi. Florence: G. C. Sansoni.

————. 1943. *Canti del popolo Greco.* Ed. Guido Martellotti. Turin: Giulio Einaudi.

————. 1953. *Lettere inedite a Emilio de Tipaldo.* Ed. Raffaele Ciampini. Brescia: Morcelliana.

Trærup, Birthe. 1970. *East Macedonian Folk Songs: Contemporary Traditional Material from Maleševo, Pijanec and the Razlog District Collected and Transcribed by the Author.* Dansk Folkemindesamling, Skrifter 2, Acta Ethnomusicologica Danica 2. Copenhagen: Akademisk Forlag.

Traves, Piero. N.d. *Lo Studio dell'Antichità Classica nell'Ottocento.* La Letteratura Italiana, Storia e Testi, vol. 72. Milan & Naples: Ricciardi.

Tuffin, Paul. 1972-73. "The Whitening Crow: Some *Adynata* in the Greek Tradition." *Epet, Kentr. Episrimonikon Erevnon* 6: 79-92.

Tylor, Edward Burnett. 1865. *Researches into the Early History of Mankind and the Development of Civilization.* London: John Murray.

————. 1871. *Primitive Culture: Researches into the Development of Mythology, Philosophy, Religion, Art, and Custom.* London: John Murray.

————. 1924. 7th edition of Tylor 1871. New York: Brentano's.

Vacalopoulos, Apostolos E. 1970. *Origins of the Greek Nation: The Byzantine Period, 1204-1461.* Rev. ed. Tran. Ian Marks. New Brunswick, N.J.: Rutgers University Press.

Valetas, G., ed. 1950. *Iak. Polilas, Collected Literary and Critical Works*. Includes introductory essay by the editor: "The Life and Work of Polilas." Athens: Piyi.*

Valvis, Stamatios. 1877. "On the Distich of the Hero Athanasios Diakos." *Athinaion* 6 (3): 129-151.*

Vasdravellis, John K. 1975. *Klephts, Armatoles and Pirates in Macedonia during the Rule of the Turks, 1627-1821*. Thessaloniki: Society for Macedonian Studies, Scientific Treatises, Philological and Theological Series 43.

Veloudis, Georg. 1968. *Der neugriechische Alexander-Tradition in Bewahrung und Wandel*. Munich: Institut für byzantinistik and neugriechische Philologie der Universität München.

Venizelos, J. 1846. *Popular Proverbs*. Athens: Vlassaridis.* 2d ed., Ermoupolis: Patris, 1867.

Vico, Giambattista. 1744. *Principi di scienza nuova*. 3d ed. Naples: Stamperia Muziana.

Vivilakis (Bybilakis), Emmanuel. 1840. *Neugriechisches Leben, verglichen mit dem Altgriechischen: Zur Erlauterung beider*. Berlin: Wilhelm Besser.

Viziinos, George, 1949. "The Last Palaeologos." Poem published in *Elliniki Dhimiouryia* 4: 545-547.*

Vlakhoyannis, Yannis. 1935. *Klefts of the Morea: Historical Study Drawn from New Sources* . . . Athens: privately published "through the patriotic grant of Mr. Alex. Pallis."*

Vlastos, Pavlos G. 1909. *Digenes: Ancient Giant and Great Hero of Crete*. Fascicle of *The Cretan People*. Iraklion.*

Voutier, Olivier. 1826. *Lettres sur la Grèce et chants populaires: Extraits du portefeuille du colonel Voutier*. Paris: Firmin Didot.

Vryonis, Speros, Jr. 1976. "The Greeks under Turkish Rule." In Diamandouros et al. 1976: 45-58.

Wace, A. J. B., and M. S. Thompson. 1914. *The Nomads of the Balkans: An Account of Life and Customs among the Vlachs of Northern Pindus*. London: Methuen/New York: E. P. Dutton. Reprint 1972, London: Methuen/New York: Biblo & Tannen.

Wachsmuth, Kurt. 1864. *Das alte Griechenland im neuen*. Bonn: Max Cohen.

Wills, Garry. 1979. *Inventing America: Jefferson's Declaration of Independence*. New York: Random House/Vintage. Originally published in 1978.

Wilson, William A. 1976. *Folklore and Nationalism in Modern Finland*. Bloomington: Indiana University Press.

Winner, Irene Portis. 1977. "The Question of the Zadruga in Slovenia: Myth and Reality in Žerovnica." *Anthropological Quarterly* 50 (3): 125-134.

————, and Thomas G. Winner. 1976. "The Semiotics of Cultural Texts." *Semiotica* 18 (2): 101-156.

Xenos, Stefanos. 1865. *East and West: A Diplomatic History of the Ionian Islands to the Kingdom of Greece*. London: Trübner.

Xydis, Stephen G. 1968. "Medieval Origins of Modern Green Nationalism."
    Balkan Studies 9: 1-20.
Yangas, Athanasios Kh. N.d. [1953.] *Epirote Folksongs, 1000-1958.* Athens:
    Pirros, for Institute of Epirote Studies.*
Zakhos, Emmanuel. 1966. *Poésie populaire des grecs.* Paris: Maspéro.
Zakythinos, Denis A. 1975. *Le Despotat grec de Morée: Vie et institutions.*
    French-language edition of the original (Athens 1953), revised and sup-
    plemented by Chryssa Maltezou. London: Variorum.
Zambelios, I. 1902. "Autobiography." Ed. D. Kambouroglou. *Armonia* 3:
    225-237.*
Zambelios, Spyridon. 1852. *Folksongs of Greece, published with a Study of*
    Medieval Hellenism. Corfu: Ermis (A. Terzakis & Th. Romaios).*
——————. 1856. "Some Philological Researches on the Modern Greek Lan-
    guage." *Pandora* 7: 369-380, 484-494.*
——————. 1859. *Whence the Vulgar Word* Traghoudho? *Thoughts Concerning*
    Hellenic Poetry. Athens: P. Soutsas & A. Ktenas.*
——————. 1880. *Parlers grecs et romans: Leur point de contact préhistorique.*
    Vol. 1 (no other published). Paris: Maisonneuve.
Zannetos, George. 1883. *The Homeric Phrase in Our Folk Poetry.* Athens.*
Zoras, George Th. 1953. "Ideological and Political Directions Formulated be-
    fore the Fall." In *1453-1953: The Quinquecentenary of the Sack of*
    Constantinople: Commemorative Volume. Athens: *L'Hellénisme Con-*
    *temporain.**

Index